THE ORIGINS OF THE OWNERSHIP SOCIETY:

How the Defined Contribution Paradigm Changed America

THE ORIGINS OF THE OWNERSHIP SOCIETY:

How the Defined Contribution Paradigm Changed America

Edward A. Zelinsky

OXFORD
UNIVERSITY PRESS

OXFORD

UNIVERSITY PRESS

Oxford University Press, Inc., publishes works that further Oxford University's objective of excellence in research, scholarship, and education.

Copyright © 2007 by Oxford University Press, Inc.
Published by Oxford University Press, Inc.
198 Madison Avenue, New York, New York 10016

Oxford is a registered trademark of Oxford University Press
Oceana is a registered trademark of Oxford University Press, Inc.

Library of Congress Cataloging-in-Publication Data

Zelinsky, Edward A.
The origins of the ownership society: how the defined contribution paradigm changed America / Edward A. Zelinsky
    p. cm.
Includes bibliographical references and index.
ISBN: 978-0-19-533935-2 (alk. paper)
1. Social security—Law and legislation—United States. 2. Social security individual investment accounts—United States. 3. Retirement income—United States. 4. Internal revenue law—United States. 5. Spendings tax —Law and legislation—United States. 6. Taxation of articles of consumption—Law and legislation—United States. I. Title
    KF3649.Z45 2007

                                                                    344.7302'3—dc22

Note to Readers:

This publication is designed to provide accurate and authoritative information in regard to the subject matter covered. It is based upon sources believed to be accurate and reliable and is intended to be current as of the time it was written. It is sold with the understanding that the publisher is not engaged in rendering legal, accounting, or other professional services. If legal advice or other expert assistance is required, the services of a competent professional person should be sought. Also, to confirm that the information has not been affected or changed by recent developments, traditional legal research techniques should be used, including checking primary sources where appropriate.

(Based on the Declaration of Principles jointly adopted by a Committee of the American Bar Association and a Committee of Publishers and Associations.)

You may order this or any other Oxford University Press publication by visiting the Oxford University Press website at www.oup.com

To the memories of my grandfather,

Barney Brotman,

and the son I named after him,

Barak Joseph Monrad Zelinsky

Table of Contents

Foreword

Edward A. Zelinsky is the Morris and Annie Trachman Professor of Law at the Benjamin N. Cardozo School of Law of Yeshiva University.

I thank the many individuals who reviewed prior drafts of parts of this book including the participants in the Harvard Law School tax seminar, the Cornell Law School faculty seminar, the University of Michigan Law School tax workshop, the William and Mary School of Law faculty seminar, and the UCLA tax policy colloquium. For reading such prior drafts, I also thank Alvin D. Lurie, Esq., and Professors Ellen P. Aprill, Steven Bank, Jeremy Bulow, Eric D. Chason, Mitchell L. Engler, Jonathan Barry Forman, John H. Langbein, David A. Pratt, Paul M. Secunda, Kirk Stark, James A. Wooten, and Eric M. Zolt.

For research assistance, I thank Megan Burrows and Benjamin Takis of the Cardozo Law School Class of 2006, Jaime A. Espinoza of the Cardozo Law School Class of 2007, and Aaron S.J. Zelinsky of the Yale Law School Class of 2010. I also thank Doris Zelinsky who, as usual, caught many (though probably not all) of my foibles.

Earlier versions of parts of this book appeared in Edward A. Zelinsky, *The Defined Contribution Paradigm* and are reprinted by permission of The Yale Law Journal Company and William S. Hein Company from THE YALE LAW JOURNAL, Volume 114, pages 451–534; in Edward A. Zelinsky, *Defined Contribution Plans After Enron: Exploring a Paradigm Shift* in Alvin D. Lurie (ed.), NEW YORK UNIVERSITY REVIEW OF EMPLOYEE BENEFITS AND EXECUTIVE COMPENSATION (2004); and in Edward A. Zelinsky, *The Defined Contribution Paradigm: Why It Happened and Why Social Security Accounts Didn't (At Least Not Yet)* in Alvin D. Lurie (ed.), NEW YORK UNIVERSITY REVIEW OF EMPLOYEE BENEFITS AND EXECUTIVE COMPENSATION (2006).

Introduction

Central to President Bush's vision of an "ownership society" are his proposals to introduce private accounts to Social Security, to revise the individual account provisions of the Internal Revenue Code and to expand the tax advantages of health savings accounts (HSAs).[1] To some, these proposals represent radical departures from the status quo. I offer a different perspective: The President's proposals continue the process of the last three decades by which the defined contribution paradigm has become the primary framework for retirement savings and, more broadly, a fundamental tenet of tax and social policy. In its own way, the emergence of the defined contribution paradigm has been a revolution, a revolution without a mastermind and without a cataclysmic event, but a revolution nonetheless which has, step-by-step, without fanfare, cumulatively transformed tax and social policy in fundamental ways.

Pension mavens (myself included) have framed the choice between the defined benefit and the defined contribution formats as a matter of risk allocation in the design of retirement savings programs.[2] The defined benefit configuration principally assigns risk to the employer (since the employer guarantees the employee a specified benefit) while the more privatized defined contribution approach

---

1   *See, e.g.*, Edmund L. Andrews, *Bush Promotes Earlier Proposals for Tax-Advantaged Savings Accounts*, N. Y. Times (January 21, 2004) at A16; Timothy Catts, *Personal Savings Account Proponents Mobilize On Bush's Cue*, 2004 TNT 14–3; Arleen Jacobius and Vineeta Anand, *Huge Implications*, 31(4) Pensions & Investments (February 17, 2003) at 1; Hal R. Varian, *Economic Scene*, N. Y. Times, March 13, 2003 at C2; Martin A. Sullivan, *Does the Trickle-Down Theory for Pensions Hold Water?* 98 Tax Notes 1180 (February 24, 2003). *See also, Bush to Streamline Pension Rules With New Tax-Free Savings Plans*, 2003 TNT 22–1 (February 3, 2003); Mary Williams Walsh, *Savings Plans Are Intended For Simplicity*, N.Y. Times (February 1, 2003) at B1; J. Christine Harris, *Simplifying Retirement Accounts Still Priority, Says Treasury Official*, 100 TAX Notes 1373 (September 15, 2003).

2   *See, e.g.*, David Millon, *Worker Ownership Through 401(k) Retirement Plans: Enron's Cautionary Tale*, 76 St. John's Law Rev. 835, 838 (2002) ("This development is important because defined-benefit and defined-contribution plans differ in how they allocate investment risk.").

apportions risk to the employee (since the adequacy of the employee's retirement resources in his individual account is the employee's problem). This remains an important truth as far as it goes.

However, the defined contribution society as it has emerged entails more considerations than this and can justly be called a paradigm shift, a fundamental transformation of the way Americans think about and implement tax and social policy (and, in this context, tax and social policy are largely the same). In a defined contribution society, the policies more likely to be adopted are those which channel government subsidies for retirement, health care and educational savings through individual accounts controlled by the taxpayer himself. In contrast, defined benefit arrangements—as exemplified by the traditional pension plan and the federal Social Security system—are less likely to be proposed, adopted or expanded.

I have four objectives in the discussion which follows. The first is empirical, to record how far we have traveled down the defined contribution road. Parts of this story are well-known, such as the rise of individual retirement accounts (IRAs) and of 401(k) arrangements as central features of American life. These defined contribution devices did not exist three decades ago. Today, it is difficult to imagine contemporary America without them. However, the story goes beyond these arrangements and involves elements which are often viewed in isolation but which, when pulled together, indicate how far we have become a defined contribution society. Some of these less well known elements, like the more familiar IRAs and 401(k)s, involve the private retirement system. The growth of cash balance pensions and their cousins, new comparability plans, are best understood as reflecting the prevailing defined contribution ethos. Equally striking is the extent to which the defined contribution format has, in the last several years, reconfigured many state retirement programs, which are correctly perceived as among the last bastions of the traditional defined benefit pension.

However, central to understanding the contemporary defined contribution culture is the extent to which individual accounts have spread beyond the realm of retirement savings to other arenas of social and tax policy. Section 529 accounts are today the predominant instrument by which Americans save for college. The path by which Section 529 accounts emerged in their current form is particularly revealing since, in their original incarnation, the arrangements which gave rise to Section 529 were conceived in defined benefit terms. The subsequent transformation of Section 529 into the individual account format testifies to the strength of the defined contribution culture.

We are now in the early stages of a comparable transformation of medical coverage, the flexible spending account (FSA), the health reimbursement arrangement (HRA) and the health savings account (HSA) emerging as important devices for financing routine medical care. In short, in the defined contribution society, the prototypical middle or upper-middle class American family funds its retirement through 401(k) accounts and IRAs, funds its children's college educations through Section 529 accounts, and finances its routine medical care through FSAs, HRAs and HSAs—all defined contribution devices nonexistent a generation ago.

My second goal in this book is to explore the causes of this transformation of tax and social policy. Again, parts of this story are well-known: the regulatory impact of the Employee Retirement Income Security Act of 1974 (ERISA);[3] economic and demographic forces including the decline of union membership and of traditional industries as well as the changing nature of work and the perception of a more mobile work force; employers' desire to shift the risks inherent in the provision of retirement savings from themselves to their employees. All of these forces have pushed employers and workers from traditional defined benefit plans toward defined contribution arrangements.

However, here again important elements of the story are not as well-known as they should be. To an important degree, the rise of the defined contribution framework reflects a story of unintended consequences and of path dependence. No one set out *ab initio* to create a defined contribution society. Initial decisions reinforced each other, leading us toward that society. Each early step made increasingly costly and thus unlikely the restoration to preeminence of the defined benefit format. The defined contribution paradigm, with its emphasis upon the individual account holder's ownership and control of his own resources, fits comfortably with the values of American society which privilege private ownership, individual control and personal self-sufficiency. Moreover, individual accounts have, in practice, worked well for many Americans, particularly middle-class and upper-middle-class Americans.

As part of this discussion, I explore the reasons for the failure (so far, at least) of proposals to incorporate private accounts into the federal Social Security program.

---

3   P.L. 93–406, 88 Stat. 829 (1974). Many ERISA provisions have repeatedly been amended since its adoption. Perhaps the most important of these amendments was the addition to the Internal Revenue Code of Section 401(k).

That failure reflects the limit (for now, at least) of the defined contribution paradigm and does not presage the imminent revival of traditional defined benefit plans.

My third goal is to speculate about the future of the defined contribution paradigm. Such speculation is, by its nature, speculative and thus error-prone. A comparable prognostication a generation ago could not have foreseen the rise of the defined contribution paradigm as we know it today.[4] Nevertheless, some possibilities can reasonably be ventured. As a matter of tax policy, the most plausible prediction for the future is the continuation and adaptation of the status quo, i.e., the current federal income tax, with heavy use of tax expenditures including what are widely considered to be tax subsidies for retirement savings and for other socially favored objectives. The defined contribution society is both a product of and a contributor to that status quo.

Another distinct possibility is that the defined contribution culture will, in piecemeal fashion, lead to the transformation of the federal income tax into a cash flow consumption tax.[5] In many quarters, the federal income tax is today characterized as a hybrid between a true levy on income, taxing all savings and consumption, and a tax on consumption only. From this vantage, the proliferation of individual accounts pushes the tax further down the road to an explicit consumption base by expanding the tax-favored treatment for different kinds of savings. President Bush's proposal for consolidating and reforming the various individual accounts now authorized in the Internal Revenue Code reflect the drive toward a consumption tax model of federal taxation.

As a political matter, the defined contribution paradigm, initiated in a bi-partisan, almost casual, fashion, will prove more contentious in the years ahead as focus increases upon public defined benefit arrangements, in particular, public employees' traditional defined benefit pensions. In contrast, in the private sector, the defined contribution model for retirement, health care and educational savings is entrenched and will continue to expand with little resistance.

---

[4]   In 1973, ERISA and the creation of the individual retirement account were a year away and by no means certain of passage.

[5]   Mitchell L. Engler and Michael S. Knoll, *Simplifying The Transition to a (Progressive) Consumption Tax*, 56 SMU Law Rev. 53, 62 (2003) (parenthetical in original) ("The principal change required to the existing tax base is the expansion of the current tax treatment of qualified accounts – such as IRAs, 401(k)s, etc. – to all investments, in effect providing an unlimited deduction for new savings.").

My final goal is to advance my own normative prescriptions for the defined contribution paradigm. Within the constraints of that paradigm, we have limited, albeit potentially important, choices, some more politically realistic than others. My final objective is to identify those choices and to indicate the ones I think best for a society which, for better or worse, has committed itself to the individual account framework for retirement, tax and social policy. Among the best choices we can make is to resolve to do no harm, i.e., to avoid heavy-handed regulation of defined contribution plans and the risks of unintended consequences stemming from such regulation. Among the judicious possibilities which I favor are changing the 401(k) rules so that employees, instead of affirmatively electing participation in 401(k) plans, must affirmatively opt out from such plans. Another proposal I endorse is expanding the federal income tax credit which subsidizes the retirement savings of low income employees to include contributions to educational and medical accounts as well. I would also extend to defined contribution plans the ceiling on holdings of employer stock which ceiling now applies only to defined benefit pensions.

The initial chapter of this book describes the differences between defined benefit and defined contribution plans as retirement savings devices. In this chapter, I emphasize the characteristics of the traditional defined benefit pension, which pays a deferred retirement annuity based on the participant's salary and work history, and the contemporary defined contribution plan, which is largely self-funded by the participant's salary reduction contributions and pays a single, lump sum to the participant. The second chapter discusses these differences as a matter of retirement plan design. Defined benefit arrangements principally allocate risk (and reward) to the sponsoring employer while defined contribution devices assign such risk and reward to the participant. In these initial chapters, pension cognoscenti are likely to find much that is familiar although I hope even some of the cognoscenti will find something here to chew on.

In the third chapter, I identify the major features of the contemporary defined contribution paradigm and its development to this point. The fourth chapter explores the causes of that development. In this chapter, I emphasize the themes of path dependency, unintended consequences, and cultural receptivity which help explain the emergence of the defined contribution paradigm.

In the fifth chapter, I place the defined contribution paradigm in the context of contemporary tax policy topics including consumption taxation and tax expenditures. I conclude that, under the most likely scenarios, the individual accounts of the defined contribution paradigm will persist as central features of federal tax law. As a matter of tax policy, individual accounts are likely to endure as prominent features of the federal income as we know it today, heavily laden with tax expenditures. Alternatively, the defined contribution paradigm may facilitate the transformation of the Internal Revenue Code into an explicit cash flow consumption tax by acclimating the public to tax-advantaged accounts. Either way, the defined contribution paradigm will persist as a central feature of federal tax policy.

In the sixth chapter, I speculate as to the future of the defined contribution society. In the private sector, the individual account paradigm will continue to expand with little controversy. In contrast, the defined contribution model will be a source of increasing contention in the public sector as state and municipal decisionmakers seek to emulate their private sector counterparts by shifting funding, investment and longevity risk to public employees. Such employees and their unions will resist the consequent termination of traditional defined benefit arrangements and their replacement with individual account plans.

Central to the resulting debate about individual accounts in the years ahead will be the basic concerns raised by the defined contribution paradigm: the benefits of individual ownership and control, the dangers of adverse selection, and the advantages of risk pooling.

Finally, I explore the choices presented to us by the defined contribution paradigm and identify those which I think are best.

Among the conclusions I draw from all of this is that I and others concerned about the stagnation of the defined benefit system have underestimated the magnitude of the forces underlying that stagnation and the concomitant rise of the defined contribution paradigm. The regulatory burdens imposed by ERISA on defined benefit plans were an initial, important cause in the creation of the defined contribution culture as we know it today. However, we are now far down the defined contribution road. Alleviating the overregulation of defined benefit plans will not resuscitate the defined benefit format. The individual account model both reflects and reinforces cultural norms of private ownership and control. That model has worked well for many individuals. For the foreseeable future, tax and retirement policy will be shaped by the limits and opportunities of the defined contribution paradigm.

While the emergence of the defined contribution society has been a quiet, largely unheralded, revolution, a revolution it has been, incrementally but fundamentally changing the manner in which Americans think about tax and social policy and the manner in which their governments formulate such policy. In an important sense, it does not matter whether President Bush implements his ownership society proposals for Social Security or expanded savings accounts. Even if these proposals are not enacted into law, the defined contribution paradigm is and will remain deeply ensconced in American life.

Like any other paradigm shift, the emergence of the defined contribution society has both opened opportunities and foreclosed possibilities. As the members of the Baby Boom generation provide for their retirements, educate their offspring and prepare for the medical costs of their older years, the defined contribution format will be the framework governing their choices.

CHAPTER ONE

How Are They Different? The Defined Benefit and Defined Contribution Formats Contrasted As A Matter of Plan Design

In the often opaque morass of pension terminology, the distinction between defined benefit and defined contribution plans is surprisingly transparent. A defined benefit pension, as its name implies, specifies an output for the participant. Traditionally, such plans defined benefits for particular employees based on the employees' respective salary histories and their periods of employment.[1] Thus, for example, a prototypical defined benefit formula specifies that a participant is entitled at retirement to an annual income equal to a percentage of his average salary times the number of years of his employment with the sponsoring employer.[2]

---

[1]   Union-sponsored plans often use service only in determining the participant's retirement benefits, e.g., $20 of monthly retirement income for each year of covered employment. *See, e.g., Schweizer Aircraft Corporation v. Local 1752*, 29 F.3d 83 (2nd cir. 1994) (describing a typical union pension under which the participant's monthly annuity at retirement is solely a function of the number of her covered years of service with the employer).

[2]   *See* Edward A. Zelinsky, *The Cash Balance Controversy*, 19 VA. TAX REV. 683 (2000) at 687–691 (hereinafter, *Cash Balance Controversy*); John H. Langbein, Susan J. Stabile and Bruce A. Wolk, PENSION AND EMPLOYEE BENEFIT LAW (4th ed. 2006) at 43; Dan M. McGill, Kyle N. Brown, John J. Haley, and Sylvester J. Schieber, FUNDAMENTALS OF PRIVATE PENSIONS (7th ed. 1996) at 201–210; Ken Vollmer, 33(1) THE ASPA JOURNAL (Jan.-Feb. 2003) at 7.

In contrast, a defined contribution arrangement, as its equally apt moniker indicates, specifies an input for the participant. Commonly, the plan defines the employer's contribution for each participant as a percentage of the participant's salary for that year. Having made that contribution, the employer's obligation to fund is over since the employee is not guaranteed a particular benefit, just a specified input. In a defined contribution context, the participant's ultimate economic entitlement is the amount to which the defined contributions for him, plus earnings, grow or shrink.

Defined contribution plans classically took the form of employer-sponsored pensions (often denoted "money purchase pensions") and of employment-based profit sharing arrangements. In the pension incarnation, the employer sponsoring a defined contribution arrangement has a fixed annual obligation to contribute, typically a percentage of the participant's salary. The profit sharing alternative, on the other hand, gives the employer flexibility in determining its contribution. Most obviously, the sponsoring employer need not contribute anything in a year without profits, unlike a pension obligation which is a fixed cost unrelated to profitability.[3] Profit sharing plans can also be designed to permit the employer to decide annually how much of its profits it wants to contribute. The great flexibility of profit sharing plans explains their increasing popularity in recent years, particularly when that flexibility is contrasted with the regulatory rigidities surrounding defined benefit pensions.

Historically, defined benefit arrangements have promised participants benefits at retirement in the form of periodic (typically monthly) annuity-style payments for the duration of the retired participant's life. Amounts to fund these benefits (paid by the employer, sometimes augmented by employee contributions) are invested in a trust fund supervised by trustees. At retirement, the fund pays the (now retired) employee his defined benefit or purchases an annuity contract for him to provide such periodic benefit.

---

[3] Defined benefit plans are, by definition, pensions since the employer is obligated to fund the benefit promised to its employees. *See* Treas. Section Reg. 1.401–1(b)(1)(i) ("A pension plan within the meaning of section 401(a) is a plan established and maintained by an employer primarily to provide systematically for the payment of definitely determinable benefits to his employees over a period of years, usually for life, after retirement."). *Cf.* Treas. Reg. Section 1.401–1(b)(1)(ii) ("A profit-sharing plan is a plan established and maintained by an employer to provide for the participation in his profits by his employees or their beneficiaries.").

Thus, traditional defined benefit pensions have four major characteristics as a matter of plan design. First, they provide income on a deferred basis at retirement and not before then.[4] Second, traditional defined benefit plans provide such retirement income as periodic, annuity-type payments, rather than as single lump sums. Third, traditional defined benefit plans are funded collectively, the employer's contributions being pooled in a common trust fund from which all participants receive their benefits. Finally, the defined benefit format places on the employer (rather than the employee) the obligation to fund the benefit promised to the participating employee. If the funds in the trust are inadequate to pay promised benefits, the employer is obligated to make up the shortfall. Thus, as I shall discuss in the next chapter, the risks associated with funding a defined benefit pension fall principally[5] on the employer.

In all four respects, the prototypical defined contribution retirement plan is today different. The contemporary defined contribution arrangement distributes to an employee when he leaves employment, even if the employee is well short of retirement age.[6] Typically the distribution from a defined contribution plan today takes the form of a single, lump sum payout of the employee's account balance, rather than an annuity or other periodic distribution spread over time.[7] By its nature, a defined contribution plan does not pool resources like a defined benefit pension but, rather, establishes for each participant his own individual account. Allocated to that account are the employer's contributions for the employee, the employee's own contributions (if any), and the earnings (or losses) generated by the investment of all those contributions. For this reason, defined contribution plans are synonymously known as individual account plans.[8]

---

4   Defined benefit plans often pay a death benefit to the employee's spouse if the employee dies while working and pay a disability payment if the employee becomes disabled while working. However, as to a living, healthy employee, the typical traditional defined benefit plan starts payments at retirement and not before then.

5   If an employer fails financially with an underfunded defined benefit plan, the funding shortfall may be the responsibility of the Pension Benefit Guaranty Corporation (PBGC), the federal corporation which provides FDIC-type insurance to defined benefit plans. If the employer is insolvent and the employee's benefit exceeds the level insured by the PBGC, the employee may be out of luck. On balance, however, the observation in the text is correct: the sponsor of a defined benefit plan undertakes to guarantee a specified output at retirement and thus bears the principal risk of a funding shortfall.

6   *See* Patrick J. Purcell, *Pension Issues: Lump-Sum Distributions and Retirement Income Security*, CRS Report for Congress, RL30496 (June 30, 2003) (hereinafter, *Lump-Sum Distributions*) at Summary ("Thus, most recipients of lump sums were more than 20 years away from retirement.").

7   *Id.* at CRS-6 ("Almost all defined contribution plans offer a lump-sum payment option.").

8   *See* ERISA Section 3(34). In this book, I shall use the terms "defined contribution plan" and "individual account plan" interchangeably.

Since the employee's entitlement under the plan is the balance of his individual account, good investment performance redounds to the employee's benefit (because the account balance will be larger) while, symmetrically, poor investment performance hurts the employee (because the employee's account balance will be smaller and the employer has no obligation to fund a defined benefit). Thus, as I also emphasize in the next chapter, defined contribution plans, in contradistinction to defined benefit arrangements, shift investment risk and reward from the employer to the employee.

Increasingly, defined contribution assets, while formally held in trust funds, are invested by each employee himself. Under such "self-directed" arrangements,[9] the employee chooses the investments for the amounts in his individual account. For many participants, self-directed accounts solidify the participants' sense of ownership and control and are thus more consonant with American norms of private property than are defined benefit arrangements, financed by pooled funds invested by the employer.

In short, the label "defined benefit," standing by itself, is in important ways incomplete. The traditional defined benefit plan specified a quite particular kind of benefit, a deferred annuity, starting at retirement, typically measured by the employee's work and salary history. Similarly, today the moniker "defined contribution" predominantly refers to a profit sharing plan with a salary reduction (401(k)) arrangement[10] and participant-directed investing, a plan which distributes to a participant as a lump sum upon the severance of employment[11] (which, in a world of employee mobility,[12] takes place often before retirement age). Thus, as we shall see, the shift from the defined benefit modality to the defined contribution format has altered in a fundamental manner the way in which Americans experience and think about retirement savings. That shift has also altered the ways in which other areas of tax and social policy are today approached.

---

[9] Such self-directed accounts are authorized under ERISA Section 404(c)(1).

[10] Congressional Budget Office, *Utilization of Tax Incentives for Retirement Saving,* (August, 2003) at 5 (hereinafter, "Utilization") ("All of the growth in participation in defined-contribution plans between 1975 and 1997 can be attributed to 401(k) plans.").

[11] Sometimes a defined contribution distribution may occur even before the participant's separation from service. *See* Treas. Reg. Section 1.401–1(b)(1)(ii) (permitting in-service profit sharing distributions as long as "the funds accumulated under the plan" for "a fixed number of years").

[12] *See* Purcell, *Lump-Sum Distributions, supra* note 6 at Summary ("A typical 25-year-old today will work for seven or more employers before reaching age 65 . . . . ").

Why Does It Matter? Allocating Risk and Reward Between Employer and Employee

In this chapter, I probe the basic features of defined benefit and defined contribution plans in terms of the allocation of risk and reward in the design of retirement arrangements. This is the traditional way of contrasting defined benefit and defined contribution plans. As I discuss in Chapter Four, there are broader cultural implications in the choice between defined benefit and individual account plans: Defined contribution plans, with their individual accounts, fit more comfortably with norms of private ownership and control than do defined benefit arrangements. However, in terms of retirement planning, there are a variety of risks which the defined benefit arrangement assigns to the employer and which a defined contribution plan allocates to the employee. In assigning those risks to the employer, the defined benefit model also pools such risks by centralizing them with the employer.

As an initial matter, it is useful to divide these retirement-related risks into three broad categories—investment risk, funding risk and longevity risk—although, as we shall soon see, within these categories there are important subclasses which could plausibly be treated themselves as separate categories of risk.

A. Investment Risk

Consider initially investment risk,[1] the risk that retirement resources will earn an inadequate rate of return. Defined benefit arrangements impose investment risk upon the sponsoring employer since the employer, having promised specified retirement benefits, must provide the additional contributions to fund those promised benefits even if the plan's assets earn disappointing returns. In contrast, defined contribution arrangements shift the risk of poor (and the rewards of better) investment performance to the employee since his entitlement under the plan is his account balance, however low (or high) that balance might be.

For several reasons, it is often advantageous for the employer to absorb investment risk via a defined benefit arrangement.[2] An employer, investing a single large pool of pension assets through a trust holding defined benefit assets, can obtain economies of scale unavailable to the employees each investing for himself, particularly since the employees are often investing relatively small amounts. By spreading transaction costs over a single large pool of capital, the employer sponsoring a defined benefit arrangement can achieve a higher net rate of return than can his employees, each investing on his own. Assigning investment risk to the employer (as defined benefit arrangements do) also pools with the employer the risks, assets and investment rewards which individual accounts assign to individual account holders.[3]

For example, employers (or, to be precise, the pension trustees appointed by employers) may negotiate lower brokerage commissions because, in the defined benefit context, they are investing a single, common pool of capital from which guaranteed benefits will be paid. In contrast, the individual participant, investing his own funds in an IRA or other individual account, has less bargaining leverage over commissions because he has less to invest on his own. Even if (as is typically

---

[1]   Langbein, Stabile and Wolk, *supra* chap. one note 2 at 43.

[2]   *See* Daniel I. Halperin, *Employer-Based Retirement Income—the Ideal, the Possible, and the Reality,* 11 ELDER L.J. 37, 61 ("Employers have much greater capacity than employees to absorb the risks associated with investment performance. Besides benefiting from economies of scale, the employer can average out investment results among cohorts of retirees, so it need not worry about a temporary market downturn.").

[3]   For an insightful discussion of the relationship among risk assignment, risk pooling and risk reduction, see David A. Moss, WHEN ALL ELSE FAILS: GOVERNMENT AS THE ULTIMATE RISK MANAGER (2002) at 17–20.

the case) an employer, as plan sponsor, hires an investment manager to help each employee manage his own retirement funds in self-directed accounts, the investment manager, in pricing his services, must consider the costs of the multiple transactions which occur when investment decisions are dispersed among the employees rather than centralized in the plan's trustees.

Similar concerns arise in the context of investment advice and education. It is now widely perceived that, when employees invest their own funds, they need professional advice and education.[4] The cost of this advice and education must come from somewhere. Even if the employer nominally pays for these services, ultimately the employees themselves likely bear the cost in the form of reduced employer contributions to the plan or lower cash wages, or some combination of the two. Even if the firm hired to provide advice and education to employees does not explicitly charge for these services, the costs will be built into the overall fee structure which, in the final analysis, falls upon the employees.

While the trustees managing defined benefit assets may also want advice and assistance, it is cheaper to provide that help once to the managers of a centralized pool of capital rather than separately and repeatedly to myriad employee-investors.

In theory, economies of scale can be achieved when investing defined contribution assets since these assets too can be controlled on a centralized basis by the plan's trustees. In that case also, the costs of commissions and investment advice can be spread over a larger pool of employer-managed capital with resulting economies of scale.

In practice, however, today defined contribution plans typically take the form of self-directed 401(k) plans under which the employee invests his own resources, even if his investment choice is simply to leave his funds in the plan's default investment option. Thus, the realistic choice today is between defined benefit plans,

---

4   See, e.g,., Jayne Elizabeth Zanglein, *Investment Without Education: The Disparate Impact on Women and Minorities in Self-Directed Defined Contribution Plans*, 5 EMPL. RTS. & EMPLOY. POL'Y J. 223, 268 (2001) ("All participants, including women, men, minorities, low-income workers, part-time employees, youth, and the elderly must be taught the fundamentals of investments.") Janice Kay Lawrence, *Pension Reform in the Aftermath of Enron: Congress' Failure to Deliver the Promise of Secure Retirement to 401(k) Plan Participants*, 92 KY. LAW J. 1, 13 (2003–2004) ("Finally, meaningful pension reform must include the mandatory provision of independent, individually-tailored investment advice as a cost of transferring investment decisions to participants.") As noted below, I am skeptical about mandating such investment education until there is evidence that it works.

with the economies of scale they can achieve through centralized investment of a single pooled fund, and self-directed defined contribution plans which, in contrast, entail proportionately higher transaction costs because retirement resources are managed on a dispersed basis by individual employees in their own separate accounts.[5]

And even with expense and effort devoted to employee education, it is unclear how successful such education can be. Astute observers conclude that, even when investment education is provided to rank-and-file employees, such employees rarely match the investment performance of the typical defined benefit trustee.[6]

A less formal statement of this analysis is that many employees in self-directed defined contribution arrangements are poor investors, regardless of how much is spent educating and advising them.[7] While not all employers (or, to be precise, not all trustees designated by employers) are great investors, on balance, the average defined benefit trustee is likely to be a more sophisticated investor than is the typical 401(k) participant, even with education and professional advice provided to that participant. Indeed, there is mounting empirical evidence that many 401(k) investors accept whatever default investments are designated under the plan.[8] This passivity might be viewed as evidence that employers tend to select default

---

5   *See* Colleen E. Medill, *Challenging The Four 'Truths' of Personal Social Security Accounts: Evidence From the World of 401(k) Plans*, 81 NORTH CAR. L. REV. 901, 907–908, 937–946 (2003) (discussing the impact of "mutual fund fees" on "the worker's account balance at retirement"). *See also* Alicia H. Munnell, *Comments*, in Benjamin M. Friedman (ed.), SHOULD THE UNITED STATES PRIVATIZE SOCIAL SECURITY (1999) at 137 (noting that "IRA-type account(s)" are "extremely costly" in terms of "transaction costs"). As I discuss *infra*, the extra costs associated with the individual's investment of his retirement account are, from the perspective of the financial services industries, service-based profits.

6   Norman Stein, *Three and Possibly Four Lessons About ERISA That We Should, But Probably Will Not, Learn From Enron*, 76 ST. JOHN'S LAW REV. 855, 861–868 (2002) ("investment education" "is problematic"). *See also* Medill, *supra* note 5 at 908, 947–953 ("These studies predict that a program of investment education aimed at workers who invest in personal accounts will have little influence on their investment behavior.")

7   *See, e.g.*, David M. Cutler, *Comments*, in Friedman, *supra* note 5 at 129 ("many people [particularly the poor] may not be good investors.") (parenthetical in original). *See also* Jeff Sommer, *Chilly Reception for Savings*, N.Y. TIMES (June 8, 2003), Section 3 (Money & Business) at 6 ("Most Americans spend less time making investment choices for their 401(k) accounts than they do buying household appliances, according to a survey released last week by Putnam Investments.").

8   *See, e.g.*, James J. Choi, David Laibson, Brigitte Madrian and Andrew Metrick, *For Better or For Worse: Default Effects and 401(k) Savings Behavior*, National Bureau of Economic Research Working Paper 8651 (December, 2001) at 5 ("Under automatic enrollment, 65–87% of new plan participants save at the default contribution rate and invest exclusively in the default fund.") James J. Choi, David Laibson,

options which correspond to employees' investment preferences. I think it is more realistic to view that passivity as a sign that many rank-and-file 401(k) participants are disengaged investors.

The notion that many rank-and-file plan participants are poor investors is reinforced by the increasingly influential body of literature associated with the seminal writings of the late Amos Tversky and Daniel Kahneman, writings today often denoted as "behavioral economics".[9] In the Tversky-Kahneman world, individuals, among other cognitive biases, irrationally value items which they currently own in comparison to the items they do not (the "endowment effect"),[10] make substantively inconsistent decisions depending upon the fashion in which the inquiry is posed (the "framing effect"),[11] become stuck in their original (now incorrect) assessments of values ("anchoring")[12] and procrastinate in implementing investment decisions they know are best.[13] One need not accept the broadest claims made in the name of behavioral economics to agree that a significant number of rank-and-file employees will be poor investors of their retirement savings because of these kinds of cognitive biases[14] and that such investors would,

---

Brigitte Madrian and Andrew Metrick, *Defined Contribution Pensions. Plan Rules, Participant Decisions, and the Path of Least Resistance*, National Bureau of Economic Research Working Paper 8655 (December, 2001) ("[E]mployer choices of default savings rates and default investment funds strongly influence employee savings levels. Even though employees have the opportunity to opt out of such defaults, few actually do so."). *See also* Medill, *supra* note 5 at 909, 968–970 ("The research concerning automatic enrollment 401(k) plans indicates that a high percentage of participants are invested exclusively in the plan's designated default investment fund."); Cass R. Sunstein and Richard H. Thaler, *Libertarian Paternalism is Not an Oxymoron*, 70 U. OF CHICAGO LAW REV., 1159, 1172–1173 (2003); Peter K. Swisher, *Automatic 401(k) Opportunities and Challenges: Using Behavioral Finance to Make 401(k) Plans More Successful*, 36(2) THE ASPPA JOURNAL 9 (March-April 2006).

[9] *See, e.g., Empirical Legal Realism: A New Social Scientific Assessment of Law and Human Behavior*, Symposium, 97 NORTHWESTERN UNIV. L. REV. 1075 (2003).

[10] Russell Korobkin, *The Endowment Effect and Legal Analysis*, 97 NORTHWESTERN UNIV. L. REV. 1227 (2003).

[11] David Fetherstonhaugh and Lee Ross, *Framing Effects and Income Flow Preferences in Decisions about Social Security* in Henry J. Aaron, BEHAVIORAL DIMENSIONS OF RETIREMENT ECONOMICS (1999); Edward A. Zelinsky, *Do Tax Expenditures Create Framing Effects? Volunteer Firefighters, Property Tax Exemptions, and The Paradox of Tax Expenditure Analysis*, 24 VIRGINIA TAX REV. 797 (2005).

[12] Jeffrey J. Rachlinski, *The Uncertain Psychological Case For Paternalism*, 97 NORTHWESTERN UNIV. L. REV. 1165, 1171 (2003); Sunstein and Thaler, *supra* note 8 at 1177–1178 ("anchors have an effect—sometimes a startlingly large one").

[13] Ted O'Donoghue and Matthew Rabin, *Procrastination in Preparing for Retirement*, in Aaron, *supra* note 11 at 149 (people "plan to invest wisely but then procrastinate in carrying out these plans.").

[14] Rachlinski, *supra* note 12 at 1182–1187 (discussing "the role cognitive errors play in the regulation of financial decisions").

for the long run, be better off with their retirement resources invested by an employer-engaged trustee, as under a defined benefit arrangement.[15]

Moreover, investment skills are not distributed randomly throughout the population. Women, for example, tend to be poorer investors than men;[16] the uneducated tend to invest less well than do those with more schooling.[17] Thus, the movement to the defined contribution paradigm, with the resulting shift of investment risk to employees, is not neutral in its impact but rather harms certain segments of the populace while yielding upside possibilities to other portions of the population.

David F. Swensen succinctly summarizes the argument that few 401(k) and IRA account holders invest their retirement assets well:

> Most individuals lack the specialized knowledge necessary to succeed in today's highly competitive investment markets. Poor asset allocation, ill-considered active management, and perverse market timing lead the list of errors made by individual investors. Even with a massive educational effort, the likelihood of producing a nation of effective investors seems small.[18]

A component of investment risk (possibly thought of as a separate kind of risk altogether) stems from employers' longer time horizons which permit employers (or, again, to be precise, plan trustees engaged by employers) to invest in riskier but ultimately more profitable investments than can many employees, particularly older persons with shorter time horizons to retirement and thus less ability to make riskier investments. The basic considerations are now well known under

---

[15] As noted above, theoretically, defined contribution plan assets can be invested by trustees selected by employers. However, in practice today defined contribution plans entail participants' self-direction of their respective individual accounts.

[16] *See, e.g.,* Dana M. Muir, *The Dichotomy Between Investment Advice and Investment Education: Is No Advice Really the Best Advice?* 23 BERKELEY J. EMP. & LAB. L. 1, 16 (2002) ("Studies of plan investor behavior uniformly find that women have a lower tolerance for risk than do male investors.") and Zanglein, *supra* note 4 at 226 ("Studies show that women and minorities bear a disproportionate risk of earning lower returns on their investments because, on average, they make more conservative investments than white males.").

[17] *See* Muir, *id.* at 16 ("{M}ore net worth and greater education both are predictors that a plan investor will allocate more assets to equity securities.").

[18] David F. Swensen, UNCONVENTIONAL SUCCESS: A FUNDAMENTAL APPROACH TO PERSONAL INVESTMENT (2005) at 4.

the rubric of portfolio theory:[19] Most[20] investments entail risk, i.e., variability in the investment's return. Some risk is specific to the particular firm; other risk arises from the movement of the market as a whole. Firm-specific risk can be eliminated by diversifying investments among firms. A rainy summer may be good for umbrella manufacturers but bad for sun screen makers. If an investor invests some of her 401(k) account in each, she has eliminated the firm-specific effects of rain on her portfolio.

On the other hand, market risk cannot be eliminated by diversifying investments since all firms are part of the market. Both umbrella manufacturers and sun screen makers have lower sales in periods of high unemployment. However, some investments entail greater market risk than do others. For example, Firm A's economic performance, while affected by overall economic conditions, may swing within relatively narrow parameters while Firm B's economic performance may oscillate over a greater range, depending upon prevailing economic conditions.

In order to attract capital, an investment in Firm B must yield a higher expected return to compensate for the greater market risk associated with Firm B. Consequently, for the long run, an investor in Firm B expects a higher return—often denoted an "equity premium"[21]—than if he had deployed his capital to an investment in less risky Firm A. However, the long run may be very long.

A thirty-year-old investor, with retirement as a distant eventuality, might comfortably expose his portfolio to the risk associated with Firm B to earn Firm B's greater, long run expected return. In contrast, a seventy year-old, on the verge of retirement, might eschew Firm B for Firm A since the variability associated with Firm B looks more daunting to someone about to retire, with the shorter time horizon imminent retirement entails. A drop in the value of Firm B, a minor blip for the thirty-year-old, could be a financial disaster for the seventy-year-old.

---

[19] For a technical presentation of these ideas, see Zvi Bodie and Robert C. Merton, FINANCE (2000) at 255–257, 272–277, 299–303, 318–337. For a presentation aimed at a general audience, see M. John Sterba, Jr., FUNDAMENTALS OF PERSONAL INVESTING (1997) at 8–43. *See also* Swensen, *supra* note 18 at 87–90.

[20] Only the debt instruments of the U.S. Treasury are considered riskless.

[21] *See, e.g.,* Swensen, *supra* note 18 at 38–40; Shannon P. Pratt, Robert F. Reilly and Robert P. Schweihs, VALUING A BUSINESS, THE ANALYSIS AND APPRAISAL OF CLOSELY HELD COMPANIES (4th ed. 2000) at 161–162.

However, if the seventy-year-old participates in a defined benefit plan, that plan might well invest in Firm B since the plan's time horizon is, if not infinite, much longer than the participant's. The plan, as an institution, is financing benefits for an entire workforce. Indeed, the plan typically anticipates providing benefits well after the seventy-year-old has died. Here, again, we see that assignment of investment risk to the employer also entails the centralized pooling of risk which would otherwise be diffused among individual investors.

To approach the matter from another vantage, for a seventy-year-old on the verge of retirement, a prolonged bear market can be a disaster, depressing his 401(k) account just when he will start to live off of it. In contrast, for his employer's defined benefit plan, that bear market may be a buying opportunity for the common pool of assets financing the benefits promised by that plan.

From this perspective, the older 401(k) participant's choice of a riskier investment with a higher long run return is potentially problematic since he may not have the time to wait for the investment's rebound—assuming that rebound will occur.[22] In contrast, with a longer time horizon, a defined benefit plan can more comfortably make this riskier but (for the long term) more profitable investment. This sub-category of investment risk can be denoted as "temporal risk," the time-based danger associated with riskier investments because such investments' variability may strike on the downside at an inopportune time in the individual's life span, namely, when he needs his retirement resources to live.

The participant can respond to this temporal risk by eschewing riskier investments, but a more conservative strategy reduces his long-term rate of return as he limits himself to less aggressive possibilities. Alternatively, a defined contribution participant concerned about the temporal risk of aggressive investments but sensitive to the lower returns earned by more conservative deployments of his capital can use his individual account resources to purchase an annuity contract. The insurer issuing that annuity contract (like a defined benefit plan) has a longer (arguably infinite) time horizon which permits the insurer to invest

---

[22]   If the seventy-year-old conceives of his retirement resources as testamentary in nature, his perspective may be different since, in that case, he may think in terms of the longer life expectancies of his younger heirs, intended to be the ultimate recipients of those resources. However, insofar as retirement resources are for financing retirement, the seventy-year-old has a far shorter time horizon than does the thirty-year-old.

more aggressively. The insurer's consequently superior long-run investment return will be reflected in the terms of the annuity contract purchased by the participant.

However, this private response to temporal risk carries with it many of the shortcomings identified earlier in the context of participant-directed investing: There are diseconomies of scale when myriad defined contribution retirees purchase annuities individually. Many of those retirees may be unsophisticated investors who are either ignorant of temporal risk or of their ability to contract out of it by purchasing annuity policies from companies with longer time horizons. Paying to educate these investors costs money and is not always successful. This is another argument for the defined benefit plan which, by imposing temporal risk on the employer, facilitates better long-term investment performance of retirement savings.

Some analysts suggest that, going forward, there will be less of a bonus for risky investments than there has been in the past, or perhaps none at all.[23] Among other reasons, more investors, the argument goes, today understand the higher return from owning risky assets and have accordingly bid up the prices of these assets. Greater demand for risky investments makes them pricier which, in turn, reduces the expected return on those investments.

For purposes of my analysis, it does not matter whether the equity premium for the future is smaller than that premium has been in the past. As long as there is some nontrivial benefit for the long run to holding riskier investments, investors who can hold for the long run are, because of the impact of interest compounding, better off than are those investors who cannot tolerate the risk associated with such higher return investments.

If, for example, a forty-year-old invests $100 for thirty years at two percent (2%), she will have $181 dollars at age seventy. If she invests that same $100 for the same thirty years at three percent (3%), she will have $243 at age seventy, over one-third (1/3) more. With compounding, an equity premium need not be large to have a significant, long-term impact on the investor's retirement resources. The trustees of defined benefit plans, as institutional investors with long (perhaps infinite) time horizons, can deploy capital for greater risk and correspondingly greater return than can many (perhaps most) individual investors managing their own retirement accounts.

---

[23]   See, e.g., Robert J. Shiller, IRRATIONAL EXUBERANCE (2000) at 192–197.

B.   Funding Risk

A second major category of risk allocated to the employer by the defined benefit format can be denoted "funding risk," i.e., the danger that the funds necessary to finance adequate retirement benefits will not be contributed to the plan. A defined benefit plan places responsibility upon the employer for financing the benefits promised by the plan. Indeed, as I will discuss in Chapter Three, ERISA imposes complex and opaque funding obligations on defined benefit sponsors to ensure that that responsibility is executed properly. In similar fashion, a money purchase pension, though a defined contribution device, is a pension plan and thus imposes upon the employer the legal responsibility to fund the contributions required under the plan. While the employee is not guaranteed that those contributions will grow to any particular level (investment risk and reward fall on the employee), the employee covered by a money purchase arrangement is assured that the employer will, as an initial matter, make the promised inputs to the plan.

In practice, however, defined contribution plans today come, not in the pension variant, but in forms which place the principal funding risk on the employee. Most[24] 401(k) plans require the employee to elect reduced salary for funds to be contributed to the plan on the employee's behalf. If an employee does not so elect, the failure to fund his 401(k) account (and thus his retirement) is the employee's problem, not the employer's responsibility.

Consider also conventional profit sharing plans under which the employer, in its discretion, may or may not contribute to the plan in any given year. Since the employer has no obligation to make discretionary profit sharing contributions in any particular year,[25] the employer's failure to make such contributions causes the employee's account to be unfunded. While the employee has no legal obligation to fund in this context, the economic risk of no or inadequate funding falls upon the employee since the employer's failure to make adequate contributions to its profit sharing plan results in a deficient account for the employee at retirement.

---

[24]   Some so-called "safe harbor" 401(k) plans provide for an automatic employer contribution equal to three percent (3%) of the employee's salary even if the employee does not contribute to the plan on his own. Code Section 401(k)(12)(C).

[25]   An employer cannot avoid profit sharing contributions indefinitely. To qualify as a profit sharing plan, there must, over the years, "be recurring and substantial contributions out of profits for the employees". Treas. Reg. Section 1.401–1(b)(2). However, as indicated in the text, there is no requirement of a profit sharing contribution in any particular year.

Here, again, the insights of behavioral economics lead to troubling conclusions: Many individuals, even those who know better, procrastinate in saving for retirement.[26] By shifting funding risk to employees, i.e., by requiring 401(k) participants to make affirmative decisions to save from current salary, the defined contribution paradigm may be pushing many employees down the path of inadequate retirement savings.

C. Longevity Risk

Consider finally longevity risk, namely, the danger that a retiree will outlive his retirement resources.[27] One can characterize this risk in a variety of ways, e.g., as the possibility that a retiree's improvidence in his initial years of retirement will diminish his resources for later. Less judgmentally, longevity risk can be understood as the possibility that a retiree will underestimate his life expectancy and will therefore overconsume in his early years of retirement, thinking (erroneously) that he has fewer years to live than he in fact does. Another characterization of longevity risk is that a retiree, while working, may save too little for retirement; that, once retired, the retiree will attempt to maintain a higher standard of living than he can afford; and that he will thereby deplete his savings with many years yet to live. To take yet another view, a retiree with a below-average life expectancy will rationally eschew the purchase of an annuity contract on the theory that his premiums are likely to subsidize those expected to live longer than him. However, some of those with lower anticipated life expectancies *ex ante* will in fact live longer than expected and thus retrospectively should have participated in an annuity pool to guarantee resources for their later years.

Whichever characterization is appropriate, the traditional, annuity-paying defined benefit plan provides at least partial protection against longevity risk since such a traditional pension disburses retirement payments periodically

---

26   *See, e.g.*, Annamaria Lusardi, *Information, Expectations, and Savings for Retirement*, in Aaron, *supra* note 11 at 82 ("as many as one-third of people aged 51–61 have not begun to think about retirement") and at 103 ("A large percentage of U.S. households that are nearing retirement age have little or no wealth. Although many explanations can be found, people have often simply not thought about retirement and they have done little or no planning."); O'Donoghue and Rabin, *supra* note 13 at 128 ("as retirement planning becomes more important, people may become *more* likely to procrastinate") (emphasis in original).

27   *See* McGill, *supra chap. one* note 2 at 444; Peter Orszag and Norman Stein, *Cross-Tested Defined Contribution Plans: A Response to Professor Zelinsky*, 49 BUFFALO L. REV. 629 (2001) at 651–656; Richard A. Ippolito, PENSIONS, ECONOMICS AND PUBLIC POLICY (1986) at 30–32.

(typically monthly) and continues such annuity-type payments until the participant's death—often with payments continuing to the participant's surviving spouse. With such a lifetime annuity, it is, by definition, impossible for the retiree to outlive his pension income, though that income may decline in real value if not increased to reflect increments in the cost of living.[28]

The defined contribution participant can, on his own, eliminate his longevity risk by annuitizing his account balance. In particular, a retiree can use his account balance from a 401(k) or other kind of profit sharing plan, a money purchase plan or an IRA to buy an individual commercial annuity policy for himself (and, perhaps, his spouse). That annuity policy will replicate the periodic, lifetime payout from a defined benefit arrangement.

However, such individualized solutions to the problem of longevity risk entail adverse selection[29] for the insurers selling individual annuity policies, i.e., the danger that those most concerned about longevity risk and purchasing protection against it will indeed be the persons who live longest. The retirees buying commercial annuities for themselves because they are concerned about longevity risk tend to be people who perceive (often accurately) that they are healthier than their peers and thus likely to live beyond their actuarial life expectancies. Consequently, commercial insurers charge a premium for the individual annuity policies they sell because the purchasers of such policies tend to be more long-lived than their peers who do not purchase such annuities.[30] The premium

---

28   William G. Gale and Peter R. Orszag, *Whither Pensions? A Brief Analysis of Portman-Cardin III*, 99 Tax Notes 573, 574 (April 28, 2003) ("annuitization is crucial to ensuring that retirees will not outlive their savings").

29   Michael J. Graetz and Jerry L. Mashaw, True Security (1999) at 16 (defining adverse selection as "the tendency of those at high risk to be overrepresented in the insurance pool.") *See also* Bodie and Merton, *supra* note 19 at 270–272. Peter H. Schuck has recently defined adverse selection as a "diversity-related impediment to market efficiency." According to Professor Schuck, "(w)here participants in an insurance pool are diverse in ways that pose significantly different risks of loss but their premiums are based on average risk rather than on their own risk, people who pose lower-than-average risks will want to avoid or abandon this pool in favor of insurance for which they can pay a premium reflecting their own, lower risk." Peter H. Schuck, Diversity in America (2003) at 58. *See also* Peter A. Diamond and Peter R. Orszag, Saving Social Security (2004) at 73 ("Adverse selection stems from the fact that those who expect to benefit more from insurance are more likely to buy it.").

30   Colleen E. Medill, *supra* note 5 at 958–959 ("The traditional explanation given by economists for the low demand for traditional annuities is the problem of adverse selection." "Annuity providers will price the traditional annuity at a higher cost to account for this systemic increased risk of longevity among purchasers of traditional annuities."); *see also* General Accounting Office, *Social Security Reform: Information on Using a Voluntary Approach to Individual Accounts*, GAO-03-309 (March, 2003)

from the insurers' perspective is a penalty from the retirees' vantage point. This penalty/premium leads many experts to prefer the defined benefit arrangement as a superior device for mitigating longevity risk.[31]

That defined benefit plans manage longevity risk particularly well highlights the relationship between the assignment of such risk to the employer and the pooling of risk which results from that assignment. As the annuity-paying defined benefit plan allocates longevity risk to the employer, such a plan also balances the longer life spans of some employees against the shorter life spans of other employees. The result is a device—the traditional defined benefit pension—which protects retirees efficiently from the danger that they will outlive their pension resources.

However, the perception that the defined benefit plan is a superior device for mitigating longevity risk prompts another inquiry: Why don't the same problems of adverse selection appear as employees sort themselves between firms with and without traditional defined benefit plans? Employees concerned about longevity risk, evaluating their employment opportunities, ought to gravitate towards firms sponsoring conventional defined benefit plans with annuity-type payouts. Employees less concerned about outliving their retirement resources will, in contrast, discount the value of annuity-paying defined benefit plans and thus migrate towards firms which do not maintain such plans. As employees sort themselves in this fashion, they should replicate the adverse selection in the commercial annuity market as the self-selected employees covered by traditional, annuity-paying defined benefit arrangements tend to be more long-lived than their peers not covered by such arrangements.

In this scenario, defined benefit plans are no more efficient at eliminating longevity risk than are policies purchased individually in the annuity market. Since the sponsors of traditional defined benefit plans should attract more long-lived employees than do their competitors without such plans, those sponsors must fund for the longer life expectancies of their self-selected workforces. This extra funding, in turn, reduces the current cash wages of the defined benefit participants, implicitly

---

(hereinafter, GAO, *Voluntary*) at 18 ("As a result" of adverse selection, "annuity prices can be as much as 14 percent higher than they would be if every retiree purchased an annuity, according to one study."); *see also* Henry J. Aaron, *Retirement, Retirement Research and Retirement Policy*, in Henry J. Aaron, *supra* note 11 at 47 ("In practice, few people voluntarily, purchase annuities because the prices are 10 to 20 percent higher than they would be if they were priced for the average person.").

31 Medill, *supra* note 5 at 960 (discussing how adverse selection "can be easily avoided" with "defined benefit plans sponsored by private employers").

resulting in the same payment of a longevity premium by those participants as when they buy individual annuity policies for themselves.

Labor economists have devoted much attention to the processes by which employees sort themselves according to their preferences and the work options available to them. Much of this scholarship has been conducted under the rubric of "compensating wage differentials."[32] One much discussed example is the willingness of some employees to incur greater risks on the job to extract higher cash wages in compensation for those risks. Risk accepting employees gravitate towards firms which pay more but which entail greater danger in the workplace. Conversely, risk averse employees migrate toward safer firms which pay lower cash wages. Presumably, a similar self-sorting process should occur as employees who (often correctly) perceive that they will live longer move to employers sponsoring traditional, annuity-paying defined benefit plans to abate longevity risk.

If this sorting process were perfect, defined benefit plans would indeed be no better remedies for longevity risk than are commercial annuities since, in both cases, adverse selection would lead to the payment of a longevity premium by the participants. In the case of a commercial annuity policy purchased individually by a participant, that premium would be embedded in the price he pays for the policy. In the case of a traditional, annuity-paying defined benefit pension plan, that premium would be extracted by the employer in the form of lower cash wages to offset the employer's higher pension costs. In either case, the result would be the same, an extra cost to offset longevity risk because of adverse selection.

However, so far at least, there is no evidence of such adverse selection among firms sponsoring defined benefit plans, i.e., longer lived employees gravitating disproportionately to such firms. Indeed, the consensus among commentators in this area is, if anything, the opposite, namely, that defined benefit plans are superior means of eliminating longevity risk than are individual purchases of commercial annuities because the latter, and not the former, confront the adverse selection problem.[33]

The question then becomes: Why? Why don't employees sort themselves between firms with and without traditional defined benefit plans in the same way that

---

[32] *See, e.g.*, Ronald G. Ehrenberg and Robert S. Smith, MODERN LABOR ECONOMICS (7th ed. 2000) at 251–284.

[33] *See, e.g.*, Medill, *supra* note 5.

individuals do (and do not) purchase personal commercial annuities based on their reasonably accurate assessments of their prospects for long life?

The best answer is that employees' career options are, in practice, limited, requiring employees to subordinate more distant objectives and concerns to more immediately pressing considerations. In a theoretical world in which every employee confronts an infinite number of firms, each slightly different from the other, the employee concerned about longevity risk could choose to work for an employer which meets all of his other needs and which also maintains a traditional defined benefit plan. In practice, however, an employee's choices are fewer and less perfectly calibrated. One firm may dominate over the employee's other alternatives because the commute to work is easier, given the location of his home. Although, all things considered, the employee would prefer an employer with a defined benefit plan, he may nevertheless subordinate that preference to work closer to his residence. By the same token, another employee, totally indifferent to an employer's defined benefit arrangement, might choose to work there because of superior medical coverage or working environment.

As a result, the employee sorting process is imperfect because employees have "lumpy," limited choices among firms. An employee who, ceteris paribus, would prefer to work for a company sponsoring a traditional defined benefit plan may nevertheless go to a firm without such a plan because other factors are more pressing in the short run. Similarly, an employee indifferent to an employer's defined benefit plan may work for that employer for other reasons. Hence, defined benefit plans reduce longevity risk for covered employees without extracting from them any premium because employees' ability to sort themselves by life expectancies is imperfect. Consequently, the pool of employees covered by defined benefit plans (unlike the pool of purchasers for individual commercial annuities) resembles the workforce as a whole in terms of life expectancies.

Ironically, then, traditional defined benefit plans mitigate longevity risk best because parts of the workforce covered by such plans don't care about longevity risk and thus balance the rest of covered workforce which does. Put less charitably, many (perhaps most) employees may not think seriously about retirement until later in their careers. As a result, the longevity sorting process may be weak or nonexistent for much (perhaps the bulk) of the workforce.

This analysis suggests that conventional, annuity-paying defined benefit plans are less successful at reducing longevity risk when employees are older (and thus more concerned about retirement savings) and mobile (and thus more capable of acting upon that concern). Suppose, for example, that an employee concerned about longevity risk, while younger, subordinates that concern for other considerations. Suppose this hypothetical employee works for a company which has no defined benefit plan but which is located in a community which allows the employee to live in a better school district for his children. Once his children have completed their educations, the (now older) employee is then free to relocate and work for an employer with a traditional, annuity-providing pension. As he ages, the priorities which controlled when he was younger become less important to his job location decision while his retirement concerns, previously subordinated, become more urgent. In an environment where job switching is acceptable, he can move later in life to a new firm with a defined benefit plan as retirement considerations become more salient to him.

Consequently, in a more mobile labor market, some (perhaps many) older employees, joining firms in middle age or later, presumably make decisions which resemble those of the purchasers of commercial insurance policies. Among these older employees, those concerned about longevity risk will move to employers maintaining traditional defined benefit plans to mitigate that risk. Hence, in a world of greater employee mobility among older workers, companies maintaining traditional, annuity-providing defined benefit plans can expect an adverse selection problem, that is, can expect to attract older employees with greater than average life expectancies and to thereby incur the extra costs of providing traditional annuity benefits for such employees.

In the absence of laws prohibiting age discrimination in the hiring decision, some employers maintaining traditional defined benefit plans might refuse to hire older employees on the theory that such employees are too costly from a pension perspective. Given the existence of laws precluding age discrimination in the hiring process, some employers maintaining defined benefit plans likely resort to more subtle measures to avoid hiring older persons. Alternatively, in the absence of legal prohibitions on employment-based age discrimination, employers sponsoring traditional defined benefit pensions might pay older employees lower cash wages to reflect the greater pension costs stemming from the longer life expectancies of the older workers attracted by traditional pensions.[34]

---

[34] Federal and state law generally prohibit age discrimination in employment. For example, Section 4(a)(1) of the Age Discrimination in Employment Act of 1967 (ADEA) makes it "unlawful for an employer – (1) to fail or refuse to hire or to discharge any individual or otherwise discriminate against an individual with

Again, some employers, confronted with statutory prohibitions on lower wage payments for older employees, likely resort to disguised forms of discrimination to compensate for the higher pensions costs generated by older participants in defined benefit plans.

On the other hand, even in the absence of laws proscribing age discrimination, refusing to hire older employees might be economically unattractive, given the skills and experience such older employees have obtained and the potential paucity of younger workers in many fields. Employers' increasing willingness to accommodate the trend often labeled as "phased retirement"[35] suggests that some, perhaps many, employers do not have the luxury of eschewing older hirees. From this vantage, the traditional, annuity-paying defined benefit plan might, in some cases, be desirable (despite possible adverse selection problems) if an employer seeks to attract and retain older workers.

On balance, however, the twin realities of an aging work force and higher pension costs for older defined benefit participants will tend to reinforce the other demographic and regulatory trends underpinning the stagnation of defined benefit plan coverage, since employers recruiting and retaining older workers will find their traditional annuity paying defined benefit pensions increasingly expensive to fund as such plans attract those aging Baby Boomers most concerned about longevity risk. Indeed, such adverse selection problems may well be a factor fueling the conversion of traditional defined benefit plans to the cash balance format which I discuss in Chapter Three, because cash balance plans, though defined benefit arrangements, usually pay lump sum distributions and thus assign longevity risk to the plan participants.

---

respect to his compensation, terms, conditions, or privileges of employment, because of such individual's age". 29 U.S.C. Section 623 (a) (1).

35 *See, e.g.*, Patrick J. Purcell, *Older Workers: Employment and Retirement Trends*, Congressional Research Service, RL30629 (October 8, 2003) at CRS-15 ("[E]mployers may find it necessary to alter their employment practices and pension plans to induce some of those who would otherwise retire to remain on the job, perhaps on a part-time or part-year schedule. This process is sometimes referred to as *phased retirement*.") (italicized in original). *See also* Patricia L. Scahill and Jonathan Barry Forman, *Protecting Participants and Beneficiaries in a Phased Retirement World*, in Alvin D. Lurie (ed.), NEW YORK UNIVERSITY REVIEW OF EMPLOYEE BENEFITS AND EXECUTIVE COMPENSATION (2002); IRS Requests Comments on Phased Retirement Arrangements, 2002 TNT 116–17 (June 17, 2002); *Phasing into retirement*, USA TODAY, January 27, 2000, Section B (Money) at 1; Colleen T. Congel, *Phased Retirement Draws Mixed Reaction; Pomeroy Drafting Bill to Permit Approaches*, BNA DAILY TAX REPORT, 30 DTR J-1 (February 14, 2000); Elizabeth A. White, *Phased Retirement Proponents Urge Congress to Increase Flexibility*, BNA DAILY TAX REPORT, 65 DTR G-5 (April 4, 2000).

In theory, defined contribution plans can be designed in a fashion which pools and ameliorates longevity risk in the same fashion as defined benefit arrangements. In particular, if a defined contribution plan provides only for the annuitization of distributions and furnishes no other distribution option (e.g., no lump sum payments), the plan will purchase annuity contracts which do not reflect a premium for adverse selection since the group of covered employees will have a normal distribution of life expectancies. In practice, however, this option rarely exists; today, virtually all defined contribution plans pay participants' account balances to them as lump sums, rather than as annuities. This leaves each retiree concerned about longevity risk to purchase her own annuity contract which, in turn, leads to an adverse selection problem as the retirees who purchase such contracts tend, as a group, to be more long-lived than those who do not.

While the universal, compulsory nature of federal Social Security is often justified in redistributive terms (Social Security provides proportionately more retirement income for lower-paid workers)[36] and in paternalistic terms (Social Security compensates for workers' short-sighted failure to save),[37] longevity risk is, in important respects, the most compelling defense of a mandatory, annuity-providing public pension program like Social Security. By definition, there can be no adverse selection when no one can opt in (or out) of a compulsory, universal pension pool.

Even if there were no adverse selection problem in the market for individually-purchased annuities, there is substantial market-based risk for the 401(k) or IRA holder who purchases an individual annuity upon her retirement. If that retiree is lucky enough to terminate employment during a bull market, her lump sum distribution will be large and the resulting gains will be locked in when she converts her substantial lump sum into an annuity contract. On the other hand, if a 401(k) participant or IRA holder retires and purchases an annuity during a bear market, her smaller lump sum distribution will translate into a permanently smaller annuity. True, that retiree could try to wait out the bear market and purchase an annuity later. However, that wait entails its own risks as the market might go even lower.

---

[36] *See, e.g.,* Shoven in Friedman, *supra* note 5 at 15 (Social Security's "redistribution from those with higher lifetime earnings to those with lower earnings is entirely appropriate and worth preserving.").

[37] *See, e.g.,* Munnell, *Comments* in Friedman, *supra* note 5 at 144 ("the rationale for the current Social Security system is that individuals are myopic and would not save an adequate amount on their own."), see also Diamond and Orszag, *supra* note 29 at 73 ("Social Security's mandatory character also protects individuals and their families from myopically undersaving and underinsuring themselves.").

Moreover, the defined contribution participant purchasing her own annuity upon retirement bears the risk associated with the purchase rates of annuity contracts. If the participant buys her annuity contract when insurers are assuming higher returns, her lump sum will purchase a more generous annual income than if the participant retires when annuity contracts are less favorable.

In sum, even absent adverse selection in the market for privately-purchased annuities, the ability of an individual account retiree to shift longevity risk to the issuer of an individually-purchased annuity contract entails market risk (and possible reward) for that retiree. The historic evidence indicates that, because of varying market conditions including the fluctuating interest rate assumptions used by annuity issuers, returns to annuity-purchasing retirees can "vary enormously and over relatively short periods of time."[38]

In contrast, a traditional defined benefit plan can self-annuitize, providing annual payments to retirees from its common pool of funds. Alternatively, the traditional defined benefit pension can purchase annuity contracts throughout the retiree's career and thereby avoid the need to buy one large annuity at a single (potentially unfavorable) moment. While a well-informed individual account holder might similarly purchase annuity policies throughout her career, there is, to date, no evidence that that investment pattern is in fact widespread. Even if it were, myriad purchases of individual annuities would entail diseconomies of scale (for example, fees and administrative costs) avoided by pension trusts' centralized purchases of annuities for groups of employees.

D. Qualifications

None of this is to say that defined benefit plans are risk-free for their participants; no financial arrangement can be devoid of risk for the parties.[39] For example, a defined benefit participant whose annuity entitlement is specified in nominal rather than real dollars bears the risk that inflation will erode the purchasing power of his retirement distribution. In this sense, the defined benefit participant

---

[38]   Aaron in Friedman, *supra* note 5 at 63–64. *See also* Diamond and Orszag, *supra* note 29 at 40–41.

[39]   Even U.S. Treasury debt, universally considered the benchmark for safe investment, carries with it the (remote) possibility that the federal government could suspend its debt payments as well as market risk from interest rate fluctuations.

is the holder of a fixed claim (like a bondholder) and, as such, is exposed to the dangers of inflation.[40]

Even if a defined benefit plan provides cost-of-living increases for retirees, inflation represents an important risk for the defined benefit participant who terminates employment prior to retirement entitled to a deferred annuity fixed in nominal terms. In such instances, even if a cost-of-living adjustment kicks in at age sixty-five (65), there is no compensation for inflation before then.

Similarly, in the event of catastrophic default, i.e., the insolvency of both the plan and its sponsoring employer, the participant, to the extent his benefits exceed the level insured by the Pension Benefit Guaranty Corporation (PBGC), bears the loss.[41] Again, in this context, analogizing a defined benefit participant to a bondholder is instructive. Insofar as the participant's pension claim is insured by the PBGC, the participant (like the owner of an insured debenture) has recourse to the PBGC if the employer/issuer becomes insolvent and the collateral (that is, the pension trust assets) becomes inadequate. However, to the extent a defined benefit participant's claim exceeds the amount covered by the PBGC, employer default is a risk which falls on the participant as pension trust assets may be insufficient to pay promised benefits after the employer's insolvency. For such a participant, employer default represents undiversifiable risk since the participant's job and his pension (to the extent noninsured and inadequately funded) both depend upon the employer's continued viability.

There is an important intergenerational element to the risk of employer default; such risk is concentrated most heavily upon younger plan participants who are neither withdrawing funds from the plan nor close to starting such withdrawals. As current retirees receive their payments and thus extract the funds of the pension trust ahead of active (typically younger) participants, the risk of employer

---

[40]   Or the possible benefits of deflation.

[41]   Some pension analysts use the term "default risk" more broadly than I do in the text. *See, e.g.,* James A. Wooten, THE EMPLOYEE RETIREMENT INCOME SECURITY ACT OF 1974: A POLITICAL HISTORY (2004) at 4–5. While a more expansive concept of default risk is useful in certain settings, for purposes of my analysis, it is helpful to distinguish the circumstances which can cause an employer to default on its pension promise, i.e., pension assets earn an inadequate rate of return, the employer funds inadequately, or the employer goes out of business before financing promised benefits. The first possibility is subsumed within the concept of investment risk while the second scenario goes to funding risk. I think it makes sense to limit the concept of "default risk" to the situation identified in the text, when the employer goes out of business, leaving behind an inadequately funded pension.

default diminishes for these retirees since they have their retirement resources in hand and, to that extent, are protected against employer default. If the plan terminates, these current retirees, by statute, have a higher claim on the assets of the defined benefit pension trust [42] than do participants who have not yet retired.[43] These mostly younger participants are the ones who will be left holding the proverbial bag if the plan and the employer are both insolvent.

The intergenerational quality of default risk can be seen most clearly when employers sponsoring defined benefit plans grant credits for past service, i.e., when employers bestow retroactive increases under which pensions are augmented for prior years' of employment.[44] Typically, these retrospective increases are funded over several decades into the future.[45] However, the payout of these larger benefits commences immediately as older participants find their pensions increased for their earlier years of employment. Consequently, retirees, because of the increase in benefits for their past service, dig deeper into the existing assets of the pension trust to the detriment of younger employees. Younger employees are accordingly left more vulnerable to the risk that the trust and the employer will default on their pension obligations.

Such increases for past service were an important cause of the famous default of the Studebaker pension plan, a default which played in key role in the passage of ERISA.[46]

The intergenerational quality of default risk can be seen in the widespread skepticism of many younger persons that they will ever collect Social Security payments. As their taxes fund the payments received and to be received by the generations ahead of them in the Social Security queue, younger workers perceive of themselves as confronting an empty cupboard when the time comes for them to retire.[47]

---

[42]   ERISA Section 4044 (a) (3).

[43]   ERISA Section 4044 (a) (4).

[44]   *See* McGill, *supra chap. 1* note 2 at 521 (defining past service liability in terms of "any additions to the actuarial liability brought about by retroactive benefit increases"); Langbein, Stabile and Wolk, *supra chap. one* note 2 at 159–160.

[45]   Prior to the adoption of the PPA, Code Section 412 (b) (2) (B) (iii) provided for pension funding obligations attributable to past service liabilities to be funded over as many as thirty (30) years.

[46]   Langbein, Stabile and Wolk, *supra chap. one* note 2 at 72–76; Wooten, *supra* note 41 at 51–79.

[47]   This is a perception with a strong basis in fact. See, e.g. Government Accounting Office, *Social Security Reform, Analysis of a Trust Fund Exhaustion Scenario* (GAO-03-907, July, 2003) at 6 ("The Trust

To the extent the PBGC insures pension payments in the face of plan and employer default, the risk for younger participants shifts from the solvency of the plan and the employer to the solvency of the PBGC. Here again, there are reasonable bases for worry, given the deficits the PBGC itself confronts.[48] Younger participants, from one perspective, are the greatest beneficiaries of PBGC coverage (since they are farthest away from claiming pension trust assets) and are consequently at greatest risk if the PBGC itself is ultimately incapable of meeting its obligations.

The "backloaded" nature of defined benefit plans creates another kind of risk for the participant, namely, that he will lose his employment (and thus his plan coverage) just as the participant is about to earn the most valuable benefits under the plan. Since older employees tend to be higher paid, their salary-based pension entitlements escalate late in their careers. An employee may work for an employer sponsoring a defined benefit plan in anticipation of earning significant pension benefits toward the end of his career and then be fired on the cusp of those high pay years.

Even for an employee whose compensation does not increase in his later years, the pension accruals of those final years have greater present value, since the employee is closer to retirement than before and a pension dollar to be received shortly has greater present value than does a pension dollar to be received far in the future. As I discuss in the next chapter, early retirement formulas often create particularly dramatic instances of backloading. If, to take a typical example, lucrative early retirement benefits accrue to a long-term employee at age fifty-five (55),

---

Fund Exhaustion scenario raises significant intergenerational issues. Specifically, due to the timing of the reductions under the Trust Fund Exhaustion scenario, younger generations would bear much greater benefit reductions.").

[48] Mary Williams Walsh, *U.S. Insurer Of Pensions Says Its Deficit Has Soared*, N.Y. Times (January 16, 2004) at C1; Mary Williams Walsh, *Pension Troubles = S.&L. Collapse? Some Say Bank on It*, N.Y. Times (December 7, 2003) (Week in Review) at 4; Steven A. Kandarian, *PBGC Head Testifies at Senate Aging Panel On Pensions*, 2003 TNT 199-28 ("During FY 2002, PBGC's single-employer insurance program went from a surplus of $7.7 billion to a deficit of $3.6 billion—a loss of $11.3 billion in just one year. The $11.3 billion loss is more than five times larger than any previous one-year loss in the agency's 29-year history".); Keith Naughton, *Business's Killer I.O.U.*, 142(14) Newsweek 42 (October 6, 2003) ("Already, the federal Pension Benefit Guaranty Corporation (PBGC) is $5.7 billion in the hole, thanks to a string of costly pension failures in steel and airlines. And its administrator is warning that the PBGC could be headed for a taxpayer bailout akin to the $150 billion S&L debacle.") (parenthetical in original); General Accounting Office, *Single-Employer Pension Insurance Program Faces Significant Long-Term Risks*, (GAO-04-90) (October 1, 2003) (hereinafter, GAO, *Single Employer*) (as to PBGC single-employer insurance program, "the long-term viability of the program is at risk.").

the last years of plan participation which bring the employee to that age are particularly valuable to him.

The Code and ERISA preclude particularly egregious forms of backloading by proscribing plan formulas which delay pension accruals until the end of the employee's work life.[49] However, even with these statutory safeguards, as a matter of economics, the most valuable pension accruals under traditional[50] defined benefit formulas occur late in the employee's career when his salary is higher and/or he is closer to retirement.[51] The defined benefit participant thus bears the risk that he will be fired on the eve of those more valuable accruals.

A variation of this risk is the danger that the employee, while retaining his job, will lose defined benefit coverage as he is about to enter his most valuable years of employment. In this scenario, the employer terminates its traditional defined benefit plan just as the employee embarks upon his late career years of high pay (and therefore of valuable pension accruals). Even if the employer replaces the terminated defined benefit pension with an individual account plan, the employee will have lost the particularly lucrative late career years of defined benefit coverage.

As its core, this is the source of the controversy surrounding cash balance plans, which I discuss further in Chapter Three. Employees who work in anticipation that they will earn valuable pension benefits late in their careers instead find themselves covered by cash balance arrangements. It understates to say that this disappoints these employees' expectations of significant backloaded pension accruals in their later years.

In light of all of this, I think it fair to criticize some defined benefit advocates (myself included) for tending to ignore or understate the financial risks of defined benefit arrangements for their participants. However, the fundamental point remains valid: Defined benefit pensions impose upon the employer the predominant risks of providing adequate retirement income, i.e., funding, investment and longevity risks. While the risks to the defined benefit participant are

---

[49] Code Section 411(b)(1); ERISA Section 204(b)(1).

[50] Note that even union-sponsored plans tend, as a matter of economics, to be backloaded since $20 of monthly pension income earned by a worker who is sixty years old, in present value terms, is more valuable than that same $20 of monthly pension income earned by a worker who is thirty.

[51] *See* Zelinsky, *supra* chap. one note 2 at 688–691.

not de minimis, they are not as large as the risks assumed by the employer sponsoring a defined benefit plan nor are they as substantial as the funding, investment and longevity risks assigned to the employee under individual account arrangements.

E.   Summary

To summarize: A strong case can be made that it is efficient to place various risks associated with retirement planning upon the employer, as defined benefit plans do. Investment risk, funding risk and longevity risk all present challenges for the individual investor. And, in the final analysis, today's prototypical defined contribution participant, who finances his retirement savings through salary reduction and self-directs the investment of his individual account, is an individual investor.

In contrast, when a workforce and its retirement resources are pooled and invested collectively, as in the case of the classic defined benefit arrangement, economies of scale and other efficiencies are achieved by investing that single common pool. When the onus is placed on employers to provide defined benefits to their respective employees, investment risk (including temporal risk) and funding risk fall on employers, on balance more likely handle those risks well than is the average employee. Similarly, an annuity-paying defined benefit plan, because it covers a more representative swath of the workforce, is a better answer to the challenge of longevity risk than is the individual purchase of annuity policies, subject to the problems of adverse selection and diseconomies of scale. An employer sponsoring a defined benefit plan is well-positioned to pool risks for the population of its employees.

Offsetting these considerations is the reality that the allocation of risk carries with it the entitlement to reward. If, in the defined benefit context, investment performance is good, the employer, having absorbed the risk, reaps the profit. The employer sponsoring a defined benefit has promised its employees an output, assuming a particular rate of return on the plan's assets. Investment performance that is better than assumed means the employer need contribute less (perhaps even nothing) to fund the promised benefits. Similarly, the benefits promised by the plan are premised on certain mortality assumptions. If employees and their beneficiaries are less long-lived than has been assumed, the employer need put less into the plan.

Conversely, in the defined contribution context, the reward to the employee for absorbing risk is the potential profit of superior investment gain in his own account. In a prolonged bull market, the allocation of risk and reward to the participant looks attractive as he sees his account balance climb with seeming inevitability. When the bears return and individual account balances stagnate or decline, the employer's promise to pay a defined benefit acquires new appeal—ironically at the same time that the cost of providing that benefit increases for the employer because declining or stagnant values of plan assets require the employer to contribute more to remedy the shortfall and thereby pay promised benefits.[52]

In light of these considerations, retirement savings specialists (myself included) have tended to view the choice between the defined benefit and the defined contribution configurations as a matter of allocating risk and reward among employers and employees. Many of these specialists (again, myself included) have been concerned that assigning risk and reward to employees, while working well for some of them, might nevertheless, for the long run, prove problematic for many plan participants.[53] However, this story of risk/reward allocation increasingly appears to me to be only part of truth, a large, indeed, the predominant part of the truth but not the totality. At its core, the defined contribution paradigm reflects an individualized conception of retirement savings, a conception which

---

[52] *See, e.g.,* Steven A. Kandarian, *PBGC Head Testifies at Senate Aging Panel On Pensions,* 2003 TNT 199 28 (As of the end of 2002, "the total underfunding in single-employer plans exceeded $400 billion, the largest number ever recorded. Even with recent rises in the stock market and interest rates, PBGC projects that underfunding still exceeds $350 billion today."); *See also* Danny Hakim with Jonathan Fuerbringer, *G.M. to Raise $10 Billion For Pension Gap,* N.Y. TIMES, ("Company pension plans have been battered by more than three years of poor investment returns combined with low interest rates. Because pension calculations involve estimating returns to cover long-term obligations, lower interest rates mean that more cash contributions are required."); *see also* Cassell Bryan-Low and Robin Sidel, *The Pension-Plan Pit: Major Companies Face Shortfall of Billions of Dollars,* WALL ST. J., October 11, 2002 at C1 ("The contributions holiday of the late 1990s that many companies enjoyed as a result of the long bull market is now grinding to a halt."); *see also* Naughton, *supra* note 48 at 42 ("Companies that offer workers traditional pensions are suddenly facing a yawning $350 billion deficit in those plans.").

[53] *See, e.g.,* Patrick Purcell, *Pension Issues: Cash Balance Plans,* Congressional Research Service (August, 2003) (hereinafter, *Cash Balance*) at CRS-2 (Under defined benefit plans, "[r]etirement benefits are paid from the pension fund, and the employer is *at risk* for the benefits that have been promised to retired employees and their surviving spouses.") (emphasis in original); *see also* Purcell, *Pensions and Retirement Savings Plans: Sponsorship and Participation,* Congressional Research Service No. RL30122 (October 22, 2003) at CRS-4 ("In a defined benefit plan, it is the *employer* who bears the financial risk of the plan, while in a defined contribution plan it is the *employee* who bears the financial risk.") (emphasis in the original) (hereinafter, *Sponsorship and Participation*).

carries tremendous appeal in a culture which, like ours, places a high value on private property, individual autonomy, and self-sufficiency. Indeed, as I shall argue in Chapter Four, the initial steps down the defined contribution path had a pronounced and unintended effect because the individual account format comports so well with American cultural norms about private property and individual ownership.

CHAPTER THREE

How Did It Happen?

In this chapter, I identify[1] the major steps by which the defined contribution paradigm became entrenched in American retirement, tax, and social policy. As a preliminary matter, it is important not to overstate the decline of defined benefit plans. Many such plans remain in existence, holding roughly $2 trillion in assets and covering approximately one-fifth of all full time, private sector employees.[2] Almost three-quarters (3/4) of the companies listed in the S&P 500 sponsor defined benefit plans.[3] Nevertheless, the defined benefit system today stagnates; both the number of such plans and the number of participants in them have declined.[4] "Since 1986, 97,000 (defined benefit) plans with 7 million participants have terminated."[5] The continuing travails of the defined benefit system have

---

[1] This chapter is a Cook's tour of the major features of the defined contribution universe, focusing upon the most salient features of the most important devices which today constitute that universe. Much excellent literature is available for the reader interested in a greater level of detail. In appropriate footnotes, I introduce the reader to a small sampling of that literature.

[2] David Wessel, *The Big Pension Bill: Is That All There Is?*, WALL ST. J., August 3, 2006 at A2 ("Private sector defined benefit plans had $1.9 trillion in assets at year-end 2005. . ."); *See also* Joint Committee on Taxation, *Present Law and Background Relating to Employer-Sponsored Defined Benefit Plans and the Financial Position of the Pension Benefit Guaranty Corporation ("PBGC")* (March 10, 2003), 2003 TNT 47–18 (hereinafter, JCT, *Present Law*).

Different estimates vary in detail but not in substance. For example, Federal Reserve data indicate that "(a)t the end of 2002, there was $2.1 trillion in corporate defined contribution plans, compared with $1.59 trillion in corporate defined benefit plans". See Arleen Jacobius, *Rollover money to eclipse DB and DC plans' assets*, 31(7) PENSIONS & INVESTMENTS (March 31, 2003) at 3. Data developed by the Society of Professional Administrators and Record Keepers paints a similar picture. See *id*.

[3] *Administration Drafting Proposals to Preserve Pension Plans*, N.Y. TIMES, March 12, 2003 at C17. The numbers in the text underestimate the relative strength of the defined contribution paradigm since many surviving defined benefit plans have adopted the cash balance format which mimics in important respects defined contribution arrangements.

[4] JCT, Present Law, *supra* note 2.

[5] Statement of Steven A. Kandarian, Executive Director, Pension Benefit Guaranty Corporation Before the Committee on Finance, United States Senate, March 11, 2003, 2003 TNT 48–30. *See also* Testimony of Henry Eickelberg, Staff Vice President for Benefit Programs for the General Dynamics Corporation on behalf of the American Benefits Council Before the Finance Committee, United States Senate,

become routine news stories as one major corporation after another freezes or terminates its defined benefit plan.[6] Many of the defined benefit plans which survive have abandoned the traditional, annuity-paying format and have instead switched to the cash balance configuration which mimics the individual account paradigm.

In contrast, defined contribution devices, most prominently 401(k) plans and IRAs, have, by all indicators, grown rapidly. Today, significantly more private sector employees participate in defined contribution retirement arrangements than in defined benefit plans. Indeed, the percentage of full-time, private sector employees participating in defined contribution plans (roughly 40%) is essentially double the percentage of private sector employees covered by defined benefit arrangements (approximately 20%).[7] The assets held by employer-sponsored defined contribution plans (almost $3 trillion)[8] exceed by a wide margin the assets of defined benefit arrangements. If amounts held in IRAs ($3.7 trillion)[9] are added to the amounts in defined contribution plans, the margin of individual account

---

Washington, D.C., March 11, 2003, 2003 TNT 48–33 ("The total number of defined benefit plans has decreased from a high of 170,000 in 1985 to 56,405 in 1998 (the most recent year for which official Department of Labor statistics exist), and most analysts believe there are fewer than 50,000 plans in the U.S. today. There has been a corresponding decline in the percentage of American workers with a defined benefit plan as their primary retirement plan from 38% in 1980 to 21% in 1997.") (parenthesis in original).

See, also, House Workforce Committee Release on Decline of Defined Benefit Pension Plans, 2003 TNT 108–43 (June 5, 2003) ("According to the Pension Benefit Guaranty Corporation (PBGC), there were 32,321 defined benefit plans insured by the agency last year, down from 114,000 in 1985. Furthermore, the percentage of active workers covered by these plans is down from 38 percent in 1985 to 23 percent today.")

[6] *See, e.g.,* Theo Francis, *DuPont Aims to Slash Pension Plan,* WALL ST. J., August 29, 2006 at A2; John D. Stoll, *GM to Freeze Pension Plans of White-Collar Workers,* WALL ST. J., March 8, 2006 at A10; *Delta Asks Bankruptcy Court To Let It Cancel Pilots'* Pensions, N.Y. TIMES, August 5, 2006 at C2; Evan Perez, *Delta Moves to Shed Pensions,* WALL ST. J., June 20, 2006 at A13; Hubert B. Herring, *Those Incredible Vanishing Pension Plans,* N.Y. TIMES, Section 3, July 2, 2006 at 2; *More Companies Freezing, Terminating Plans,* PENSIONS & INVESTMENTS, July 10, 2006 at 21.

[7] *See* Patrick Purcell, *Retirement Savings and Household Wealth in 2002: Analysis of Census Bureau Data,* 29 J. OF PENSION PLANNING & COMPLIANCE 48, 53–54 (2003) ("Over the past 25 years, there has been a shift in the distribution of pension plans and of pension plan participants from defined benefit plans to defined contribution plans."); *see also* Congressional Budget Office, "Utilization" *supra* chap. one note 10 at 4 ("In 1975, 39 percent of private-sector workers were covered by defined-benefit plans. By 1997, that figure had dropped to 21 percent. Over the same period, the percentage participating in defined-contribution plans increased from less than 15 percent to 40 percent.").

[8] Wessel, *supra* note 2.

[9] *Id.*

assets over defined benefit assets grows even wider.[10] All of this represents a significant reversal of historic patterns under which the traditional defined benefit plan was the dominant paradigm for the provision of retirement income.[11]

A. The Underlying Decline of the Defined Benefit Plan: Economic and Demographic Factors

How did the defined benefit plan go from the behemoth of the private retirement system to a secondary player in that system? The story starts with the economic and demographic forces which in the 1960s and 1970s eroded these once-dominant pension plans and thereby set the stage for the emergence of the defined contribution paradigm.

Among the forces depressing the defined benefit system have been diminishing union membership and the decline of traditional manufacturing, extractive and transportation firms.[12] Even if there had been no ERISA or Section 401(k), reduced union membership and the stagnation and demise of the firms in these traditional industries[13] would have depressed defined benefit pension participation and sponsorship. Unions in these industries have been important advocates of defined benefit pensions while employers in these declining industries have been pre-eminent sponsors of such pensions.

For a variety of reasons, unions like defined benefit pensions in contradistinction to individual account plans: A collectively-bargained defined benefit plan reinforces the group solidarity of the union by subjecting all participants to a single, union-negotiated formula to receive uniform benefits. Such a plan also emphasizes the importance of the collective bargaining services the union supplies to its members since augmentation of a participant's retirement income must be

---

[10]   *Id. See also* Jacobius, *supra* note 2.

[11]   And these numbers do not reflect the assets held in individual accounts for educational and medical purposes.

[12]   Steven A. Sass, THE PROMISE OF PRIVATE PENSIONS 229 (1997) ("This rapid union decline produced a sharp contraction on both the asset and liability sides of the pension ledger.").

[13]   Steven A. Kandarian, *PBGC Head Testifies at Senate Aging Panel On Pensions*, 2003 TNT 199–28 ("Many defined benefit plans are in our oldest and most capital intensive industries.") *See also* Lee A. Sheppard, *Pension Benefit Obligations: Twilight of the Household Names*, 2003 TNT 198–5 (October 13, 2003) (discussing the financial problems of defined benefit plans maintained by "the steel companies, the automobile and parts companies, and the airlines.").

achieved through such bargaining, rather than through the participant's superior investment performance with his own individual account. When traditional defined benefit plans are jointly-governed by both management and union trustees, the union as an entity has more economic clout than when individual participants make their own decentralized investment decisions 401(k)-style. Consequently, the erosion of union membership and influence diminished a key constituency for traditional defined benefit plans.

Moreover, as service and high tech industries, with no strong history of unionization or of defined benefit sponsorship, grew in relative importance, ERISA, as we shall see, pushed the firms in those industries toward defined contribution, rather than defined benefit, plans for their employees.

Further reinforcing the underlying decline of the defined benefit system have been the changing nature of work, an aging workforce, and increased acceptance of employee mobility. These forces have transformed the workplace from one to which the traditional defined benefit pension was well-adapted to a workplace in which these once-conventional plans are ill-suited.

Traditionally, defined benefit plans have implemented a quite precise pattern of worker retention and superannuation. In particular, such plans have been structured to retain older employees until specific times in their careers and to encourage these employees to retire once they reach those specified points.

As a reward for long service with the sponsoring employer, traditional defined benefit pensions frequently offer an early retirement benefit commencing upon an early retirement date. This early retirement date is typically age fifty-five (55), provided the employee has completed a designated number of years of service with the employer sponsoring plan. The early retirement benefit payable at that date is usually quite valuable and thus incents the employee to stay with the employer to reach that lucrative milestone.[14] Similarly, normal retirement benefit

---

[14] Such early retirement benefits are often denoted as "subsidized" early retirement to reflect the extra pension earnings that employees accrue by working for the sponsoring employer until their respective early retirement dates. *See* McGill, *supra* chap. one note 2 at 218 (7th ed. 1996)("The general practice of using early retirement factors more favorable than the actuarially equivalent ones is referred to as 'subsidized early retirement.'").

formulas often provide strong financial incentives for an employee covered by a traditional pension to stay with the employer until that retirement date.

After attaining these financially rewarding milestones under the traditional defined benefit pension, the employee, if he continues to work, typically accrues retirement benefits at an economically reduced rate. Under some circumstances, the employee, in real economic terms, actually loses benefits by continuing to work past the traditional plan's normal retirement date.[15]

This traditional defined benefit structure was well-adapted to an economy in which employers valued experienced workers, work was often physically taxing, and many young workers stood ready to take the places of their elders. As I noted in Chapter Two, the traditional defined benefit plan is often characterized as "backloaded" since late-career participation is particularly lucrative for the employee. This is especially the case when late-career participation brings the employee to the proverbial brass ring that is the plan's early and/or normal retirement benefit.[16] In such instances, the employee, incented to remain with a single employer through this late-career, backloaded period, provides continuity to the employer's workforce.

However, once the employee reaches the point at which the employee's declining capabilities outweigh the value of his experience, i.e., early or normal retirement,

---

[15] See Jonathan Barry Forman, *How Federal Pension Laws Influence Individual Work and Retirement Decisions*, 54 TAX LAW. 143, 148 (2000) ("[T]raditional defined benefit plans provide large financial incentives for workers to stay with their employers until they become eligible for early retirement. . . . [T]raditional defined benefit plans typically impose large financial penalties on workers who stay past the plan's normal retirement age.").

In the Omnibus Budget Reconciliation Act of 1986, P.L. 99–509, Congress added Section 411(b)(1)(H) to the Code and Section 204(b)(1)(H) to ERISA. These parallel provisions prevent age discrimination in the pattern of defined benefit accruals. To the extent those provisions successfully prevent the age-based benefit accrual pattern discussed in the text, they make the traditional defined benefit plan less attractive to an employer seeking to use that plan to implement the historic pattern of superannuation at early and normal retirement.

[16] Both ERISA and the equivalent provisions of the Code regulate rates of accrual to prevent more egregious forms of backloading. However, even with those statutory rules in place, the economics of traditional defined benefit plans entail backloading. *See* ERISA Section 204 and Internal Revenue Code Section 411(b). *See also* Zelinsky, *supra* chap. one note 2 at 688–691 (2000)(discussing the backloaded nature of traditional defined benefit plans); Langbein, Stabile & Wolk, *supra* chap. one note 2 at 45 ("A defined benefit plan is intrinsically backloaded . . . .").

the defined benefit plan then encourages the employee to retire since staying further results in relatively little extra pension rights and sometimes results in an actual decline in the economic value of the employees' pension entitlement.

Most of us know a military or civilian government worker who stayed in service until his pension rights matured and who then left shortly thereafter, to retire or to pursue a second career.[17] Such pension-sensitive career choices were, at one time, part of a broader defined benefit culture which encouraged this pattern of superannuation, to wit, long careers with a single employer to earn valuable, late-career benefits followed by retirement upon the attainment of these backloaded benefits, or shortly thereafter.

For a variety of reasons, this pattern of stable, single-employer careers is today less desirable for employers and employees than in the past. Much contemporary work is not physically taxing.[18] Hence, employers today have less incentive to encourage older workers to quit as they age, while some older workers find themselves stretching their careers beyond traditional retirement ages in a less physically challenging workplace. As the Baby Boomers grow older, a smaller cohort of young workers stands ready to take their places in the workplace. The practice today labeled "phased retirement,"[19] under which older workers transition to retirement via part-time work, reflects these realities of today's employment market, namely, that work is less physically taxing; in light of a smaller pool of younger workers, employers often need to retain older employees they would in the past have encouraged to retire at early or normal retirement dates. A principal means of encouraging that retirement has been the design of the traditional

---

[17] Richard A. Ippolito, PENSION PLANS AND EMPLOYEE PERFORMANCE: EVIDENCE, ANALYSIS AND POLICY 39 (1997) ("The data are consistent with the hypothesis that the extraordinarily low quit rates evinced in the federal sector can be explained by the unusually large quit penalties imparted by its pension plan. And retirement tends to occur within a short period of workers' eligibility age.").

[18] Eugene Steuerle, Christopher Spiro, and Richard W. Johnson, *Can Americans Work Longer?*, URBAN INSTITUTE, STRAIGHT TALK ON SOCIAL SECURITY AND RETIREMENT POLICY, Aug. 15, 1999, at 1 ("we estimate that the percentage of workers in physically demanding jobs has dropped substantially – from about 20 percent in 1950 to almost 8 percent in 1996"); Richard W. Johnson, *Trends in job demands among older workers, 1992–2002*, MONTHLY LABOR REVIEW, July, 2004, at 48, 51 ("In general, the share of older workers reporting that their jobs entail physical demands all or almost all of the time did not change much over the past 10 years, while the share reporting virtually no physical demands on the job increased significantly.").

[19] The IRS has issued proposed regulations to formalize phased retirement programs for traditional defined benefit pensions. *See Distributions from a pension plan under a phased retirement program*, 69 Fed. Reg. 9754 (proposed Nov. 10, 2004).

backloaded defined benefit plan which encourages employees to stay to accrue lucrative late-career benefits and then leave once those benefits are earned.

Moreover, few contemporary employees expect to have the kind of long, single-employer careers experienced (in theory, at least) by their fathers and grandfathers. For these contemporary employees, the traditional defined benefit plan, with its backloaded, late-career benefits as early and normal retirement dates are approached, makes little sense since today's workers have no intention of staying with a single employer long enough to earn such late-career benefits. By the same token, today's employer neither expects nor desires to encourage the single-employer careers fostered by the design of the traditional, backloaded defined benefit plan.

Whether employee mobility has actually increased is a matter of controversy.[20] However, undoubtedly real are both the perception of greater employee mobility and the loss of stigma attached to frequent job changes. Hence, defined contribution devices have come to be favored by many employers and employees as better adapted to a world of greater (or, at least, more acceptable) employee mobility.

Finally, as the defined benefit system matured, employers sponsoring traditional defined benefit plans increasingly sought to reduce or eliminate the funding, investment and longevity risks stemming from their sponsorship of such plans. As more employers confronted the reality of these risks, defined benefit plans looked increasingly unattractive.

In sum, the traditional defined benefit pension has become something of a dinosaur in the contemporary world. The decline of the traditional benefit plan set the stage for the emergence of the defined contribution paradigm. Had the defined benefit system remained robust, the defined contribution paradigm would not have emerged as or when it did.

Nevertheless, the decline of the traditional defined benefit pension, while it enabled the rise of the defined contribution paradigm, did not make that rise inevitable. It took affirmative congressional decisions to inaugurate the defined contribution paradigm as we know it today.

---

[20] *See* Zelinsky, *supra* chap. one note 2 at footnote 79.

B.   The Role of ERISA

The first of these affirmative congressional decisions was the adoption of ERISA in 1974.[21] Defined contribution arrangements—money purchase pensions, profit sharing plans, Section 403(b) plans[22]—existed before ERISA. Nevertheless, in four ways, ERISA (without anyone planning it that way) started the trend towards the defined contribution society as we know it today.

First, ERISA created the individual retirement account, a device which played a critical role in acclimating Americans to the notion of tax-advantaged[23] individual accounts.

Second, ERISA placed regulatory burdens upon defined benefit plans in a fashion making the more flexible defined contribution devices, particularly profit sharing plans, more attractive to employers than traditional defined benefit arrangements.

---

[21]   The origins of ERISA are well explored in Wooten, *supra* chap. two note 41.

[22]   Section 403(b) is the provision of the Code under which tax-exempt employers and their employees have traditionally undertaken retirement savings.

[23]   It is important to distinguish between the tax-advantages under current law of qualified plans and the view that current law constitutes a tax subsidy or, to use the more conventional term, tax expenditure. The Code's treatment of qualified plan earnings (i.e., the deferral of tax until the distribution of such earnings to the plan participants) is undoubtedly more advantageous than current law's approach to investment earnings arising outside qualified plans (i.e., immediate taxation as earned). This advantage is commonly labeled as a tax subsidy or a tax expenditure. For two reasons, I am skeptical of these labels as applied to qualified plans. First, current law's treatment of qualified plans falls within the range of plausible choices for a normative income tax. A rational legislator, seeking not to subsidize retirement plans but to tax them properly, could plausibly have made the choices embodied in current law considering such criteria as administrability, popular acceptance and taxpayer liquidity. Second, current law's treatment of qualified plans is normatively correct if one favors cash flow consumption taxation, that is, deferring taxation of savings until savings are used for consumption. From either vantage, it misleads to call the Code's treatment of qualified plans a tax expenditure since that treatment implements tax norms rather than subsidizes. For elaboration of the argument that the current tax treatment of qualified plans is not a tax subsidy but, rather, is consistent with choices which can be properly be made in designing a normative income tax, see Edward A. Zelinsky, *Tax Policy v. Revenue Policy: Qualified Plans, Tax Expenditures and the Flat, Plan Level Tax*, 13 VA. TAX REV. 591 (1994); Edward A. Zelinsky, *Qualified Plans and Identifying Tax Expenditures: A Rejoinder to Professor Stein*, 9 AM. J. TAX POLICY 257 (1991); Edward A. Zelinsky, *The Tax Treatment of Qualified Plans: A Classic Defense of the Status Quo*, 66 N. CAR. L. REV. 314 (1988). Professor Wooten, analyzing the historic origins of the tax treatment of qualified plans, concludes that those who crafted that treatment in fact did not intend to subsidize but, rather, sought to tax such plans properly. That conclusion reinforces my skepticism about the application of the tax expenditure label to the current tax treatment of qualified plans. *See* James A. Wooten, *The "Original Intent" of the Federal Tax Treatment of Private Pension Plans*, 85 TAX NOTES 1305 (1999).

Third, ERISA's fiduciary rules incented employers to shift to self-directed defined contribution arrangements under which participants control the investment of their own retirement resources.

Finally, ERISA permitted defined contribution plans to hold more stock of sponsoring employers than defined benefit arrangements.

Cumulatively but inadvertently, these regulatory choices, embodied in ERISA, started America down the path to the contemporary defined contribution society.

i. The Creation of the Individual Retirement Account

Among the many issues confronted by the drafters of ERISA, none was knottier than the two topics labeled "portability" and "coverage"[24] for those not participating in employer-sponsored plans. Under the rubric of portability, those who crafted ERISA addressed the situation of the vested, but younger, participant who leaves employment prior to his retirement age. Under pre-ERISA practice, it was common (particularly under traditional defined benefit plans) for the (now terminated) employee to receive nothing at the time he severed employment. Rather, he remained entitled to a deferred benefit, payable on a delayed basis upon the subsequent attainment of retirement age. For both administrative and economic reasons, this delay was often problematic, particularly as to relatively young employees. As an administrative matter, the plan and the terminated participant had to stay in touch with one another, for the participant to receive information about the plan and his benefit, and, ultimately, for the participant to get paid. Such participant tracking could be (and still is) resource-consuming.[25]

Moreover, there was (and still is) no requirement for defined benefit plans to adjust a terminated participant's benefit to reflect either inflation or the time value of money between the participant's termination of his employment and his eventual retirement from the workforce, when he finally starts to receive that defined benefit. Suppose, for example, that a forty-year-old vested participant quit his job in 1950, entitled to an annuity of $100 per month at his retirement

---

24   The term "coverage" is also used to address situations where an employer maintains a plan and the issue
        is how much of the workforce must be included within the plan. *See* Code Section 410(b).
25   *See* Halperin, *supra* chap. two note 2 at 60 (discussing the "difficulties in requiring employers and employ-
        ees to keep track of each other").

twenty-five years hence. Twenty-five years later, then ready to retire, the participant was entitled to this same payout of $100 per month. While in nominal terms the participant's benefit had remained steady for two decades, in economic terms, his entitlement had eroded over the years.

Even before ERISA, there was, if the plan elected, an alternative approach, namely, to pay the employee his benefit as a lump sum on his termination of employment rather than wait to commence payment upon his future attainment of retirement age. Even prior to ERISA, such pre-retirement distributions were common from defined contribution plans. However, this approach suffered from serious drawbacks. In particular, prior to ERISA, an employee had to pay tax on his pre-retirement distribution and on the subsequent earnings generated by this distribution.[26] While this early taxation often occurred at relatively favorable rates,[27] such early taxation was (often correctly) viewed as diminishing the ultimate resources available for the participant's retirement.[28]

In light of these considerations, the drafters of ERISA, under the rubric of "portability," sought a device which enabled the employee to carry his benefit with him from job to job on a tax-advantaged basis and which allowed him to earn additional income on that benefit as he moved toward retirement. The mechanism ultimately devised to achieve such portability was the individual retirement account.[29] In particular, under ERISA, the employee receiving a pre-retirement distribution from a qualified plan is given the "rollover" option, the right to transfer his distribution tax-free to an IRA.[30] Once in the IRA, those

---

[26] The recipient of a pre-retirement distribution could have invested the proceeds of such distribution in tax-favored investments, e.g., municipal bonds. However, that kind of investment choice typically entails an implicit tax in the form of a lower rate of return. *See* e.g., William A. Klein, Joseph Bankman and Daniel N. Shaviro, FEDERAL INCOME TAXATION (14th ed. 2006) at 11, 185–187.

[27] Before the adoption of ERISA, Code Sections 402(a)(2), 402(a)(3)(C) and 402(a)(5) provided capital gain treatment to certain lump sum distributions.

[28] Much ink has been spilled analyzing the consequences of tax deferral. Suffice it for these purposes to observe that the deferral of income taxation until retirement typically generates two benefits for the retiree, i.e., a higher after-tax return on investment earnings (since these earnings are untaxed prior to retirement) and a lower tax bracket on distribution since the retiree is then no longer working. *See* Langbein, Stabile and Wolk, *supra* chap. one note 2 at 336–343; Daniel I. Halperin, *Interest in Disguise: Taxing the "Time Value of Money,"* 95 YALE L. J. 506 (1986).

[29] *See* Code Section 408.

[30] Code Section 402(c). The rollover provisions of the Code have undergone many changes since the original version enacted by ERISA, including the authorization of trustee-to-trustee rollovers under Code Section 401(a)(31). These changes do not affect the basic point in the text, the decision by ERISA's drafters to use the IRA to address the issue of portability.

funds grow tax-free; income tax is not payable until the participant finally withdraws his funds from the IRA to which those funds were previously transferred without tax.[31]

The architects of ERISA also used the IRA to address the problem of workers not covered by pensions at their workplaces. In particular, the drafters of ERISA envisioned the IRA as a mini-pension plan under which workers without employer-provided pension coverage can make tax-deductible contributions from their own earnings for their own retirements. Such tax-deducible contributions were initially limited to $1,500[32] per year and were permitted only if the taxpayer was not an "active participant" in an employer-based qualified plan.[33]

There was nothing inevitable about the creation of the IRA or about the decision, embodied in ERISA, to use the IRA to address concerns about portability and coverage. Portability, for example, could instead have been addressed by creating a federal pension clearinghouse,[34] perhaps administered by the Social Security Administration. On the employee's termination of employment before retirement age, the employer would have deposited the employee's benefit with the clearinghouse as a lump sum and would thereby have discharged the employer's obligations to its former employee. The clearinghouse would have invested all such funds committed to it and, on the employee's eventual attainment of retirement age, would have paid the employee an annuity reflecting the clearinghouse's investment experience with the funds given to it. If the employee earned vested benefits from different employers over the course of his career, the clearinghouse would have cumulated his entitlements and eventually paid him an annuity reflecting the totality of employer contributions and earnings over the course of the employee's career.

---

[31] Code Sections 408(d)(1), 408(e)(1).

[32] The original ERISA limit on IRA contributions was the lesser of $1,500 or fifteen percent (15%) of the participant's compensation. *See* Code Section 219(b) as originally enacted by ERISA. As discussed below, ERTA increased the $1,500 limit to $2,000. The $2,000 limit on IRA contributions then remained in effect until the Economic Growth and Tax Relief Reconciliation Act of 2001 (EGTRRA) provided for scheduled increases in that limit through 2008, cost-of-living increases thereafter, and additional "catch-up" contributions for persons fifty (50) years of age and older. In 2007, the basic IRA deduction is $4,000 annually and "catch-up" contributions are permitted for an additional $1,000. *See* Code Section 219(b)(5) as amended by EGTRRA, P.L. 107–16, 115 Stat. 38 (2001). For the delightful reminiscences of one who was present at the creation of the IRA, *see* Edwin S. Cohen, A LAWYER'S LIFE: DEEP IN THE HEART OF TAXES (1994) at 534–537.

[33] *See* Code Section 219(b) as originally enacted in ERISA.

[34] Professor Wooten traces the decision to address portability issues via IRA rollovers rather than a federal agency. *See* Wooten, *supra* chap. two note 41 at 94, 180, 195, 198, 251–252.

Similarly, the employee without employer-sponsored pension coverage could, in lieu of tax-deductible IRA contributions,[35] have been given the option of making additional, voluntary FICA payments to compensate for the absence of work-based pension coverage. In return, the employee would, on retirement, have received supplemental Social Security distributions financed by these extra FICA contributions.

Alternatively, the drafters of ERISA might have used the IRA to address either the portability issue or the coverage issue but not both. However, the decision embodied in the statute was to establish the IRA and to use that device to address both portability and coverage concerns. This decision proved critical on the path toward the defined contribution paradigm by acclimating Americans to individual accounts via IRA coverage.

ii. ERISA's Regulatory Burdens on Defined Benefit Plans

A second way in which ERISA proved critical on the path toward the defined contribution society was the heavier regulatory burdens ERISA imposed on defined benefit arrangements, burdens which discouraged the creation and continuation of such arrangements at a time when economic and demographic forces (e.g., the decline of unions and traditional manufacturing industries) were already depressing the defined benefit system.[36] Much of ERISA applies equally to individual account and defined benefit plans. For example, ERISA's minimum vesting rules apply to both defined contribution and defined benefit plans.[37] These rules require that employees' interests in their accrued benefits become nonforfeitable upon the completion of specific periods of employment. Such rules, by increasing employee vesting and thus employer costs, may lead some employers to eschew qualified plans altogether. However, ERISA's vesting rules do not affect the choice between the defined contribution and the defined benefit formats since the rules apply to both.

---

[35] Professor Wooten traces the origins of the IRA as a coverage mechanism in Wooten, *id.* at 171, 174–175, 260.

[36] Alicia H. Munnell and Annika Sunden, COMING UP SHORT, THE CHALLENGE OF 401(K) PLANS (2004) at 9 ("Technically, ERISA's provisions applied to both defined benefit and defined contribution plans. But the main thrust of the legislation was on the defined benefit side.")

[37] Code Section 411 and ERISA Section 203.

On the other hand, parts of ERISA burden defined benefit plans more heavily than defined contribution arrangements. Most prominently, ERISA imposes complex minimum funding requirements on defined benefit plans.[38] These rules have been tweaked repeatedly over the years, most recently in the Pension Protection Act of 2006 (PPA).[39] However, in all of their incarnations, these often opaque rules have limited employer flexibility in the financing of defined benefit plans. Consequently, in a bad year, the employer sponsoring a defined benefit plan may find itself locked into a pension funding obligation it would rationally prefer to defer to better times.

The minimum funding rules are not without their defenders who can marshall plausible justifications: Employees covered by defined benefit plans reasonably rely on the promise of future benefits and the implicit assurance that those benefits are being funded properly. The sound financing of projected pension benefits is actuarially complex, leading to complicated calculations and, thus, a complicated statute.[40] Since promised benefits are payable in the future, it is tempting to promise those benefits now and leave to one's successor the task of financing them; hence, the need for legislation to assure that promised benefits are funded currently. Whatever the merits of these arguments,[41] the minimum funding rules deprive the employer of significant flexibility in the financing of defined benefit pensions. In contrast, the employer sponsoring a profit sharing plan retains far greater flexibility[42] to contribute (or not) in any year and to decide how much to contribute.[43] Moreover, the employer's obligations in the profit sharing context are far simpler to understand.

---

[38] For plan years beginning after December 31, 2007, the minimum funding standards are found in the Internal Revenue Code in Sections 412 and 430 through 432, inclusive, and in ERISA Sections 301 and 302.

[39] *See* PPA Sections 102 and 103 (revising the ERISA version of the minimum funding rules) and PPA Sections 111, 112 and 212 (revising the Code version of the minimum funding rules).

[40] Between the often-complex formulas for determining a participant's benefit and the equally-complex actuarial formulas for funding, it is in some ways appropriate to think of defined benefit pension plans as the original complex financial instruments.

[41] Ironically, concerns about systematic underfunding were (and still are today) most compelling as to governmental defined benefit plans—which are exempted from ERISA's minimum funding rules.

[42] For the long run, the employer's discretion to contribute to its profit sharing plan is not unbridled. However, that discretion is enormous in contrast with the minimum funding requirements applicable to pension plans.

[43] A common design today is for 401(k) plans to include an employer match of the employees' salary reduction contributions. Unlike defined benefit funding requirements, employers can suspend or reduce this match in difficult economic times — as many employers do. *See, e.g.,* Arleen Jacobius, *More plan sponsors do away with 401(k) match,* 31(17) Pensions & Investments 4 (August 18, 2003); Joann S. Lublin, *Benefits: I'll Have What He's Having,* Wall St. J., May 20, 2003 at B1 ("At least a dozen major companies

Compliance with ERISA's minimum funding rules also entails significant administrative costs for defined benefit arrangements, i.e., actuarial, accounting and legal fees, costs to which many employers, particularly smaller ones, are quite sensitive.[44]

In short, the inflexibiliy, impenetrability and administrative costs associated with ERISA's defined benefit minimum funding rules are, for many employers, a significant deterrent to establishing or continuing defined benefit plans, particularly when those rules are contrasted with the greater flexibility, transparency and simplicity of the rules governing profit sharing plans including 401(k) plans.[45]

Another cost ERISA imposes only on defined benefit plans is premium payments to the Pension Benefit Guaranty Corporation (PBGC), the government-operated insurance entity which resembles the FDIC and which insures basic pension benefits.[46] Here, again, there are both plausible arguments for the existence of the PBGC as well as a serious critique against it.[47] However, my purpose is not to evaluate the pros and cons of the PBGC, but, rather, to observe the impact of PBGC premiums on an employer's choice between a defined benefit plan and a defined contribution arrangement. Since the PBGC only covers the former and not the latter, PBGC premiums impose an additional cost on the defined benefit option in contradistinction to an uninsured individual account plan.

---

have temporarily reduced or suspended matching contributions to 401(k) plans since January 2002.") See also *Firms cutting contributions to 401(k)s*, NEW HAVEN REGISTER, April 4, 2003 at E4. This flexibility stands in sharp contrast to the defined benefit funding rules.

[44] Norman P. Stein, *An Alphabet Soup Agenda For Reform of the Internal Revenue Code and ERISA Provisions Applicable to Qualified Deferred Compensation Plans*, 56 SMU LAW REV. 627, 641 (2003) ("Defined benefit plans are generally more costly to administer, in large part because of the need to engage the services of an actuary.").

[45] As Patrick Purcell has pointed out, in the years immediately after the enactment of ERISA, the number of defined benefit pensions actually increased. By some measures, the decline of the defined benefit system commenced in earnest after the adoption of Section 401(k). I find it plausible, as indicated in the text, to conclude that the subsequent adoption of Section 401(k) had a synergistic effect, compounding ERISA's regulatory impact on defined benefit plans by creating an attractive alternative (the 401(k) plan) for employers. However, it seems likely that, for the long run, ERISA's regulation of defined benefit plans discouraged the maintenance and creation of defined benefit plans, independently of the existence of the 401(k) alternative. *See* Purcell, *supra* note 7 at 54 ("Between 1975 and 1983, the number of [defined benefit] plans increased from 103,346 to 172,642.")

[46] ERISA Section 4001 et seq. *See also* Daniel Keating, *Chapter 11's New Ten-Ton Monster: The PBGC and Bankruptcy*, 77 MINN. L. REV. 803, 806 (1993) (describing the PBGC as "a wholly-owned United States government corporation modeled after the Federal Deposit Insurance Corporation.").

[47] *See, e.g.*, Richard A. Ippolito, PENSIONS, ECONOMICS AND PUBLIC POLICY (1985).

To the extent employers must absorb these extra costs, those costs deter the creation and continuation of defined benefit plans. Even if these costs can be passed on to employees in the form of reduced wages, these costs are likely to give employers pause. Insofar as employees appreciate the advantages of an insured benefit, they might accept lower cash wages as a reasonable price to pay for insured defined benefit coverage. However, insofar as employees do not presently value either their participation in a defined benefit plan or PBGC insurance coverage, lower cash wages put the employer at a competitive disadvantage in the labor market.[48]

Many employers, particularly smaller firms, responded to the regulatory burdens imposed by ERISA by abandoning qualified plans altogether. Other employers responded to the heavier burdens placed on defined benefit plans by shifting to less heavily-regulated defined contribution devices. This shift gave an important impetus to the defined contribution paradigm as employers and employees came to experience and thus conceive of retirement savings as individual accounts.

iii. ERISA's Fiduciary Rules and Participant-Directed Accounts

ERISA's third step down the road toward a defined contribution society was the decision embraced in the statute to permit sponsors of defined contribution plans to authorize employees to direct the investment of their own accounts.[49] Such self-directed investment largely[50] relieves the employer (or, to be precise, the trustee the employer has designated) of the otherwise substantial fiduciary obligations stemming from the responsibility for investing the plan's assets.

---

[48]   See Halperin, *supra* chap. two note 2 at 41 ("If other employers are paying compensation solely in cash, employers who establish plans must provide equal cash compensation for reluctant savers in order to compete.").

[49]   ERISA Section 404(c).

[50]   Under the Department of Labor's interpretation, ERISA Section 404(c) relieves a plan fiduciary of liability for a participant's investment decisions only if the plan satisfies certain regulatory requirements designed to ensure that such participant has a meaningful "opportunity. . . to exercise control over assets in his individual account" as well as the "opportunity to choose . . . from a broad range of investment alternatives." As long as the fiduciary satisfies the requirements of the regulations, he is relieved of liability for the participant's investment choices. See 29 CFR Section 2550.404c-1. PPA Section 624 amends ERISA Section 404(c) to authorize the Secretary of Labor to regulate the default investments in which participants' assets are to be invested if the participant gives no direction as to such investments.

A central feature of ERISA was the imposition upon trustees managing plan assets of federal fiduciary standards based on the traditional obligations of trustees, namely, the duties of loyalty, prudence and diversification.[51] In some states, state law, even without ERISA, imposed upon pension trustees the traditional duties of trustees and the time-honored sanctions for violating those duties.[52] However, even in those states, ERISA's federalization of the fiduciary obligations of pension trustees gave those obligations a new salience. Moreover, as to those states in which the fiduciary responsibilities of pension trustees were less well-articulated, ERISA was reasonably perceived as imposing new burdens on such trustees.

However, offsetting these burdens was an important safety valve: Under ERISA Section 404(c), if a defined contribution plan permits each employee to direct the investment of the funds in his own account, the plan's trustee bears no[53] liability to the employee for investments, on the apparent assumption that the employee is deciding for himself. Such participant direction of plan investments is not feasible in the defined benefit context since the defined benefit participant has no discrete subset of assets earmarked for him which he can manage for himself. Rather, the defined benefit participant has a claim for future benefits against the totality of a common fund. Hence, in the defined benefit context, it would make little sense for the employee to invest funds since the employer, promising a specified benefit, bears the consequences of investment performance by the total pool.

Consider in this context the owner of a closely-held corporation who, before ERISA, acted as trustee of his company's defined benefit pension plan. With ERISA heightening the salience (and perhaps the substance) of his fiduciary obligations, this owner had three alternatives: continuing to serve as trustee with those obligations, hiring a professional trustee for the plan, or terminating the defined

---

51   ERISA Code Section 404(a)(1). *See also* Langbein, Stabile and Wolk, *supra* chap. one note 2 at 556–559; John H. Langbein, *What ERISA Means By "Equitable": The Supreme Court's Trail of Error in Russell, Mertens and Great-West*, 103 Columbia L. Rev. 1317, 1321–1338 (2003).

52   *See, e.g., Board of Trustees v. Mayor and City Council of Baltimore City*, 317 Md. 72, 102; 562 A.2d 720, 734 (1989) (as to governmental pension plan, not regulated by ERISA, "the pension contracts incorporate the Trustees' common-law duties of prudence and loyalty.").

53   Subject to compliance with the regulatory requirements to insure the participant a meaningful opportunity to make his investment choices and to provide for proper default investments if the participant gives no directions for his account. *See* 29 CFR Section 2550.404c-1 and ERISA Section 404(c)(5) added by PPA Section 624.

benefit plan and replacing it with a self-directed defined contribution plan. For some employers, the self-directed defined contribution plan proved the best choice since it shifted the investment function to the plan participants and consequently shifted fiduciary liability away from the owner/trustee.

iv. The Ten Percent Limit on Employer Stock

Finally, ERISA established a numerical limit on the amount of the sponsoring employer's stock which may be held as a defined benefit plan investment. Generally, employer stock may constitute no more than ten percent (10%) of total defined benefit plan assets.[54] In contrast, ERISA enacted no such numerical limit on the employer stock held by individual account plans.[55] As the Enron saga demonstrated, this difference was grasped by many employers who established defined contribution plans, loaded such plans with employer stock, and encouraged employees to direct the investment of their 401(k) resources into employer stock. The upshot was (and still remains) defined contribution arrangements which hold quantities of employer stock far beyond the limits permitted for defined benefit plans.[56]

---

[54] ERISA Section 407(a)(2).

[55] ERISA Section 407(b)(1).

[56] Susan J. Stabile, *Enron, Global Crossing, and Beyond: Implications for Workers,* 76 St. John's Law Rev. 815, 820–821 (2002) ("In addition, we have reached a point where the 401(k) plan accounts of a significant number of employees are bloated with company stock.") Millon, *supra* intro. note 2 at 838–840 ("At a number of companies, however, the percentage of 401(k) assets invested in company stock is even higher.") Sharon Reece, *Enron: The Final Straw & How to Build Pensions of Brick,* 41 Duquesne L. Rev. 69, 116 (2002) ("Other companies have 401k assets similarly invested in a high percentage of company stock.")

The question why employers contribute their stock to qualified plans is not as simple as first appears as the economic effects of contributing newly-issued stock directly to the plan are identical to the impact of contributing cash to the plan and then having the plan itself purchase new stock from the corporation with that contributed cash. The employer derives no additional cash savings from a direct stock contribution as opposed to a cash contribution followed by the plan's purchase of newly-issued stock from the corporation with that cash.

If, for example, an employer contributes $100 to its plan and the plan immediately uses that $100 to buy new stock from the employer, the plan ends up with stock and the employer ends up with its $100 back – exactly the same result obtained by the employer contributing the stock directly to the plan and forsaking any cash contribution. Either way, there is no net cash outlay by the corporation.

Why, then, do corporations contribute their stock to their 401(k) plans rather than contribute cash for stock purchases? I believe that such contributions are primarily intended to encourage employees to invest their salary reduction contributions in the employer's stock. The employer's direct contribution

The post-ERISA period saw the termination of defined benefit pension plans as employers reassessed such plans in the new legal environment created by the statute. In many instances, employers created defined contribution plans to replace their terminated defined benefit arrangements. Moreover, employers seeking to establish new qualified plans from scratch eschewed the defined benefit configuration and instead opted for individual account arrangements, particularly profit sharing plans.

Many of the defined benefit plans terminated in the wake of ERISA were maintained by small and professional employers. Some observers dismissed these defined benefit pensions as tax shelters for high income earners and consequently viewed the demise of these plans with equanimity.[57] However, for two reasons, the death of the small employer defined benefit plan had important long-term consequences. First, small firms, in the aggregate, employ much of the workforce.[58] Second, some small employers become large employers; when firms establish money purchase pension and profit sharing plans in their early years, they tend to stay with such plans later.

In short, ERISA, without anyone intending it that way, laid the ground work for the defined contribution society, both by authorizing the IRA and by placing

---

endorses its stock as an investment. That endorsement, in turn, influences employees to put their salary reduction contributions in the same investment. In short, the corporate contribution of stock signals to the employees that they should direct their funds into stock purchases.

There are three reasons why corporate management wants employees to invest their salary reduction amounts in the employer's stock. First, when employees purchase newly-issued stock, they in effect rebate part of their compensation back to the employer. Suppose an employee is paid $10 and elects salary reduction for $1. If that $1 is returned to the corporation for newly-issued stock, the corporation has in practice paid the employee $9 and has the other $1 back to spend for corporate purposes.

Second, if the employees' salary reduction amounts are used to purchase stock in the open market, those purchases increase demand for the employer's stock and thus elevate the price of that stock. It is attractive to corporate management, particularly managers with stock options, to increase the price of the employer's stock in this fashion.

Third, corporate management perceives (often with good reason) that stock owned by employees is in friendlier hands than if that stock were in the hands of third parties.

[57] This attitude persists among influential commentators today. *See, e.g.*, Stein, *supra* note 44 at 654 (small employer defined benefit "plans are inconsistent with the justification for the tax subsidy, since they operate to weight benefits toward highly compensated employees and away from the lower and middle-income employees, who are the primary target of the tax expenditures.").

[58] Purcell, *Sponsorship and Participation, supra* chap. two note 53 at CRS-4 ("Encouraging sponsorship of retirement plans by small firms is an important issue to Congress in part because of the large number of people employed by small businesses. In 2002, for example, more than 34 million people worked for firms with fewer than 25 employees.").

burdens on defined benefit plans which discouraged the creation and maintenance of such plans. ERISA thereby, unintentionally but decisively, shifted employers toward the defined contribution model.

C.   Section 401(k)

The next critical event for the emergence of the defined contribution paradigm was the adoption of Code Section 401(k) and the regulations implementing that section. Today, we are so used to thinking of the now ubiquitous 401(k) account as a retirement savings device that it is easy to forget Section 401(k)'s origins in the tax problem of constructive receipt. An endemic problem of the federal income tax is taxpayers' manipulation of the cash method of accounting.[59] In its classic incarnation, that manipulation takes the form of a high bracket, cash method taxpayer ignoring income available to him in the current year to shift that income into subsequent years in which the taxpayer's marginal rate will be lower. To combat perceived abuses along these lines, the doctrine of constructive receipt taxes this cash method taxpayer in his high bracket year when the income was constructively received, that is, when he could have taken it had he not manipulated the cash method.[60]

In the context of qualified retirement plans, consider an employer who establishes a plan with what is sometimes called a "cash-or-deferred" provision, sometimes also called a "salary reduction" arrangement. Under such an arrangement, the employer gives the employee an election between full salary (all currently taxable to the employee as current compensation) or reduced salary with the difference contributed by the employer to the qualified plan. If the tax system respects the employee's election to receive reduced salary and for the employer to make a corresponding plan contribution, the employee shifts a portion of her otherwise available income from the current year to the future, when she eventually receives her plan distribution and is likely to be in a lower tax bracket. Such shifting of

---

[59]   That manipulation and the doctrines developed to combat it (including constructive receipt) are important topics in virtually all introductory casebooks on the federal income tax. *See, e.g.*, Klein, Bankman and Shaviro, *supra* note 26 at 253–281.

[60]   *See, e.g.*, Treas. Reg. Section 1. 451–2(a) ("Income although not actually reduced to a taxpayer's possession is constructively received by him in the taxable year during which it is credited to his account, set apart for him, or otherwise made available so that he may draw upon it at any time, or so that he could have drawn upon it during the taxable year if notice of intention to withdraw had been given.").

income to a lower future tax bracket is precisely the harm at which the doctrine of constructive receipt is aimed.

For this reason, the IRS and the Treasury had serious misgivings about elective salary reduction provisions while employers naturally defended them as reasonable devices for tailoring employers' compensation packages to meet employees' needs. The issue proved so contentious that the drafters of ERISA postponed it for future resolution.[61] Finally, in 1978, Congress acted in a way which inadvertently but decisively accelerated the trend toward the defined contribution culture.[62]

Congress's decision—embodied in Section 401(k) of the Code—simultaneously condoned and cabined salary reduction arrangements and the tax deferral they entail. Specifically, Section 401(k) permits elective cash-or-deferred provisions in profit sharing plans if the higher paid portion of the employer's workforce participates under such provisions at levels roughly proportional to the participation rates of rank-and-file employees. For these purposes, Section 401(k) originally divided the sponsoring employer's covered employees into the highest paid one-third (1/3) and the rest. For each member of both groups, Section 401(k) required the calculation of an "actual deferral percentage," i.e., the percentage of the employee's compensation electively converted into an employer contribution to the plan. As long as the average actual deferral percentage of the high paid third of the workforce did not exceed the actual deferral percentage of the remaining employees by more than certain statutorily-permitted limits,[63] the plan and its cash-or-deferred arrangement were respected for tax purposes.[64]

---

[61] *See* ERISA Section 2006.

[62] *See* Section 135 of P.L. 95–600, adding to the Code Section 401(k). *See also* Stein, *supra* note 44 at 659 (discussing the events leading to "the Section 401(k) revolution.").

[63] Code Section 401(k)(3)(A) as originally adopted.

[64] Congress later amended 401(k) to define the group of higher paid employees as those employees who are highly compensated within the meaning of Code Section 414(q). Congress also gave Section 401(k) plans the alternative of complying with so-called "safe harbor" rules. *See* Code Section 401(k)(12). For many, particularly smaller, employers, these safe harbor rules have proved attractive.

In addition, Congress later imposed a numerical limit on each participant's annual salary deferrals. These limits were subsequently liberalized by the Economic Growth and Tax Relief Reconciliation Act of 2001 (EGTRRA) including so-called "catch-up" salary reduction contributions for individuals fifty years of age and older. See Section 1105(a) of the Tax Reform Act of 1986, P.L. 99–514, adding Section 402(g) of the Code. See also current Section 402(g) of the Code as amended by EGTRRA (increasing the annual salary reduction limit to $15,000 per individual) and Section 414(v) of the Code added by EGTRRA (permitting "catch-up" contributions).

Section 401(k) was effective for 1980 and, once implemented through Treasury regulations,[65] resulted in the rapid growth of what, quite sensibly, became known as "401(k) plans," i.e., profit sharing plans with qualified cash-or-deferred provisions. Two features of typical 401(k) plans enhanced their popularity. First, employers often augment their cash-or-deferred arrangements with matching formulas. Under such formulas, if the employee converts one dollar ($1.00) of otherwise taxable salary into one dollar ($1.00) of employer contribution, the employer matches that contribution with additional funds. Thus, the employee's decision to defer one dollar ($1.00) of salary results in, e.g., a two dollar ($2.00) plan contribution, the second dollar coming from the employer's match.[66]

Second, Section 401(k) plans typically provide for self-directed investments with the participant allocating the funds in his own account among the available alternatives. An important feature of participant directed accounts, we have seen, is that, per ERISA Section 404(c), fiduciary liability largely abates for the plan trustee since the self-directing participant is investing for himself. For the financial services industry, self-directed plans have proved an attractive product with the industry providing a panoply of services such as plan documents, investment advice to employees, and the actual investments themselves including the means for employees to switch their allocations, often quite frequently. The 401(k) plan and its self-directed accounts have accordingly become an important (perhaps the important) retail product of the financial services industry.[67]

The insurance industry had played a critical role in the early stages of the private pension system, encouraging firms to establish plans and to fund such plans with

---

[65] The regulations today appear at Treas. Reg. Section 1.401(k)-0 et seq.

[66] Congress subsequently imposed upon such matching contributions rules similar to those of Section 401(k). *See* Section 401(m). For an interesting experiment gauging the impact of matching formulas on the propensity to save, *see* Esther Duflo, William Gale, Jeffrey Liebman, Peter Orszag and Emmanuel Saez, *Saving Incentives For Low- and Middle-Income Families: Evidence From a Field Experiment with H&R Block*, NBER Working Paper 11680 (September, 2005).

[67] *See* Lawrence A. Cunningham, *Behavioral Finance and Investor Governance*, 59 Washington and Lee L. Rev. 767 (2002) at 789 ("As the Baby Boomer generation has become poised to pressure the Social Security System, self-directed retirement plans have increased in size and availability. People now want to take individual responsibility for their financial needs, particularly in retirement. The market for investment services eagerly meets the demand.") *See also* Fareed Zakaria, The Future of Freedom (2003) at 200–201 ("Anyone with a pension account knows that the entire financial business now revolves around selling products to people like him or her.").

the industry's insurance and annuity products.[68] Banks have long served as trustees and financial advisors for corporate pension and profit sharing plans.[69] Thus, at one level, the role of the financial services industry in promoting 401(k) arrangements merely extended an historic pattern. At another level, however, the role of that industry hastened the shift toward the defined contribution paradigm as the financial services industry became a major advocate of and advertiser for 401(k) plans and IRAs.

One way of characterizing the services provided to 401(k) plans and their participants is that these services are the diseconomies of scale which result from decentralized investing, the diseconomies avoided under the defined benefit format with its centralized investment of a common pool of capital. That, needless to say, has not been the perspective advanced by the financial services industry which has instead emphasized the investment autonomy of the individual 401(k) participant and IRA holder. That emphasis, I suggest in Chapter Four, strongly appeals to prevailing norms of private property, self-sufficiency and individual control.

D. ERTA and TRA86: Expanded Availability of IRAs and the Financial Services Industry

As Section 401(k) accelerated the shift to the defined contribution paradigm, the Economic Recovery Tax Act (ERTA) of 1981,[70] championed by President Reagan, further reinforced that shift by converting the IRA into something approximating a universal savings vehicle. President Reagan was committed, depending upon one's perspective, to the encouragement of tax-favored savings or to the elimination of the income tax bias against savings. Reflecting these concerns, ERTA liberalized ERISA's rules for tax-deductible IRA contributions by permitting any person with earned income (even if covered by a qualified plan at work) to establish an IRA and to make tax-deductible contributions to that IRA up to $2,000 per person.[71] ERTA thus transformed the IRA from a response to the

---

[68] *See* Sass, *supra* note 12 at 154 ("the insurance companies were the most active providers of pension services through the years of depression and war . . .").

[69] *Id.* at 154–155.

[70] P.L. 97–34.

[71] ERTA limited IRA contributions to the amount of the individual's compensation for the year. Thus, IRA contributions were only available to taxpayers with earned income. *See* Code Section 219(b) as amended by ERTA.

coverage and portability problems to a virtually[72] universal savings vehicle, even as the IRA continued to address the portability issue via the rollover rules.

It is interesting to speculate how ERTA would have passed Congress had ERISA not created the IRA seven years earlier. Perhaps, in deference to President Reagan's views, something like the IRA would have been created from scratch in 1981 to serve as a general, tax-favored savings vehicle. Alternatively, in a world without the IRA, perhaps President Reagan would not have succeeded in extending taxpayers' ability to save on a tax-deductible basis. From this vantage, that the IRA both existed and was easily adaptable to President Reagan's vision may have facilitated an otherwise unobtainable alteration of the tax law; what would have seemed an abrupt change instead appeared incremental given the pre-existence of the IRA. In any event, the IRA was at hand and became the vehicle for President Reagan's goal of a more saving-friendly tax code.

Even without the enactment of ERTA, the amounts held in IRAs would, with the passage of time, have increased as more individuals received plan distributions and rolled them over into IRAs. However, ERTA, by permitting anyone with earned income to contribute to an IRA on a tax-deductible basis, caused an immediate and explosive growth in the number of IRAs and in the amounts they held—which, of course, is what President Reagan and those who supported this aspect of ERTA intended.

Between the adoption of ERISA in the mid-1970s and the effective date of ERTA (January 1, 1982), relatively few individuals had established IRAs for coverage purposes, that is, to make tax-deductible contributions in the absence of pension participation at the workplace. This is not surprising given the correlation among higher incomes, pension coverage, and ability to save. Those covered by qualified plans tend to be the better paid participants in the workforce. Correspondingly, those without employment-based pension coverage tend to be lower paid workers who, by virtue of their lesser incomes, are poorly positioned to save via IRA contributions or otherwise.[73] Moreover, the IRA was then a novel device and

---

[72]   As noted above, the taxpayer needed earned income to make deductible IRA contributions.

[73]   Jonathan Barry Forman, MAKING AMERICA WORK (2006) at 220 ("the probability of participating in a pension plan increases significantly with income level"); Medill, *supra* chap. two note 5 at 919 ("higher income workers with greater amounts of discretionary income are better positioned financially to defer the receipt of some current income than lower income workers, who are more likely to need all of their compensation for immediate consumption needs.") *See also* David A. Pratt, *Pension Reform*

initially lacked Treasury regulations to clarify the inevitable concerns which arise under a new and complex statute. The upshot was that, in the period immediately after ERISA's adoption, relatively few persons availed themselves of the opportunity to make deductible contributions to IRAs since persons without work-based pension coverage (before ERTA, the only persons permitted tax-deductible IRA contributions) tend to be low income individuals who find it difficult to save, even with a tax incentive. In addition, the novelty and uncertainties of the IRA initially deterred some, perhaps many, individuals who might otherwise have established such accounts.

ERTA radically changed the dynamic of the IRA, making tax-deductible contributions available to middle-income and upper-income taxpayers even if they had employment-based pension coverage. This caused a quantum growth in the number of persons with IRAs and in the amounts held in those accounts. In 1981, the last year before ERTA became effective, slightly over three million taxpayers had IRAs. In 1982, the first year ERTA was in force, the number of taxpayers with IRAs almost quadrupled to twelve million.[74] The corresponding increase in total IRA assets was even more dramatic, from slightly less than $5 billion in 1981 to over $28 billion in 1982.[75]

Much ink has been spilled arguing whether this growth in IRA assets reflected new, additional savings or, rather, the diversion to IRAs of existing savings or of savings which would have occurred anyway.[76] However, for the emergence of the defined contribution paradigm, this dispute is irrelevant: Whether the ERTA-stimulated growth of IRA assets in the early 1980s reflected new net savings or not, that growth turned the IRA from a device of limited utility into a national

---

Proposals, at section 3.05 in Alvin D. Lurie (ed.), NEW YORK UNIVERSITY REVIEW OF EMPLOYEE BENEFITS AND EXECUTIVE COMPENSATION (2003) (noting that "upper-income taxpayers . . . are the ones who have sufficient disposable income to be able to save more than minimal amounts.") Patrick J. Purcell, *Sponsorship and Participation, supra* chap. two note 53 at Summary ("Workers who earned less than $20,000 in 2002 were just one-third as likely as those who earned $60,000 or more to have participated in a retirement plan at work.").

74 *See* Edward A. Zelinsky, *ERISA and the Emergence of the Defined Contribution Culture,* Chapter 6 in Alvin D. Lurie (ed.), NYU 57TH INSTITUTE ON FEDERAL TAXATION- EMPLOYEE BENEFITS AND EXECUTIVE COMPENSATION (1999) at footnote 33.

75 *Id.* For a discussion of the background of ERTA's expansion of IRA availability and the consequences of that expanded availability, *see* Cohen, *supra* note 32 at 621–624.

76 *See, e.g.,* James M. Poterba, Steven F. Venti and David A. Wise, *The Transition to Personal Accounts and Increasing Retirement Wealth: Macro and Micro Evidence,* National Bureau of Economic Research Working Paper 8610 (November, 2001).

institution, widely used by middle-income and upper-income taxpayers. As a result, millions of Americans for the first time experienced retirement savings as individual accounts, rather than as employer-guaranteed defined benefits. This spread and reinforced the defined contribution paradigm.

Moreover, the ERTA-based growth of the IRA further ensconced the financial services industry as a key support of the defined contribution paradigm as it exists today.[77] With ERTA's embrace of near universal IRA availability and the simultaneous emergence of the self-directed 401(k) account, the financial services industry aggressively promoted the retirement savings business on a retail basis, serving individuals as IRA owners as well as 401(k) participants. As Fareed Zakaria has observed:

> Introduced only twenty-five years ago, IRAs and 401(k) plans are now the mechanisms through which most Americans participate in the stock and bond markets.[78]

The promotion of IRAs by the financial services industry did not diminish when Congress, in the Tax Reform Act of 1986[79] (TRA86), severely curtailed ERTA's expansion of taxpayers' ability to make tax-deductible IRA contributions. The central policy of TRA86, again Reagan-inspired, was a significant reduction of federal income tax rates in return for a broadening of the tax base. As part of that policy, TRA86 restricted, on the basis of income, the ability of taxpayers covered by employment-based qualified plans to make tax-deductible IRA contributions.

In particular, under TRA86,[80] a married couple filing jointly with an annual adjusted gross income in excess of $50,000 was precluded altogether from making deductible IRA contributions if either spouse was covered by a qualified plan. If married taxpayers filed jointly, if either was covered by a workplace plan and if their adjusted gross income was between $40,000 and $50,000 per year, the statute

---

[77] See Cunningham, *supra* note 67, Zakaria, *supra* note 67.

[78] Zakaria, *supra* note 67.

[79] P.L. 99–514, P.L. 99–514, 100 Stat. 2085 (1986).

[80] See Code Section 219(g) as added by TRA86. These rules were subsequently liberalized. *See* the current version of Code Section 219(g).

progressively diminished their ability to make tax deductible IRA contributions as their income increased. Under TRA86, only married taxpayers without employment-based plan coverage and married taxpayers with such coverage but earning less than $40,000 annually were permitted the full IRA contribution deduction of $2,000 per year.

For single taxpayers, the equivalent figures established in TRA86 were $35,000 (no deductible IRA if covered by a qualified plan and annual adjusted gross income exceeded that amount), $25,000 and $35,000 (the amount of deductible contributions phased out as yearly income rose between these levels), and $25,000 (below this annual income level, IRA contributions were fully deductible even if the single taxpayer was covered by an employment-based qualified plan).

Taxpayers not permitted deductible contributions under these TRA86 rules were allowed to make IRA contributions up to $2,000 without a deduction or, in the case of taxpayers whose incomes fell within the phase-out zones, a deduction limited by the phase-out formula.

TRA86 thus restored the IRA to a role closer to that originally embodied in ERISA: Taxpayers without employment-based qualified plan coverage could, regardless of income, use the IRA on a tax-deductible basis as a substitute for workplace pension coverage. The IRA's rollover function continued unimpaired. However, nondeductible IRA contributions did not prove particularly attractive for higher income households while lower income families generally could not afford the savings entailed in deductible IRA contributions.

For the emergence of the defined contribution paradigm, TRA86's restoration of the IRA to something closer to its original role was less important than might have been predicted. During the five year period (1982 through 1986) during which ERTA expanded to near universality the availability of deductible IRA contributions, enormous sums were placed into IRAs. These sums had to be managed even if no further amounts were being contributed. Even if IRA owners were precluded from further tax deductible contributions (as many were by TRA86), they continued to hold and manage those accounts. Between Congress's decision to condone cash-or-deferred arrangements under Section 401(k) and ERTA's five year expansion of the IRA, the defined contribution genie was out of the bottle.

In this context, consider again a theoretical retiree who received a monthly annuity check from his defined benefit plan starting in 1970. Consider also his granddaughter who entered the workforce in the early 1980s. While the grand-father, during his working life and on his retirement, experienced retirement savings in the traditional defined benefit form, his granddaughter increasingly experienced such savings in the defined contribution format, as 401(k) participation, IRA coverage or both. As a union member during the 1940s and 1950s, the grandfather was taught to conceive of retirement income in traditional defined benefit terms, namely, as a deferred annuity based on salary and service history, starting at retirement. His granddaughter, more likely employed in a nonunion-ized service or high-tech industry, was introduced to a different paradigm based on individual accounts.

During the prolonged bull market of the 1980s and 1990s, an employer's promise to pay a guaranteed benefit seemed increasingly stodgy as the granddaughter's IRA and 401(k) account balances rose with seeming inevitability. That same bull market stimulated employers to terminate their defined benefit plans which, in light of superior investment performance, became overfunded. To recoup those surplus funds, many employers eliminated their defined benefit arrangements and, after paying promised benefits, kept the remaining resources for themselves, net of corporate income tax.[81]

Reality, of course, was often more complex than this simple vignette suggests. The grandfather might have had a profit sharing plan at his work place, supplement-ing his defined benefit coverage, and thus had some experience with the defined contribution format. Some younger people became participants in defined benefit plans. Many younger people eligible for 401(k) participation failed to elect salary reductions to fund their accounts or contributed minimal amounts to their 401(k) accounts.[82]

Nevertheless, this idealized example captures important truths: By the mid-1980s, the defined benefit system was stagnating. Virtually no new defined benefit plans were being created. Many had been (and were being) terminated or frozen. Simultaneously, less heavily regulated defined contribution devices—in particular, 401(k) arrangements and IRAs—were thriving. For many individuals, the

---

[81]   *See* Langbein, Stabile and Wolk, *supra* chap. one note 2 at 251 et seq.

[82]   In 2001, families headed by persons between the ages of 21 and 34 had a mean balance in their retirement accounts of $19,123 and a median balance of $7,000. Only slightly more than half of such families had retirement accounts at all. *See* Patrick J. Purcell, *Retirement Savings and Household Wealth: A Summary of Recent Data*, Congressional Research Service (December 11, 2003) at CRS-8.

individual account format worked well. A paradigm shift was under way which, by the end of the twentieth century, would transform the way in which Americans save for retirement. As Patrick Purcell has observed:

> Considering that IRAs were first authorized by Congress in 1974, and that the first 401(k) plan was established just 22 years ago in 1981, some might find it quite astonishing that by 2000 more than 47 million Americans owned one or more of these retirement savings accounts.[83]

In some ways, the most interesting manifestation of the growing grip of the defined contribution paradigm was the legislative response to employers' increasingly vociferous complaints that Congress, by its cumulative regulation of qualified plans, had made such plans too complex for many (particularly smaller) employers. Rather than embracing the most straightforward response to the problem of overregulation, i.e., deregulating, Congress instead added to the Code provisions for "simplified employee pensions"[84] and "simple retirement accounts."[85] These devices authorized employer contributions to employees' IRAs as a substitute for regular pension contributions—and thereby further extended employers' and employees' experiences with such accounts.

E.   Extending the Defined Contribution Paradigm: FSAs, MSAs, Educational Savings Accounts, Section 529, and Roth IRAs

Given the shift to the individual account paradigm for retirement savings, it was a natural progression for Congress to extend this paradigm to other areas of tax and social policy. An initial step in that direction occurred in the early 1980s with the institutionalization of the "flexible spending account" (FSA). Like the 401(k) plan, the origins of the FSA can be traced to the question of employment-based constructive receipt: If an employer offers an employee a choice of either a tax-free fringe benefit or taxable cash compensation, does the employee electing the fringe benefit constructively receive taxable income because he could have taken taxable cash? As a statutory matter, Congress answered with a qualified "no,"

---

[83]   Purcell, *supra* note 7 at 66.
[84]   Code Section 408(k).
[85]   Code Section 408(p).

decreeing in Code Section 125 that, pursuant to a nondiscriminatory "cafeteria plan," an employer can offer employees the choice between cash compensation and certain fringe benefits with the fringe benefits retaining their tax-free status.

Thus was born the FSA, an individual account by which the employee can elect to reduce his taxable compensation by diverting a portion of such compensation to certain tax-favored fringe benefits. Notwithstanding the Treasury's efforts to restrain FSAs,[86] these have become popular, particularly as a way of permitting employees to defray their co-payments and deductibles for medical coverage on a pre-tax basis.[87] The FSA thus further acclimated working Americans to the individual account experience, broadening that experience beyond retirement savings. Today, "FSAs are available to more than one-fifth of private-sector workers (typically in larger establishments) and nearly half of government workers (including federal employees), though participation rates are substantially lower."[88]

In 1996 and 1997, Congress took further, indeed decisive, steps in the expansion of individual accounts. Again, no one heralded these steps as furthering a significant transformation of tax and social policy. Each step was taken as a discrete response to a particular problem. Cumulatively, however, the results were the

---

[86]　Long-pending Treasury regulations under Section 125 embody the so-called "use it or lose it" principle. As originally implemented by the proposed regulations, the holder of an FSA had to use the balance in her account by the end of the year for the fringe benefit she selected or forfeited any remaining funds in the account. *See, e.g.,* Prop. Treas. Reg. Section 1. 125-1, A-7 ("For example, a plan that offers participants the opportunity to purchase vacation days [or to receive cash or other benefits under the plan in lieu of vacation days] will not be a cafeteria plan if participants who purchase the vacation days for a plan year are allowed to use any unused days in a subsequent plan year.")
Technically these proposed regulations have been pending since 1984. De facto these regulations today serve as part of the legal framework governing FSAs. *See* Julie A. Roin, *United They Stand, Divided They Fall: Public Choice Theory and the Tax Code,* 74 Cornell L. Rev. 62, 101–108 (1988).
In Notice 2005–42, the IRS modified the "use it or lose it" rule to permit an additional two and one-half month period to use unexpended funds in FSAs. *See* Notice 2005–42, 2005–23 IRB 198. In 2006, Congress authorized one-time rollovers of unused FSA funds to health savings accounts (HSAs). *See* Code Section 106(e) as amended by Section 302(a) of the Tax Relief and Health Care Act of 2006.

[87]　*See, e.g.,* Eileen Alt Powell, *Flexible spending accounts help consumers cover health, child care costs,* New Haven Register, October 20, 2003 at A6.

[88]　Bob Lyke and Chris L. Peterson, *Tax-Advantaged Accounts for Health Care Expenses: Side-by-Side Comparison,* Congressional Research Service, Order Code RS21573, Dec. 26, 2006, available at 2007 TNT 17–27 (Jan. 25, 2007) (parentheticals in original).

extension of the defined contribution configuration to the funding of education and of medical care, and the adaptation of the individual account design to provide for tax-free withdrawals coupled with nondeductible contributions. The devices which thus extended and adapted the defined contribution format in the mid-1990s were the medical savings account (MSA), the 529 program, the educational savings account, and the Roth IRA.

Congress added the MSA to the Code as part of the Health Insurance Portability and Accountability Act of 1996.[89] The MSA adapts the IRA model to medical care. An employee or self-employed person maintains an MSA by making tax deductible contributions to an MSA, subject to dollar limits; those contributions grow tax-free; amounts are withdrawn tax-free from the MSA to defray the medical expenses of the employee and his family. In retrospect, the MSA paved the way for more robust medical-financing arrangements in the form of health reimbursement arrangements (HRA) and health savings accounts (HSA), both discussed later in this chapter.

While the MSA adapts the IRA model to medical care, the MSA differs from the IRA in ways which reflect, *inter alia*, the vagaries of tax policy, interest group influence, and ideological concerns. Withdrawals from MSAs for medical expenses are (unlike distributions from conventional IRAs) tax-free. In this way, MSAs mimic the highly favorable tax treatment of employer-provided medical care under which premiums are tax-deductible to the employer[90] and tax-free to the employee[91] while the payments received by the employee for medical outlays are tax-free also.[92] In addition, MSAs are available only to self-employed persons who purchase "high deductible" medical insurance to cover large, nonroutine medical outlays and to persons whose employer purchases such insurance for them.[93] Thus, in the final analysis, the MSA is a device for defraying day-to-day medical expenses with insurance coverage triggered for larger expenditures. An employee can maintain an MSA only if he works for a small employer, generally defined as a firm with fifty or fewer employees. Except for employees who work

---

[89] *See* Section 301 of P.L. 104–191, 110 Stat. 1936 (1996), adding Section 220 to the Code. Congress subsequently renamed these accounts "Archer Medical Savings Accounts."

[90] Code Section 162(a).

[91] Code Section 106.

[92] Code Sections 105(b).

[93] Code Section 220(c)(1)(A)(iii). An individual can establish an MSA if his spouse is employed by a small employer maintaining a high deductible policy or if his spouse is self-employed.

for employers already sponsoring MSAs and high deductible health coverage, no new MSAs can be established after December 31, 2007.[94]

This network of limitations reflects both the clash of interest groups and the ideological tensions between the individualized vision underlying the defined contribution paradigm and the preference for group risk-pooling embodied in the defined benefit format. Opponents of MSAs often decry the political influence of insurers offering high deducible insurance coverage.[95] MSAs, permitted only if the insured has such coverage, obviously stimulate such insurers' business. On the other hand, full service insurance companies must consider the MSA a threat to their routine claims processing business since the MSA shifts responsibility for paying such claims to the account holder who withdraws from the MSA what he needs to pay, without the claims processing services of the insurer. One need not be a devotee of public choice theory to see that, just as the establishment in the Code of the MSA reflected the political heft of the insurers which sell high deductible coverage, the statutory limits on MSAs similarly protect other insurers' claims processing businesses, by limiting both the size of MSAs and the number of MSAs which can be established.

These statutory limits on MSAs also reflect the ideological fault lines of the defined contribution society. Medical insurance (whether of the indemnity or managed care variety) is the health care analogue to a defined benefit pension. Just as defined benefit plans pool employees and their claims and assign risk and reward to the sponsoring employer, medical insurance[96] pools the insureds into a covered group and allocates risk and reward to the insurer. If those covered by medical insurance in the aggregate spend less on medical care than had been predicted,

---

[94]   Code Section 220(i) as amended by Section 117 of the Tax Relief and Health Care Act of 2006.

[95]   *See, e.g.*, Edwin Park and Iris J. Lav, *Proposed Expansion of Medical Savings Accounts Could Drive Up Insurance Costs and Increase the Number of Uninsured*, 2003 TNT 85–56 (April 30, 2003) ("These MSA expansions have long been pushed by insurance companies that sell MSA policies and conservative policy institutions.") *See also* Martin A. Sullivan, *Economic Analysis: The Side Effects of Health Savings Accounts*, 2003 TNT 140–8 (July 21, 2003) ("To this day, Rooney and the Golden Rule Insurance Co. are the leading supporters of efforts to expand medical savings accounts. The company has spent millions of dollars on lobbying expenses and campaign contributions – mostly to Republicans.")

[96]   This is true whether medical insurance takes the form of traditional indemnity insurance or HMO or other managed care arrangements. That HMOs and similar managed care devices spread risk, like classic indemnity insurance, has proved to be a critical factor in the Supreme Court's evolving jurisprudence of ERISA preemption. *See* Edward A. Zelinsky, *Against a Federal Patients' Bill of Rights*, 21 YALE LAW AND POLICY REV. 443, 450–451 (2003).

the difference inures to the insurer; conversely, greater than expected outlays for the insured group are the insurer's problem. Similarly, if the insurer generates more income than anticipated from the investment of premiums, that profit accrues to the insurer—as does poorer than expected investment experience. Within the group of insureds, insurance pools the risks of unexpectedly bad health just as defined benefit plans pool investment, funding and longevity risks for members of the covered workforce.

Just as defined contribution retirement devices (i.e., self-directed 401(k) accounts, IRAs) privatize decisions about retirement savings, MSAs assign to the individual account holder responsibility for his routine medical outlays and for investing the assets in his MSA account. Such responsibility is crucial for MSA advocates who contend that that responsibility makes consumers of health care more sensitive to the cost of such care, leading them to economize their use of medical resources and to shop for less expensive medical services.

In light of these similarities, it is not surprising that debates about MSAs tracked the arguments in the retirement context about the relative merits of the defined benefit and defined contribution formats and presaged the subsequent debate about health savings accounts (HSAs). Opponents of MSAs argued that such accounts will be utilized by relatively healthy persons who feel that they can, via the MSA, handle their routine medical issues alone. Thus, in a world of MSAs, conventional, full service medical insurance will be subject to an adverse selection process as less healthy persons pursue conventional insurance to pool risk with others. The premiums for such insurance will rise as the insurance pool reflects the poorer health of the remaining participants in the pool. A vicious cycle ensues as relatively healthy persons respond to higher premiums by shifting to the MSA format which, in turn, further isolates those less healthy in the conventional insurance system and increases the costs to those who remain in that system.[97]

---

[97] *See, e.g.*, Park and Lav, *supra* note 95 (discussing "spiraling premium costs due to adverse selection" caused by MSAs). Professor Roin raises the possibility that fundamental tax reform in the form of a value-added tax (VAT) could trigger a similar process for group health insurance in general as healthy persons opt for cash wages rather than insurance coverage. *See* Julie Roin, *The Consequences of Undoing the Federal Income Tax*, 70 U. OF CHICAGO L. REV. 319, 326 (2003) ("A vicious cycle may ensue that in the end virtually eliminates the insurance function of group health insurance . . .") *See also* Schuck, *supra* chap. two note 29 at 58 (Adverse selection "will leave only relatively high-risk people in the first insurance pool, unable to afford that high-cost coverage") and Sullivan, *supra* note 95 (discussing how adverse selection in the context of health accounts creates "(t)he possibility that widespread availability of healthaccounts would substantially increase premiums for less healthy individuals who are likely to retain traditional, low-deductible health insurance.") Similar observations are often made about proposals to expand

The critique advanced by MSA opponents and their defense of conventional medical insurance is analogous to the justification of the defined benefit plan as a risk pooling device and its alleged superiority to the defined contribution alternative. Just as individual accounts shift the financing of retirement from a common pool to the employee himself, the MSA similarly privatizes the financing of routine medical care. Just as the defined benefit plan is a superior device for reducing longevity risk only if the relevant workforce includes persons unconcerned about outliving their retirement resources, conventional medical insurance works best when it covers a broad swath of the workforce, rather than a self-selected group which is sensitive to its health needs and is thus likely less healthy than a random cross-section of workers.

On the other hand, MSA proponents tout the price sensitivity engendered by MSAs and the more efficient consumption of medical services said to result from requiring consumers to confront the costs of their care. Moreover, MSA advocates point to the benefits of eliminating the insurance company middleman when the health care provider and the MSA holder contract with each other without the intervention between them of a third party payer. Advocates of individual medical accounts often analogize to other forms of insurance, noting that home and auto insurance policies do not cover routine house repairs or gasoline purchases but are reserved for true emergencies of an unpredictable nature. So too, they contend, medical insurance should only pay for health care costs that are unforeseeable and expensive while routine medical outlays (like everyday home expenses and oil changes) should be paid by the consumer himself from funds he controls.[98]

Initially, the opponents of the MSA won this debate; relatively few MSAs were established, nowhere near the number triggering the statutory cap.[99] However, at

---

health accounts along the MSA model. *CBPP Says HSAs Could Threaten Fiscal Policy, Employer-Based Insurance*, 2003 TNT 208–35 (October 27, 2003) ("When this process (known as 'adverse selection') occurs, premiums for comprehensive insurance rise. That, in turn, can drive still more of the healthier workers to MSAs, which then makes the pool of workers left in comprehensive coverage even more expensive to insure.") (parenthetical in original).

[98] *See, e.g.*, Sally C. Pipes, MIRACLE CURE: HOW TO SOLVE AMERICA'S HEALTH CARE CRISIS AND WHY CANADA ISN'T THE ANSWER (2004) at 24 ("It's as if automobile insurance paid for the 3,000-mile oil change and the 30,000-mile tune up, or if homeowners' insurance paid to replace burnt out light bulbs and repair leaky faucets.") Amy B. Monahan, *The Promise and Peril of Ownership Society Health Care Policy*, 80 TULANE LAW REV. 777, 805 (2006) ("Analogies to auto and homeowners' insurance can be helpful in understanding insurance in the health context.")

[99] *See* Sullivan, *supra* note 95 (reporting that "(t)here are fewer than 100,000 Archer MSAs now existence" out a total authorized of 750,000).

another level, as we shall see later in this chapter, the introduction of the MSA model had greater influence than the numbers would indicate. The MSA encouraged many insurers to develop comparable individual account devices in the form of health reimbursement arrangements (HRAs) and presaged Congress's authorization of health savings accounts (HSAs), an MSA-type device without many of the restrictions burdening MSAs.

At roughly the same time that Congress added the MSA to the Code, Congress also added to the federal tax law Section 529 for higher education savings. The background of Section 529 is particularly revealing, as the state-sponsored prepaid tuition programs which gave rise to Section 529 were originally structured as defined benefit arrangements. That Section 529 plans have evolved into predominantly defined contribution devices testifies to both the strength of the defined contribution paradigm and to the role of the financial services industry in promoting that paradigm.

Responding to the fact that even public colleges and universities have become expensive for large segments of their populations, many states established prepaid tuition programs. Typical of these programs is the Michigan Education Trust (MET), a public corporation which the Michigan legislature established in 1986 and which entered into prepaid tuition contracts for Michigan residents attending Michigan's public institutions of higher education.[100] As was common for these programs, a purchaser (e.g., a parent or grandparent) gave the MET a sum of money as prepaid tuition for a Michigan resident (e.g., a child or grandchild). In return for that prepaid tuition payment, the MET guaranteed the resident's tuition at a Michigan institution of higher education when the resident reached college age. Thus, the risk of future tuition increases was shifted to the MET which planned, through superior investment performance and actuarial funding techniques, to use the prepaid tuition funds entrusted to it to cover future tuition increases.[101]

---

[100] *See State of Michigan v. United States*, 40 F.3d 817 (1994). *See also* Jeffrey S. Lehman, *Social Irresponsibility, Actuarial Assumptions, and Wealth Redistribution: Lessons About Public Policy From A Prepaid Tuition Program*, 88 MICH. L. REV. 1035 (1990).

[101] It has not turned out that way. *See, e.g.*, Christopher Swope, *Catch-22 for College Savings*, 16(6) GOVERNING 40 (March, 2003) ("the combination of skyrocketing tuition rates and a swooning stock market are forcing states to raise their prices and rethink their prices.") *See also* Robert Tomsho, *Prepaid College Tuition Plans Are Falling Short*, WALL ST. J. (December 16, 2002) at B1 ("many prepaid plans are projecting actuarial deficits for the first time"); Peter Schmidt, *Prepaid-Tuition Plans Feel the Pinch*, 50(3) THE CHRONICLE OF HIGHER EDUCATION A19 (September 12, 2003) ("What has left many state prepaid tuition plans financial vulnerable is their basic structure.")

If, for example, a parent living in Detroit entered into a prepaid tuition contract with the MET for her young child and the child, upon reaching college age, attended the University of Michigan, the child's tuition was covered by the parent's earlier prepayment to the MET. If the child were no longer a Michigan resident but attended a Michigan state institution of higher learning as a nonresident, the child (or the parent) paid the difference between in-state and out-of-state tuition; per the prepayment to it, the MET was responsible for the base in-state tuition. If the child did not go to college or went to college outside of Michigan, a refund formula applied.

The MET, like other such prepaid tuition programs, was thus a defined benefit-style device, pooling resources (the prepaid tuition payments from Michigan families concerned about increasing education costs), shifting the risk associated with such costs to the MET, and guaranteeing a future output in the form of in-state tuition (whatever that might be when a child was ready for higher education).

The IRS determined that the MET was not covered by the State of Michigan's tax-exempt status but was instead liable for the federal tax on corporate income. This was a serious financial blow to the MET since the MET was obligated to generate sufficient earnings from the tuition prepayments the MET received to cover future tuition increases. The District Court agreed with the IRS. However, a split panel of the Sixth Circuit Court of Appeals held that the MET was tax-exempt and thus immune from federal corporate tax.

The government did not seek Supreme Court review of the appellate tribunal's decision. Instead, the controversy shifted to Congress which, in Section 529, not merely confirmed the tax-exempt status of prepaid tuition institutions like the MET, but broadened the compass of such institutions, expanding what had been solely defined benefit-type guarantees of future tuition into defined contribution arrangements as well. Specifically, Section 529 created a new statutory category, the "qualified[102] tuition program" and declared such programs to be federally tax-exempt.[103]

---

[102] The original name was qualified State tuition program.

[103] A qualified tuition program may trigger the tax on unrelated business income. *See* Code Section 529(a) (second sentence).

Under Section 529, a qualified tuition program can come in either of two forms. Such a program can permit the "purchase (of) tuition credits or certificates on behalf of a designated beneficiary which entitle the beneficiary to the waiver or payment of qualified higher education expenses of the beneficiary." In this incarnation, the Section 529 program takes the original defined benefit configuration (like the MET) as the program, in return for a current payment, grants a future output as an in-kind "credit" or "certificate," e.g., one year of tuition at any of State X's state-sponsored colleges in 2015.

However, a qualified tuition program may also take the form of "an account which is established for the purpose of meeting the qualified higher education expenses of the designated beneficiary of the account." In this version, the Section 529 program uses the defined contribution format as an individual account is established for a particular beneficiary to pay his higher education expenses. In this incarnation, the qualified tuition program does not promise for the future a guaranteed defined benefit-style output (e.g., one year of tuition in 2015) but rather generates an individual account balance available for educational expenses. Cash from this account is withdrawn to pay such expenses. Thus, with a defined contribution Section 529 program, risk (both investment risk and the possibility of escalating tuition costs) remains with the prospective student and his family as does reward if, for example, funds in the Section 529 account grow particularly well or at least at a faster pace than future tuition increases.

As originally passed by Congress in 1996, benefits under a qualified tuition program (whether in-kind tuition or actual cash withdrawn for educational expenses) were taxable to the beneficiary.[104] In 2001, Congress, as part of EGTRRA, refined Section 529 by excusing from all federal income tax both the in-kind benefits of a defined benefit-style qualified tuition program and the cash payments from Section 529 accounts to the extent of qualified higher education costs.[105] Thus, today, neither the college student nor her parent pays any federal income tax upon the child's receipt of credits for the tuition prepaid for him or upon the

---

[104] To continue the example in the text, if the college student attended the University of Michigan using tuition credits purchased earlier, the value of those credits was taxable to the student (who was likely in a lower bracket than her parent). Similarly, if cash were withdrawn from a Section 529 account to the pay the child's tuition costs, that cash was then taxable to the child.

[105] While originally adopted as a temporary feature of Section 529, in 2006 Congress made permanent the tax-free status of cash payments and in-kind benefits received under Section 529 programs. Section 1304(a) of the Pension Protection Act of 2006.

use of the cash in a Section 529 account to defray the child's qualified education expenses.

On the face of the statute, the financial services industry has no particular role under Section 529. The reality has been otherwise; indeed, Section 529 has been a boon to the financial services industry, providing that industry with another tax-favored account to promote.[106] States have essentially subcontracted their qualified tuition programs to particular firms which have aggressively marketed Section 529 in its defined contribution form, often on a nationwide basis.

Merrill Lynch, for example, manages Maine's Section 529 program.[107] A Merrill Lynch customer in California (who has no interest in a defined benefit-style arrangement guaranteeing future tuition at Maine's public colleges) can open a Section 529 account with his local Merrill Lynch office. Maine's sponsorship of the account is of no import to the Merrill Lynch customer who is simply offered the program as an opportunity to save for college through a tax favored account. From the customer's perspective, Maine's involvement is nominal;[108] it is Merrill Lynch which offers the customer an opportunity to open a tax-favored account for the accumulation of college funding.[109]

---

[106] Swope, *supra* note 101 ("private money-management firms that run the state plans are marketing them aggressively") *See also* Lynn O'Shaughnessy, *Avoiding Fee Pitfalls as College Savings Climb*, N.Y. Times, July 13, 2003, Section 3 (Money & Business) at 8 ("More states have been embracing broker-sold savings plans, partly because of pressure from the financial industry, which wants to participate more in this growing area.") William Baldwin, *Section 529 Crime Wave*, 172(12) Forbes 24 (December 8, 2003) ("Section 529 lets states team up with fund outfits to offer college savings plans.") John Kimelman, *Fund Scandal Puts College Saving Plans on Alert*, N.Y. Times, Section 3, Money and Business at 6 ("Many fund companies, including Fidelity Investments, the Vanguard Group and Franklin Templeton Investments, have formed partnerships with state governments to offer 529 plans.")

[107] My discussion in the text of Merrill Lynch, which manages the Maine Section 529 program, is illustrative. I could as easily have discussed another state's program managed by a comparable firm. For example, Franklin Templeton manages the New Jersey Section 529 program. *See* Special Advertising Section, *Tuition Planning*," Forbes, June 23, 2003 ("Franklin Templeton 529 College Savings Plan is offered and administered by the State of New Jersey Higher Educational Student Assistance Authority and managed and distributed by Franklin Templeton Distributors, Inc.")

[108] A qualification to this observation is that many states provide a state income tax deduction for a 529 contribution but only if the taxpayer uses that state's 529 plan. *See* Ron Lieber, *A Little-Known Tuition Tax Break*, Wall St. J., June 10–11, 2006, at B1.

[109] *See, e.g.*, Nextgen College Investing Plan Client Select Series, July 28, 2003 (discussing role of Merrill Lynch as "Program Manager.") Another increasingly common format has been the rebate to Section 529 accounts of a portion of consumer purchases. *See, e.g.*, www.BabyMint.com; www.upromise.com.

This defined contribution product flows incrementally from the experience of this customer who, via 401(k) participation or IRA participation or both, has come to see tax-favored individual accounts as a standard way of saving and investing for the future. From this perspective, the Section 529 account is a natural extension of the customer's familiarity with retirement savings in similar accounts.

In short, Section 529 has come full circle from the original conception of prepaid state tuition programs like the MET which in defined benefit fashion pooled funds from state residents, shifted to the state instrumentality both investment risk and the risk of future tuition increases, and guaranteed a specified, projected output in the form of eventual tuition coverage. Today, the typical Section 529 arrangement, as promoted by the financial services industry, is an individual account for higher education outlays. The industry has merchandised these individual account arrangements aggressively. It is thus not surprising that, just as the assets held by defined contribution retirement plans have outstripped the assets of defined benefit pensions, the amounts invested in defined contribution-style Section 529 accounts now exceed by a substantial margin the amounts held by defined benefit-style prepaid tuition plans.[110]

Besides this shift to the defined contribution format, two other aspects of Section 529 are noteworthy. First, the tax treatment today incorporated in Section 529 (no deduction on contribution, investment earnings grow tax-free, no income taxation on distribution) finds increasing favor with Congress and the President in contradistinction to the traditional tax treatment of qualified plans and conventional IRAs (deductible contributions, investment earnings grow tax-free, income taxation on distribution). While the cognoscenti debate the relative utility of these differing patterns of taxation,[111] the political appeal of the newer formula is undeniable as that formula, under existing budgetary accounting rules, moves

---

[110] Swope, *supra* note 101. *See also* O'Shaughnessy, *supra* note 106 ("In a short time, the state-sponsored 529 savings plan has become one of the nation's most popular ways to invest for college. About $30 billion is now spread among more than three million accounts, and the flood of cash is rising exponentially.")

[111] *See, e.g.,* Brian H. Graff, *President's Dividend Proposal Could Affect Small Business Retirement Plan Coverage,* 33(1) THE ASPA JOURNAL 1,5 (Jan.-Feb. 2003)("assuming the same tax rates at the time of contribution and distribution, a deductible IRA and a Roth IRA are economically neutral.")

perceived revenue losses from the present (since there is no current deduction on contribution) to the future (when funds are paid out tax-free).[112]

A second noteworthy feature of Section 529 is the absence of income-based limits on participation. As we have seen, since TRA86, if a taxpayer is covered by a qualified plan, his ability to make deductible IRA contributions is limited (and eventually eliminated) as the taxpayer's income rises. As we shall see further, this type of income-based restriction has been extended to other Code provisions regulating defined contribution devices. But not to Section 529. Thus, Section 529 accounts can be marketed to affluent families, a feature of these accounts undoubtedly of interest to the financial services industry.[113]

Unlike Section 529 programs, Congress constrained the educational savings account with income-based restrictions. As originally enacted in 1997, these accounts bore the oxymoronic label "educational IRAs."[114] As a political matter, that label reflected the same strategy as ERTA's use of the IRA to create a universal savings vehicle: An arguably radical innovation instead appeared to be incremental, the modest extension of the IRA status quo.

As originally passed by Congress in 1997, the educational IRA was indeed modest in scope. In addition to the income-based limitations Congress imposed on contributions to such accounts, Congress also initially capped contributions to educational IRAs at $500 per year and made those contributions nondeductible.

---

[112] This appeal was most recently demonstrated by Congress's decision to permit, starting in 2010, high income individuals to convert their regular IRAs into Roth IRAs by agreeing to taxation upon such conversion. *See* Section 512 of the Tax Increase Prevention and Reconciliation Act of 2005, P.L. 109–222. This decision will generate short-run revenues as individuals recognize as income the amounts in their regular IRAs to transform those IRAs into Roth accounts. However, for the long run, net revenues will be lost as these new Roth IRAs grow tax-free and also yield tax-free withdrawals. *See* Wesley Elmore, *Senate Sends Tax Cut Package to President's Desk*, 2006 TNT 92–1 (May 12, 2006) ("The provision would raise about $7 billion between 2011 and 2015 as high-income taxpayers convert their traditional IRAs to Roth IRAs and pay taxes on the amount being converted. But Democrats and budget watchdog groups have said that any revenue gains would be more than offset by revenue losses incurred beyond 2015, as holders of the newly converted Roth IRAs make withdrawals on a tax-free basis.")

[113] An interesting effort to revive Section 529 savings in the defined benefit form is the Independent 529 Plan in which over 200 private colleges participate. *See* Ron Lieber, *What "Independent 529" Plans Get You When Junior Applies to Private College*, WALL. ST. J., Sept. 30/Oct. 1, 2006 at B1.

[114] *See* Section 530 of the Code as originally enacted by Section 213(a) of the Taxpayer Relief Act of 1997, P.L. 105–34, 111 Stat. 788 (1997).

Like the funds placed in Section 529 plans, the funds given to educational IRAs in their initial incarnation could only be used for higher education expenses. To the extent so used, withdrawals from educational IRAs were (and are) tax-free, thus subjecting such devices to the alternative tax pattern: nondeductible contributions, tax-free income, tax-free withdrawals.

In 2001, again as part of EGTRRA, the educational IRA was retooled in important respects.[115] The $500 annual contribution limit was raised to $2,000. The income-based limitations on contributions were liberalized. Most importantly, Congress permitted funds in educational IRAs to be used for "qualified elementary and secondary education expenses" which include costs connected with "public, private, or religious" schooling. Finally, in 2002, these accounts were given the more apt moniker, Coverdell education savings accounts, in memory of a prime advocate of these devices.[116]

It remains to be seen whether education savings accounts will become as ubiquitous as IRA and 401(k) plans. What cannot be gainsaid is that, between Section 529 plans and educational savings accounts, Congress has firmly implanted tax-favored individual accounts for education into federal tax and social policy.

The other defined contribution device introduced by Congress in 1997 was the Roth IRA. The critical difference between the Roth IRA and the traditional IRA which it adapts is the sequence of taxation. Instead of the tax pattern of a conventional IRA (deduction on contribution, tax-free earnings, taxation on distribution), a Roth IRA uses the alternative sequence, i.e., no deduction on contribution, tax-free income during the accumulation phase, tax-free distribution. While that alternative tax sequence has plausible justifications, undoubtedly the driving force behind Congress's decision to embrace that sequence for the Roth IRA (as well as for Section 529 and education savings accounts) is the budgetary accounting convention which allocates revenue losses to the future when amounts will be withdrawn tax-free from these accounts.[117]

---

[115] *See* Sections 401 and 402(a)(4) of the EGTRRA.

[116] *See* the current version of Code Section 530.

[117] The pattern of after-tax contributions, tax-free earnings and tax-free distributions has proved so appealing to Congress that in 2001 Congress extended the option of such treatment to both 401(k) and 403(b) plans. *See* Code Section 402A (establishing "qualified Roth contribution program(s)"). The Treasury proposed regulations implementing this extension on January 25, 2006. *See* 71 F.R. 4320 (REG-146459–05).

F. Cash Balance, New Comparability, and Age Weighted Plans

While Congress was, during the 1990s, reinforcing and expanding the defined contribution paradigm by establishing new kinds of individual accounts, other developments were confirming and accelerating the emergence of that paradigm. To the general public, the best known of these developments was the cash balance pension plan.

The cash balance pension is a defined benefit arrangement designed to look like an individual account plan.[118] As we have seen, the traditional defined benefit plan promises a deferred annuity at retirement age and typically determines the amount of that annuity based upon the participant's salary and service history with the sponsoring employer. This tends to favor older, long-term workers who accumulate substantial employment history with the sponsoring employer.

In contrast, a cash balance plan guarantees a benefit but specifies that benefit in terms of a theoretical account balance. This theoretical account balance is nominally credited with a portion of the participant's salary, thus mimicking the employer contributions under a true defined contribution arrangement. This theoretical account balance is also credited with a notional interest factor, again to look like an individual account arrangement.

However, in the cash balance context, no separate account for the participant actually exists. Rather, the defined benefit trustee holds a common pool of funds financing the cumulative total of all participants' theoretical account balances and the plan guarantees to the participants benefits equaling their respective theoretical account balances.

Suppose, for example, that a cash balance pension credits each participant's notional account with ten percent of his salary and augments each such account with a nominal interest factor of five percent. Suppose further that a hypothetical cash balance participant earns a salary of $50,000 in the current year. Under this cash balance plan, the participant's theoretical account is credited with $5,000 as

---

[118]   Zelinsky, *supra* chap. one note 2 at 687.

a pay credit[119] and with a notional interest credit of $250.[120] Thus, the participant has a fixed claim against the plan for a lump sum of $5,250.[121]

If, to continue the example, the trustee garners a seven percent (7%) return on the plan's assets, the cash balance participant is not entitled to any more than $5,250 since the plan is a defined benefit arrangement. Superior investment performance inures to the sponsoring employer, not to the participating employee who receives a guaranteed, defined benefit in the form of a notional account balance. Conversely, if the trustee earns only a three percent return on the plan's assets, the participant is not harmed since he is guaranteed $5,250, based on notional interest earnings of $250. Any shortfall in actual investment earnings is the employer's liability since the employer has promised a benefit based on a five percent return.

On the other hand, if this were a true defined contribution plan, the employer, once it conveyed the $5,000 to a genuine, separate account for the employee, would have no further obligation. The participant would be entitled to whatever the account grows or falls without any guarantee from the employer or the plan.

If the participant terminates his employment with the firm sponsoring this cash balance plan, he is usually entitled (in defined contribution style) to an immediate lump sum distribution of his notional account balance rather than the deferred annuity of the traditional defined benefit arrangement.[122] As a matter of law, cash balance pension plans must distribute benefits as joint-and-survivor annuities unless the participant elects otherwise. The participant's spouse must consent to this election. In practice today, most payments from cash balance pensions take the form of lump sum distributions.

In short, the cash balance plan is a defined benefit pension; the plan and the employer guarantee a benefit; the risk and reward of investment performance accrue to the plan and the employer, not to the employee; funds are invested with

---

[119]   i.e., $50,000 × 10\% = $5,000.

[120]   i.e., $5,000 × 5\% = $250.

[121]   Subject to the satisfaction of the minimum vesting rules of Code Section 411(a) and ERISA Section 203.

[122]   Again, subject to vesting rules. See Purcell, *Lump-sum Distributions*, *supra* chap. one note 6 at CRS-6 ("Virtually all cash balance plans offer a lump-sum distribution option to departing employees who are vested in their benefits.")

the plan trustee as a common pool from which benefits are paid. However, the benefit of a cash balance plan is defined and typically distributed as an individual account-style lump sum. This mixture of features shifts longevity risk to the employee (since the employee receives his distribution as a lump sum) while the employer incurs the funding and investment risk of a defined benefit arrangement (since the employer promises a benefit, albeit one formulated as a nominal account balance rather than a traditional deferred annuity). Given this mix, it is not surprising that cash balance pensions are often denoted "hybrid" plans.[123]

Much controversy has surrounded cash balance plans.[124] For purposes of this discussion, two aspects of this controversy are revealing, namely, employers' justifications for switching their defined benefit plans to the cash balance format and the statutory controversy about cash balance pensions and age discrimination.

Those firms that have shifted their defined benefit plans from the traditional format to the cash balance motif justify that shift via the norms of the defined contribution paradigm: Workers, particularly younger workers, today neither appreciate nor understand traditional defined benefit plans with their deferred annuity payments and benefit formulas based on salary and work history.[125] Few expect to remain with an employer long enough to accrue significant benefits under the backloaded formulas of traditional defined benefit plans.[126] To adapt to the expectations of a younger, more mobile workforce, expectations molded by 401(k) plans, IRAs and similar individual account devices, the defined benefit pension must conform to those expectations.

Hence, the cash balance plan formulates its benefits in terms of theoretical account balances and pays immediate lump sum distributions upon the employee's termination of employment because these are the expectations workers

---

[123] *See, e.g.,* Forman, *supra* chap. three note 73 at 216; Nicholas G. Apostolou, D. Larry Crumbley, and William M. VanDenburgh, Illusionary Pension Fund Returns, 99 Tax Notes 565, 567 (April 28, 2003) ("A cash balance is a hybrid type of pension plan . . . "); Purcell, *Lump-sum Distributions, supra* chap. one note 6 at CRS-6 ("These are hybrid pensions that have some of the characteristics of defined contribution plans . . . ").

[124] *See, e.g.,* Mary Williams Walsh, *What if a Pension Shift Hit Lawmakers, Too?* N.Y. Times, March 9, 2003, Section 3 at page 1.

[125] For one commentator who agrees, see Jane Bryant Quinn, *Oh, No - More Pension Blues,* Newsweek (January 20, 2003) at 35 (traditional "pensions are going the way of the dodo. They bore young workers and multiply the cost of maintaining an aging work force.")

[126] Purcell, *Lump-sum Distributions, supra* chap. one note 6 at Summary ("A typical 25-year-old today will work for seven or more employers before reaching age 65.")

have developed from their experiences with 401(k) plans, IRAs and other individual account arrangements. The hybrid features of a cash balance plan represent the best of both worlds as those features achieve the superior investment performance of a commonly-managed pool and shift investment risk to the employer. At the same time, the cash balance plan defines and pays benefits in a fashion which mimics the individual account format which has become the norm for American workers.

Even if this is not the entire story,[127] this defense of cash balance plans is instructive as it reveals how far we have traveled down the defined contribution road. A generation ago, it would have been anomalous to suggest that defined benefit plans must jettison some of their traditional features (i.e., deferred annuity payments based on salary and service formulas) to emulate defined contribution arrangements. Today, it is a compelling, if not totally complete, explanation for the popularity of cash balance plans that, to survive in the defined contribution culture, defined benefit plans must be restyled to emulate individual account plans.

---

[127] I believe it is not. Traditional pensions are more expensive to fund for older employees since these employees are closer to retirement, leaving fewer years for the pension's trust funds to earn investment returns. Older employees also tend to be more highly paid than their younger co-workers. Consequently, shifting to the cash balance format reduces the sponsoring employer's costs as to older employees by eliminating the expensive, backloaded pension benefits these employees would earn under the traditional defined benefit format. *See* Zelinsky, *supra* chap. one note 2 at 704. Employers shifting to the cash balance format may also (with good reason) be concerned that they will attract older workers if such employers retain their traditional defined benefit pensions. As the Baby Boom cohort enters its "empty nester" phase, employers maintaining traditional, annuity-paying defined benefit plans may fear that those plans will attract older, more expensive participants, now free to relocate since their child-rearing responsibilities are over. Hence, the shift to the cash balance motif to avoid attracting older Baby Boomers, now interested in traditional, annuity-paying pensions. On the mobility of empty nester Baby Boomers, see Barbara Kantrowitz and Karen Springen, *Free At Last!* 142(15) NEWSWEEK 62 (October 13, 2003).

Moreover, some sponsors of well-funded, traditional defined benefit plans shift to the cash balance format (rather than establish true defined contribution plans) to avoid the excise tax on plan reversions under Section 4980. See Zelinsky, *supra*, note at 713. IBM has been commendably candid on this score. See *Cooper v. IBM Personal Pension Plan*, 274 F. Supp. 2d 1010, 1022 (S.D. Ill. 2003) ("According to IBM," "moving to a defined contribution plan" "was impractical as the Plan surplus could not have been `tax effectively' withdrawn.")

Finally, an important factor (which I overlooked in my initial writings on this subject) is the perception that sponsors of cash balance pensions can obtain more favorable accounting treatment of plan-based liabilities than can the sponsors of traditional, annuity-based defined benefit plans. See, e.g., Mary Williams Walsh, *Changes Discussed in Accounting for Some Pension Fund Obligations*, N.Y. TIMES, (September 25, 2003) at C1.

Equally revealing is the controversy concerning cash balance pensions and the federal statutes outlawing age discrimination in pension plans. The Pension Protection Act of 2006 (PPA) decreed that, for "periods beginning on or after June 29, 2005," cash balance plans will be deemed nondiscriminatory as to age.[128] Prior to the adoption of PPA and, even after the adoption of PPA, for periods before June 29, 2005, there was (and still is) intense controversy over the status of cash balance pensions under the statutes preventing pensions from discriminating on the basis of age.

At the core of this age discrimination controversy is the statutory definition of an employee's "accrued benefit", i.e., the pension entitlement the employee has earned to date. For a defined benefit plan, that accrued benefit is specified statutorily as "an annual benefit commencing at normal retirement age."[129] As the U.S. Court of Appeals for the First Circuit has stated, this definition "is quite sensible as applied to traditional defined benefit plans, which provide an annual benefit upon retirement".[130]

The relevant statutes,[131] in essentially identical terms, prevent defined benefit plans from reducing "the rate of an employee's benefit accrual" "because of the attainment of any age." If the notional contributions under cash balance plans are translated into the annual annuity benefits those contributions purchase at retirement, the rate at which such benefits are earned declines with age since the same contribution for an older person has fewer years to accumulate interest before an annuity must be purchased at retirement. If, for example, an employer allocates a notional cash balance contribution of $1,000 to the nominal accounts of employees aged thirty-five, forty-five and fifty-five, that contribution will, at age sixty-five, purchase for each of them annual annuities of $1,094, $507, and $235, respectively.[132] These differences reflect the longer period contributions earn interest for younger employees and the correspondingly shorter time to retirement (and lesser interest earnings) for older employees.

---

[128] Section 701 of the Pension Protection Act of 2006 (PPA). The PPA specifically provides that it establishes no "inference with respect to" the interpretation of prior law. Section 701(d) of the PPA.

[129] Code Section 411(a)(7)(A)(i); ERISA Section 3(23)(A).

[130] *Campbell v.BankBoston, N.A.*, 327 F.3rd 1 (1st Cir. 2003).

[131] Code Section 411(b)(1)(H)(i), ERISA Section 204(b)(1)(H)(i), ADEA Section 4(i)(1)(A).

[132] These numbers come from an example developed in Zelinsky, *The Cash Balance Controversy, supra* chap one note 2 at 722. Altering the assumptions of this example would change the specifics but not the conclusion.

Thus the issue arises: How should the statutes' annuity-based definition of accrued benefit be applied to cash balance pensions? These pensions do not, in traditional defined benefit fashion, pay deferred annuities starting at retirement as described in the statute but rather distribute pseudo-account balances as lump sums immediately upon the termination of employment, often many years before the participant has attained retirement age. How should we fit this square peg (immediate lump sum distributions based on notional account balances) into the round statutory hole (a deferred annuity-based definition of benefits for defined benefit plans)?

Voluminous commentary[133] and case law[134] address this quandary. For present purposes, the relevant issue is not the correct answer to this quandary[135] but the fact that this quandary exists. Had the drafters of ERISA foreseen the emergence of a hybrid device like the cash balance plan, they might well have crafted a broader or alternate definition of accrued benefit, reflecting the possibility that a defined benefit pension might pay a guaranteed amount as a lump sum before

---

[133]   *See, e.g.,* Richard C. Shea, Michael J. Francese and Robert S. Newman, *Age Discrimination in Cash Balance Plans: Another View*, 19 VA. TAX REV. 763 (2000); Edward A. Zelinsky, *The Cash Balance Controversy Revisited: Age Discrimination and Fidelity to Statutory Text*, 20 VA. TAX REV. 557 (2001) (hereinafter, *Revisited*); Alvin D. Lurie, *Age Discrimination or Age Justification? The Case Of the Shrinking Future Interest Credits under Cash Balance Plans*, 54 TAX LAWYER 299 (2001); Alvin D. Lurie, *Murphy's Law Strikes Again: Twilight for Cash Balance Design?* 101 TAX NOTES 393 (October 20, 2003); Edward A. Zelinsky, *Cash Balance Plans and Age Discrimination*, 101 TAX NOTES 907 (November 17, 2003); Alvin D. Lurie, *Riposte to a Reply*, 101 TAX NOTES 908 (November 17, 2003). The last three of these articles are reproduced in Alvin D. Lurie (ed.), NEW YORK UNIVERSITY REVIEW OF EMPLOYEE BENEFITS AND EXECUTIVE COMPENSATION (2004).

[134]   The Courts of Appeals for the Seventh and Third Circuits have concluded that cash balance plans do not age discriminate under pre-PPA law. In contrast, district courts in Connecticut and New York have held that cash balance plans do age discriminate in violation of pre-PPA law. *Compare Cooper v. IBM*, 457 F.3d 636(7th Cir. 2006) and *Register v. PNC Financial Services Group, Inc.*, 2007 U.S. App. LEXIS 1967 (3rd Cir., Jan. 30, 2007 (no age discrimination) with *Parsons v. AT&T Pension Benefit* Plan, 2006 U.S. Dist. LEXIS 93135 (D. Conn. Dec. 22, 2006); *In re Citigroup Pension Plan ERISA Litigation*, 2006 U.S. DIST. LEXIS 89565 (S.D.N.Y. Dec. 12, 2006); *In re J.P. Morgan Chase Cash Balance Litigation*, 460 F. Supp. 2d 479 (S.D.N.Y. 2006); *Richards v. FleetBoston Fin. Corp.*, 427 F. Supp. 2d 150 (D. Conn. 2006) (cash balance pensions do age discriminate under pre-PPA law).

[135]   I should note that I agree with the district courts holding that cash balance plans discriminate under pre-PPA law. *See* Edward A. Zelinsky, Cooper v. IBM Personal Pension Plan: *A Critique* in Alvin D. Lurie (ed.) NEW YORK UNIVERSITY REVIEW OF EMPLOYEE BENEFITS AND EXECUTIVE COMPENSATION (2007, Alvin D. Lurie (ed.)). While there are strong policy arguments for cash balance plans, the language of the statutes is explicit. The proper course is the amendment of the statutes (as Congress has done in the PPA), not the disregard of the statutes' terms. I should also note, in the interests of full disclosure, that an article of mine is cited by the District Court in *Cooper* in reaching its conclusion that cash balance plans discriminate on the basis of age.

(perhaps well before) retirement. That is essentially what the PPA now does prospectively.

It is, however, anachronistic to criticize ERISA's drafters for lacking such foresight. Those drafters were pensions lawyers, not seers. In the world in which they framed ERISA, the cash balance plan was literally inconceivable. It took the subsequent emergence of the defined contribution paradigm for the cash balance pension to spring up as part of that paradigm. It is thus unsurprising that the original statutory definition of accrued benefits for defined benefit plans, drafted before the rise of the defined contribution culture, is expressed exclusively in terms of the traditional deferred annuity at retirement nor is it surprising that that definition did not anticipate the notional account balances of cash balance plans.

Equally instructive in confirming the emergence of the defined contribution culture are the hybrid plans which have earned the monikers "age weighted" and "new comparability."[136] While cash balance pensions are defined benefit plans which mimic individual account arrangements, age weighted and new comparability plans are individual account plans which mimic defined benefit pensions. In particular, under an age weighted or new comparability plan, the employer allocates contributions among employees' respective accounts, not in the typical way as a percentage of each employee's salary, but, rather, in a fashion which emulates the employer's contributions as if the plan were a defined benefit device. Such an allocation formula skews contributions towards older, higher paid employees since, in the defined benefit context, more must be contributed to fund projected benefits which are based on higher salaries and which are scheduled to begin sooner. Since older employees are closer to retirement, there is less time for the pension's trust fund to accumulate investment earnings before such employees retire. Moreover, older employees are typically higher paid than their younger colleagues and are thus entitled to higher, salary-based defined benefits. Accordingly, more must be funded by the employer to finance the benefits starting upon such employees' retirements.

---

[136] See Edward A. Zelinsky, *Is Cross-Testing A Mistake? Cash Balance Plans, New Comparability Formulas, and the Incoherence of the Nondiscrimination Norm*, 49 BUFFALO LAW REV. 575 (2001) reprinted in Alvin D. Lurie (ed.), NYU 59TH INSTITUTE ON FEDERAL TAXATION — EMPLOYEE BENEFITS AND EXECUTIVE COMPENSATION (2001). *See also* Edward A. Zelinsky, *Cross-Testing, Nondiscrimination and New Comparability: A Rejoinder to Mr. Orszag and Professor Stein*, 49 BUFFALO LAW REV. 675 (2001), also reprinted in Alvin D. Lurie (ed.), NYU 59TH INSTITUTE ON FEDERAL TAXATION — EMPLOYEE BENEFITS AND EXECUTIVE COMPENSATION (2001).

This is another manifestation of the backloading phenomenon discussed earlier: Under defined benefit plans, late-career accruals tend to be particularly valuable for employees (and commensurately expensive for employers) both because older employees are generally better paid than their younger coworkers and are also closer to retirement, when benefits must be paid.

These observations prompt the inquiry: If new comparability and age weighted plans are defined contribution arrangements under which the employer's contributions are allocated among employees to emulate backloaded defined benefit pensions, why don't employers instead establish such defined benefit plans? The answer harkens back to the burdens ERISA imposes on defined benefit arrangements, in particular, the minimum funding requirements of Section 412 and PBGC premiums.[137]

Those who decide about plan design will generally be older and better paid employees, typically the owners or managers of the firm. New comparability and age weighted formulas give these decisionmakers the advantages of backloaded defined benefit funding patterns weighted in their favor while sparing the firm the inflexibility and the costs of the minimum funding rules and PBGC premiums. In addition, new comparability and age weighted plans, since they are defined contribution devices, can permit employees to self-direct their own investments. This abates trustee liability for such investing while granting to the employees something they may view as valuable, specifically, the right to direct the allocation of their own funds with the resulting sense of ownership and control.

In short, the new comparability and age weighted designs reflect the regulatory burdens placed on defined benefit plans and constitute yet other defined contribution alternatives for firms which, a generation ago, would have utilized backloaded defined benefit pensions to skew contributions toward their older, better paid employees.

G.   Public Employee Pensions and Section 457 Plans

The discussion so far has documented the extent to which the traditional defined benefit plan has stagnated in the private sector economy while individual account

---

[137]   Smaller professional plans are not covered by the PBGC. *See* ERISA Section 4021(b)(13).

arrangements have, in their various incarnations, become predominant in the private retirement system and increasingly common for educational savings and medical outlays. Reflecting further the shift towards the defined contribution paradigm is the embrace by some states and municipalities of that paradigm for public employee pensions. Less than a decade ago, the movement to convert public employee pensions to the individual account format was nascent.[138] It has now accelerated to the point where defined contribution plans today increasingly serve as replacements for or as alternatives to many states' and municipalities' traditional defined benefit pensions.[139] Other states and localities contemplate a transition to the defined contribution format.[140] Particularly noteworthy are the (so far, unsuccessful) efforts of Governor Schwarzenegger to move California's massive and entrenched defined benefit plans for public employees to individual account arrangements.

The movement to shift public sector retirement plans to the individual account format has a variety of causes, many the same as the causes of the shift to individual accounts in the private sector: The culture of private ownership; the influence of the financial services industry and conservative ideological groups; the self-reinforcing expectations of workers and taxpayers molded by the norms of the defined contribution culture; the desire of public officials to shift funding, investment and longevity risks from the public fisc to public employees. Taxpayers who experience retirement savings as 401(k) plans are likely to agree that public employees should provide for their retirements in similar fashion.[141] For now, the important point is that this last bastion of the defined benefit plan—state and

---

[138] When I explored this issue in 1999, I was skeptical of the strength of the movement to establish public defined contribution plans. I was wrong. For those earlier observations, see Zelinsky, *supra* note 74 at Section 6.04[2].

[139] *See Profiles of the top public defined contribution plans*, 31(7) Pensions & Investments 16 (March 31, 2003). *See also* GAO, *Voluntary, supra* chap. two note 30 at 20 (discussing Florida's recent adoption of an optional individual account plan for its employees).

[140] Dave Kovaleski, *State eyes DC plan that is mandatory for new workers*, 31(6) Pensions & Investments 4 (March 17, 2003); Arleen Jacobius, *Oregon Legislature mulling new pension plan to cut state's deficit*, 31(8) Pensions & Investments 2 (April 14, 2003). However, one commentator believes that the shift to public defined contribution plans has peaked. *See* Anya Sostek, *Pension Pendulum*, 17(6) Governing 28 (March, 2004).

[141] James W. Prado, *Poll: Make public pensions more like private industry*, Ocean County Observer, Nov. 12, 2006 ("A majority of New Jersey taxpayers say government employees should have retirement plans and health benefits that mirror those of private industry, according to a Monmouth University/Gannett New Jersey newspaper poll.")

municipal employee pensions—is under assault by the advocates of defined contribution arrangements. As I discuss in Chapter Six, the status of public defined benefit plans is likely to be a contentious and salient public issue in the years ahead as many government employees and their unions resist the shift to individual account arrangements.

Many state and local governments which maintain traditional defined benefit pensions for their employees often provide a supplementary defined contribution program, known as a Section 457 plan. Congress adopted Code Section 457 in response to the perception that tax-exempt employers can offer their employees unique tax benefits via nonqualified deferred compensation.

When an individual employed by a taxable employer defers compensation outside of a qualified plan, the employer's deduction for that compensation is delayed until the employee ultimately reports the deferred compensation as income.[142] Moreover, if, prior to distribution to the employee, the deferred compensation is retained and invested by the taxable employer, the annual earnings generated by that retained compensation are themselves taxable since these earnings are assignable to a taxable person, i.e., the employer. The deferred compensation bargain between a taxable employer and its employee will reflect the employer's tax burden from the delay of the employer's deduction and the employer's possible tax liability for the earnings of deferred amounts.

In contrast, when an individual employed by a tax-exempt entity, such as a state or local government, defers otherwise taxable compensation, there is no tax cost to the employer in terms of a delayed deduction for the deferred compensation since the exempt employer pays no tax anyway and is thus indifferent as to the timing of the employee's recognition of income. Similarly, if an exempt employer retains deferred income for ultimate distribution to the employee, the earnings of those deferred amounts are free of tax since the employer itself is free of tax. The concern animating Section 457 is that tax-exempt employers and their employees can negotiate favorable deferred compensation arrangements at the expense of the federal fisc since there is no tax cost to exempt employers from participating in such arrangements.[143]

---

[142] Code Section 83(h) (employer deduction delayed until "the taxable year in which such amount is included in the gross income of the" employee).

[143] For a colloquy between two prominent members of the tax community debating the logic of Section 457, see Peter L. Faber, *It's Time To Repeal Section 457*, 100 TAX NOTES 416 (July 21, 2003); Daniel Halperin,

Section 457 was thus adopted to constrain the ability of tax-exempt employers and their employees to engage in deferred compensation arrangements. Section 457 is similar to Sections 401(k) and Section 403(b); like those other provisions, Section 457 both permits and limits employees' ability to defer compensation and thereby postpone income taxation until actual receipt of that deferred compensation. Under Section 457, employees of tax-exempt employers (including state and local governments)[144] can today defer compensation subject to an annual ceiling of $15,000.[145] The amounts deferred pursuant to Section 457, including earnings, are allocated to employees' individual accounts subsequently taxable to the employee (or his beneficiary) upon eventual distribution.[146]

Just as Section 401(k) triggered an explosive growth of profit sharing plans with cash-or-deferred features, Section 457 has catalyzed the establishment of public employee deferred compensation programs which, not surprisingly, have been denominated "Section 457 plans." Over $40 billion is now held by such individual account plans.[147] Particularly noteworthy has been Congress's recent decision to incorporate governmental Section 457 plans into the network of rules governing IRA and qualified plan rollovers. This decision firmly plants Section 457 within the statutory structure of the defined contribution paradigm.[148]

H. Health Reimbursement Arrangements

The health reimbursement arrangement (HRA) is an important response of the insurance industry to the defined contribution paradigm. As approved by the IRS

Section 457 Should Be Replaced By A Special Tax on Investment Income, 100 Tax Notes 730 (August 4, 2003); Peter L. Faber, *Arguments Against Section 457 Repeal Don't Stand Up*, 100 Tax Notes 969 (August 18, 2003); Daniel Halperin, *Section 457 Repeal Debate Continues*, 100 Tax Notes 1455 (September 15, 2003).

[144] Originally, Section 457 just applied to employees of state and local governments. Today, Section 457 applies to all employees of tax-exempt entities. *See* Section 457(e)(1)(B).

[145] Section 457(e)(15)(A). Under no circumstances can the employee defer more than the amount of his income. In the future, this limit will be increased by cost-of-living adjustments. The employee may also make additional catch-up deferrals at the end of his career. *See* Sections 415(b)(3), 415(e)(15)(B), 415(e)(18).

[146] Section 457(a). In the case of nongovernmental, nonprofit employers, amounts are also taxable when "made available to the participant" or to the participant's beneficiary.

[147] Arleen Jacobius, *Slow change: 457 plans win top spot in popularity with government; Decades-old plans hold majority of assets, but 401(a) now becoming wave of future*, Pensions and Investments (March 31, 2003).

[148] *See* Code Section 402(c)(8)(B)(v) (permitting rollover from governmental 457 plan into IRA).

in 2001,[149] the HRA is an individual account for health care controlled by the covered employee. After the employee (or his dependent) incurs a health care outlay, the HRA reimburses that cost. An employer which completely self-funds medical coverage for its employees can provide all such coverage through HRAs.[150] More typically (so far, at least) are HRAs which cover employees' routine health costs up to an amount specified by the employer.[151] Above that base level, conventional insurance is triggered when the HRA is exhausted.[152] The insurance industry is now actively promoting packages along these lines, i.e., the HRA for basic, routine medical costs coupled with insurance for larger health outlays.[153]

When linked to conventional insurance coverage, the HRA adapts the MSA model just as the MSA adapted the IRA model. Indeed, when coupled with conventional insurance, the resemblance of the HRA to the MSA (also coupled with high deductible insurance) is striking. The HRA is best understood as the insurance industry's response to the MSA model, a recognition that, in a defined contribution society, the insurance industry must offer an individual account product for routine medical care.

---

[149] Rev. Rul. 2002–41, 2002–28 I.R.B. 75; IRS Notice 2002–45, 2002–28 IRB 93. In Rev. Rul. 2003–43, 2003–21 I.R.B. 935, the IRS condoned HRAs utilizing debit and credit cards and other forms of electronic payment. For a comprehensive discussion of these rulings and the Code sections which they implement, *see* Dianne Bennett, *Health Reimbursement Arrangements: Boon or Bane for Employers?* in Alvin D. Lurie (ed.), NEW YORK UNIVERSITY REVIEW OF EMPLOYEE BENEFITS AND EXECUTIVE COMPENSATION (2003) at Section 2.02. *See also* Edward A. Zelinsky, *Against a Federal Patients' Bill of Rights*, 21 YALE LAW & POLICY REV. 443, 465–468 (2003).

[150] *See, e.g.*, Zina Moukheiber, *Give Them A Stake*, FORBES, May 13, 2002 at 171 (discussing Definity Health, an administrator of HRAs for self-funded employers).

[151] Note that an HRA is not an FSA under which the employee chooses between taxable compensation and nontaxable fringe benefits. Rather, under an HRA, the employer specifies the level of coverage for all participating employees who have no right to elect another form of benefit or cash compensation instead. *See* Brian L. Shiker and Emily C. Vitan, *Defined Contribution Health Plans: A Tool to Help Control Rising Health Care Costs*, 29 J. OF PENSION PLANNING & COMPLIANCE 53, 57 (2003) ("Further, an employee is not given a choice between the receipt of cash and a contribution to the account; an employee's salary will not be increased if the employer chooses not to offer an individual account plan."). In 2006, Congress authorized one-time rollover of unexpended HRA funds into health savings accounts. *See* Code Section 106(e) as amended by Section 302(a) of the Tax Relief and Health Care Act of 2006.

[152] Under some HRA arrangements, the employee, after exhausting her account, must herself pay some additional medical expenses before triggering insurance coverage. *See, e.g.*, Beth Kobliner, *A New Health Plan Works, at Least for the Healthy*, N.Y. TIMES, March 2, 2003, Money and Business Section at 8 (describing the HRA of CompuCom Systems).

[153] *See, e.g.*, Elizabeth White, *Defined Contribution Health Plans Emerge as Employers Face Double-Digit Cost Hikes*, BNA PENSION & BENEFITS DAILY (February 25, 2002) ("an increasing number of big-name health insurers are rolling out defined contribution products"); *Defined Contribution Product For Employers Announced By Wisconsin Blue Cross Plan*, BNA PENSION & BENEFITS DAILY (April 11, 2002).

I. Health Savings Accounts

If the MSA is best viewed as an initial defined contribution toehold in the financing of health care, the health savings account (HSA)[154] authorized by Congress in 2003 broadens and institutionalizes the individual account approach to medicine. Unlike MSAs, HSAs are neither limited to a fixed number of taxpayers nor are they restricted to those employees who work for small employers. In practical terms, the HSA, Congress's most recent embrace of the defined contribution paradigm, extends the MSA model just as the MSA extends the IRA model. Not surprisingly, the HSA, freed of many of the constraints applicable to the MSA, has already proved far more popular than the MSA. Published reports indicate that "(a)t least three million people" may currently have the kind of high-deductible health insurance which permits HSA participation and that some observers expect there to be as many as fifteen million Americans covered by HSAs in 2010.[155]

Any individual who is covered by a "high deductible health" plan and who is generally[156] not covered by any other insurance or health plan may establish and make tax deductible contributions to an HSA. For these purposes, a high deductible health plan is a health plan with a minimum annual deductible of at least $1,000 for an unmarried individual ($2,000 for a family) and a maximum annual deductible of $5,000 for an unmarried individual ($10,000 for a family).[157]

If an individual establishing an HSA is the only person covered by a high deductible health plan, he may contribute to the HSA and deduct for income tax purposes annually up to $2,250.[158] An individual who establishes an HSA and

---

[154] See Code Section 223 added by P.L. 108–173. See also IRS Issues Guidance on Health Savings Accounts, 2003 TNT 246–5; Monahan, supra note 98 at 795–800.

[155] Sarah Lueck, Tax Breaks to Boost Cost of Bush's Health Budget, WALL ST. J., Feb. 6, 2005, at A1. See also Eric Dash, Wall Street Senses Opportunities In Health Care Savings Accounts, N.Y. TIMES, Jan. 27, 2006, at A1; Sarah Rubenstein, A Hitch on Health Insurance, WALL. ST. J., June 10–11, 2006, at B4 ("a growing number of major corporations, including General Motors Corp. and Microsoft Corp., are offering HSA-linked insurance plans to employees.")

[156] An individual may be covered by certain kinds of health plans and still maintain an HSA, provided that he is also covered by a high deductible plan. These permitted forms of coverage include long-term care insurance, accident and disability coverage, dental and vision care plans, and workers' compensation insurance. See Code Sections 223(c)(1)(B) and 223(c)(3).

[157] Code Section 223(c)(2). These limits will be adjusted for inflation. Code Section 223(g).

[158] Code Section 223(b)(2)(A) as amended by Sections 303 and 307 of the Tax Relief and Health Care Act of 2006. This limit will be adjusted for inflation. Code Section 223(g). The 2006 Act also authorizes certain one-time rollovers to HSAs from FSAs, HRAs and IRAs. See Code Sections 106(e) and 408(d)(9) as amended by Sections 302(a) and 307(a) of the Tax Relief and Health Care Act of 2006.

who maintains high deductible coverage for his family may contribute to the HSA and deduct yearly up to $4,500.[159]

HSAs receive the same income tax treatment as MSAs, i.e., contributions (subject to these limits) are deductible for income tax purposes;[160] earnings of HSAs grow tax-free;[161] distributions from HSAs are tax-free as long as such distributions are used for medical expenses.[162]

It is obviously too early to know whether (as HSA proponents obviously hope) large employers (forbidden from utilizing MSAs in the design of their health care arrangements) will find attractive the combination of HSAs and high deductible coverage. At a minimum, the enactment of the HSA guarantees that traditional insurers will continue to offer insurance coordinated with HRAs as an alternative for persons who might otherwise be tempted by the HSA model. The more robust possibility (obviously sought by HSA supporters[163] and feared by HSA detractors[164]) is that HSAs, freed of the limitations and restrictions applicable to MSAs, will find broad acceptance in the medical insurance marketplace. The preliminary results indicate far greater use of HSAs than of MSAs.

J.   The Saver's Tax Credit

In 2001, Congress originally adopted the saver's credit of Code Section 25B as a temporary measure. In 2006, Congress made the credit a permanent feature of

---

[159]   Code Section 223(b)(2)(B) as amended by Sections 303 and 307 of the Tax Relief and Health Care Act of 2006. This limit will be adjusted for inflation. *See* Code Section 223(g).

[160]   Code Section 223(a).

[161]   Code Section 223(e)(1).

[162]   Code Section 223(f)(1).

[163]   *See, e.g.,* Tom Miller, *How The Tax Exclusion Shaped Today's Private Health Insurance Market,* Joint Economic Committee (December 17, 2003), 2003 TNT 243–19 ("Consumer-driven health vehicles would reacquaint individuals with the cost and quality of the choices they can manage on their own."); Newt Gingrich, *Bill sets foundation for revitalizing Medicare,* NEW HAVEN REGISTER (December 3, 2003) at A6 ("Health Savings Accounts are the single most important change in health-care policy in 60 years."); Steve Forbes, *Big Good in a Bad Bill,* 172(13) FORBES 35 (December 22, 2003) (HSAs will "put patients in charge of their own health care dollars.")

[164]   *See, e.g.,* Emily Dagostino, *Democrats Question President's Health Savings Account Initiative,* 111 TAX NOTES 526 (May 1, 2006); Robert Greenstein and Edwin Park, *HSAs in Medicare Agreement Pose "Threats," CBPP Claims,* 2003 TNT 231–13 (December 2, 2003) ("As HSA use becomes more widespread, the health policy consequences are likely to become increasingly serious, especially for older and sicker workers.")

the Code,[165] thus firmly placing the credit into the defined contribution paradigm.

Under Code Section 25B, certain persons with low and moderate incomes may obtain an income tax credit for a portion of their respective retirement contributions to any of the panoply of retirement-related individual account devices, i.e., individual retirement accounts, 401(k) plans, 403(b) arrangements, 457 deferred compensation programs, simplified employer pensions and simple retirement accounts.

The tax credit is determined by multiplying the amount of the individual's retirement savings contributions up to $2,000 by the individual's "applicable percentage."[166] Each eligible individual's applicable percentage is based upon his annual adjusted gross income. For example, under Section 25B as originally enacted, if the annual adjusted gross income of a married individual filing a joint return was $30,000 or less, the applicable percentage was 50%, yielding an income tax credit of one-half (½) of the individual's retirement contributions. The applicable percentage decreases as the individual's adjusted gross income rises. Under Section 25B as first adopted, if this married individual's yearly adjusted gross income was over $50,000, the applicable percentage was 0% and thus no credit was allowed. In 2006, Congress provided for the inflation adjustment of these income levels.[167] The first such adjustment was effective as of January 1, 2007.[168]

The credit is not refundable if the amount of the credit exceeds the individual's tax liability.[169] There is, moreover, no provision for carrying any excess credit forward or back to earlier taxable years. Nevertheless, for certain persons of low and moderate incomes, the credit provides a substantial tax subsidy for their retirement contributions to individual accounts. The IRS indicates that the saver's credit is claimed each year on more than five million income tax returns.[170]

---

[165] Section 812 of the Pension Protection Act (PPA) of 2006.

[166] Code Section 25B(b).

[167] Section 833(a) of the Pension Protection Act of 2006.

[168] Section 3.06 of Revenue Procedure 2006–53. Starting as of January 1, 2007, the statutory figure of $30,000 is inflation adjusted to $31,000 while the statutory figure of $50,000 is increased to $52,000. The other figures under Section 25B are similarly increased to reflect the cost of living.

[169] Code Section 25B(g).

[170] Patrick Purcell, CRS Report, "The Retirement Savings Tax Credit: A Fact Sheet," RS21795, August 7, 2006, available on BNA Tax Core, Vol. 6, Number 166, Aug. 28, 2006, Congressional Documents, Reports.

K. Proposals

The strength of the defined contribution paradigm is further confirmed by the many individual account proposals receiving serious attention today from policy-makers and analysts. These proposals (as well as the possibilities which are beyond the bounds of current debate) demonstrate the extent to which the individual account model defines the parameters of contemporary discussion of tax and social policy.

Chief among the proposals manifesting the power of the defined contribution format is the much-discussed suggestion that the federal Social Security program be modified to include individual accounts.[171] A generation ago, such a proposal (like the cash balance pension plan) would have been inconceivable. Today, proposals for such accounts bear the imprimatur of the President of the United States, a reflection of the way in which the norms of the defined contribution paradigm have come to set the framework for contemporary debate. One could no more imagine President Nixon discussing individual accounts for Social Security than imagining him discussing the Internet.

It now appears unlikely that President Bush's proposal for private social security accounts will be enacted into law. I discuss in Chapter Four the reasons that President Bush has failed (so far, at least) to secure enactment of this proposal. However, in terms of my underlying theme—the emergence and predominance of the defined contribution paradigm—the ultimate fate of the President's proposal is of little importance. No one, including the fiercest opponents of the Bush proposal for individual Social Security accounts, advocates an expansion of Social Security benefits. The defenders of Social Security as a traditional defined benefit program fight a defensive battle to protect the *status quo*, not a struggle for the enhancement of traditional Social Security. Furthermore, it is becoming increasingly apparent that the preservation of Social Security in its traditional defined benefit form will—if not now, later—require reduction of projected benefits through the postponement of retirement ages, the capping of cost-of-living increases, or similar measures to curtail currently anticipated benefit increases.

---

[171] *See, e.g.,* James R. Storey, *Social Security Reform: Individual Account Proposals*, Congressional Research Service (July 26, 2002); GAO, *Voluntary, supra* chap. two note 30; Martin Feldstein (ed.), Privatizing Social Security (1998); Medill, *supra* chap. two note 5; Friedman, *supra* chap. two note 5.

In short, the debate over President Bush's proposal for individual Social Security accounts has confirmed the *de facto* role of Social Security as a baseline, publicly-financed and publicly-administered defined benefit while the private pension system shifts predominantly to the individual account format.

In other ways also, President Bush has been a proponent of the defined contribution model. President Bush's budget for 2004 proposed a major expansion of MSAs.[172] That proposal undoubtedly boosted the movement which resulted in the authorization of HSAs. President Bush has been an outspoken supporter of such HSAs. President Bush also advocates IRA-style "re-employment" accounts.[173] Such accounts would replace conventional unemployment compensation and retraining programs with a lump sum controlled by the unemployed worker. When the worker obtains re-employment, any unexpended balance in the account would be the worker's to keep on a taxable basis.

President Bush has also proposed a radical modification and expansion of other defined contribution programs today embodied in the Code.[174] In addition, he has endorsed "individual development accounts," the proceeds of which would be available for higher education expenses, first-time home purchases or small business creation.[175] Such individual development accounts are now widely used

---

172 MSAs and President Bush's proposal to expand them are described (and criticized) in Park and Lav, *supra* note 95. *See also* Edwin Park and Iris J. Lav, *What's in a Name? House Ways & Means Committee Changes Name But Not the Substance of a Proposed Expansion of Medical Savings Accounts*, 2003 TNT 117–28 (June 16, 2003) (making similar criticisms of the Health Savings Account Availability Act, H.R. 2351, as "essentially the same as a proposal included in the Administration's fiscal year 2004 budget to greatly expand MSAs.") *See also* Sullivan, *supra* note 95 (discussing the Bush proposal for "an extension and expansion of Archer MSAs.")

173 *See, e.g., White House Release on Administration Efforts to Provide Jobs*, 2003 TNT 117–25 (June 18, 2003) (describing "Personal Re-employment Accounts"). *See also* George F. Will, *Once More, The Bullhorn*, Newsweek (January 20, 2003) at 84 (describing the Bush proposal for "Personal Reemployment Accounts."); Steve Lohr, *Debate Over Exporting Jobs Raises Questions on Policies*, N.Y. Times (February 23, 2004) at C1 (same).

174 For descriptions and analyses of those proposals, see Patrick J. Purcell, *Retirement Savings Accounts: President's Budget Proposal for FY2005*, (February 6, 2004); Jane G. Gravelle and Maxim Shvedov, *Proposed Savings Accounts: Economic and Budgetary Effects*, Congressional Research Service, RL32228 (June 30, 2006), 2006 TNT 134–24 (July 13, 2006); David A. Pratt, *supra* note 73 at sections 3.03 through 3.07; Gene Steuerle, *The Latest "ZITCOM" and My New Tax Shelter Bank*, 99 Tax Notes 739 (May 5, 2003); Karen C. Burke and Grayson M.P. McCouch, *Lipstick, Light Beer, and Back-Loaded Savings Accounts*, 25 va. Tax Rev. 1101 (2006); Sam Young, *IRA Flexibility Will Increase, Treasury Official Predicts*, 114 tax notes 913 (March 5, 2007) (discussing President Bush's proposal for lifetime savings accounts).

175 *See* Robert F. Manning, *Cuttings on the Conference Room Floor: Will The Grafts Take?* 100 Tax Notes 217, 225 (July 14, 2003).

by the states to encourage self-reliance and entrepreneurial efforts among the poor.[176]

Democrats have also advanced proposals to expand the defined contribution network. President Clinton, for example, advocated the creation of a "Universal Savings Account," with particular emphasis on assisting low income families to save for retirement.[177] Representative Gephardt proffered a comparable proposal to expand the defined contribution participation of lower income workers.[178] Senator Bill Nelson, a Democrat who represents hurricane-prone Florida, has proposed the creation of "Catastrophe Savings Accounts."[179] Senator Blanche Lincoln, a Democrat from Arkansas, has joined with Senator Gordon Smith, a Republican from Oregon, to propose amending the Internal Revenue Code to create "long-term care trust accounts."[180]

Influential commentators similarly propound individual account proposals. For example, David C. John of The Heritage Foundation and J. Mark Iwry of The Brookings Institution propose that certain employers who do not sponsor qualified plans for their employees be required to implement "automatic" IRAs instead. Under the John-Iwry proposal, contributions to such IRAs would come from employees' salaries unless they affirmatively elect against IRA coverage.[181] Professor Anne L. Alstott proposes "caretaker resource accounts." Parents could use these publicly-funded accounts "to purchase paid child care, to pay tuition for parents to complete their education (or retrain), or to augment retirement savings."[182] Professor Jacob S. Hacker, who takes a generally dim view of the

---

[176] See, e.g., Colorado's Individual Development Account Act, C.R.S. 26–2-1001 et seq. For a controlled study of individual development accounts by Brookings economists, see Gregory Mills, William G. Gale, Rhiannon Patterson and Emil Apostolov, *Economists Conduct Experiment to Evaluate Individual Development Accounts*, 2006 TNT 136–26 (July 11, 2006).

[177] Halperin, *supra* chap. two note 2 at 72; Martin A. Sullivan, *Pols Maneuver to Protect and Increase Pensions*, 95 TAX NOTES 822, 826 (May 6, 2002).

[178] See H.R. 4482. See also Pratt, *supra* note 73 at sections 3.13(4) and 3.13(5); Sullivan, *supra* note 95 at 825–826.

[179] See the "Catastrophe Savings Accounts Act of 2006," S. 3115, 109th Cong., 2d Session.

[180] See S. 504, 110th Cong., 1st Session.

[181] Joint Written Statement of David C. John and J. Mark Iwry Before the Subcommittee on Long-Term Growth and Debt Reduction, Committee on Finance, United States Senate, 2006 TNT 126–33 (June 29, 2006). See also Doug Halonen, *Automatic IRA motherlode*, 34(15) PENSIONS & INVESTMENTS 2 (July 24, 2006).

[182] Anne L. Alstott, *Child-Rearing and the Code: A Proposal For Caretaker Accounts*, 111 TAX NOTES 1285 (June 12, 2006) (parenthetical in the original).

defined contribution paradigm, proposes to consolidate all nonretirement accounts into a Universal Savings Account and to "create a Universal 401(k) that is available to all workers, whether or not their employer offers a traditional retirement plans."[183]

For present purposes, it does not matter whether any of these proposals will ultimately become law. Rather, the relevant observation is that today these proposals define the parameters of debate. The extent to which the defined contribution paradigm shapes contemporary thinking about tax and policy issues becomes clear when we consider the kinds of proposals which fall outside those parameters and consequently command little political support or academic interest.

Even those concerned about the decline of the private defined benefit format are, at best, proposing relatively minor reforms to resuscitate that format. One can envision proposals designed to stimulate the private retirement system back towards the traditional defined benefit pension. For example, Congress could deny tax-advantaged treatment to individual accounts, thereby requiring firms in search of tax savings to establish defined benefit pensions. To articulate such a possibility is to indicate its impossibility in the contemporary defined contribution society. No congressman today will vote to deny his constituents the tax savings associated with their IRA and 401(k) accounts. But, absent such fundamental change, it is difficult to envision any reversal of the stagnation of the defined benefit system or of the preeminence of the defined contribution paradigm.

Similarly, as I noted above, no one today proposes expansion of Social Security benefits.[184] Those opposed to incorporating individual accounts into the Social Security system wage a defensive battle for the defined benefit status quo, rather than advocate the enlargement of the payments promised by that system. Indeed, the thoughtful proponents of the current, defined benefit configuration for Social Security generally favor benefit reductions (rather than individual accounts) to

---

183 Jacob S. Hacker, THE GREAT RISK SHIFT (2006) at 184–187.

184 *See, e.g.*, Halperin, *supra* chap. two note 2 at 39 ("[I]t is unlikely that future Social Security benefits will achieve full income replacement. Because payroll tax revenues dedicated to Social Security are in the long run insufficient to provide for promised benefits, it is more likely that future benefits will be less than the level of benefits currently promised by the program.")

restore the long-term solvency of Social Security.[185] If proponents of the defined benefit status quo did suggest an enlargement of Social Security payments, it is unlikely they would be taken seriously.

Consider in this context a thought game: Assume that the Democratic Party were to take control of the Presidency with commanding majorities in both houses of Congress. Under these circumstances, the Bush proposals to expand the defined contribution model would lie dormant. Most obviously, it is improbable that a Democratic Congress would approve individual accounts for the federal Social Security system or that a Democratic president would propose them.

However, there is no chance that a Democratic president or Congress would mount a frontal assault on the major features of the defined contribution paradigm, even if they were inclined to do so. Would Democratic congressmen and senators want to justify to their constituents a vote to repeal Section 401(k) or to revoke the favorable tax treatment of those constituents' IRAs? Not likely. A Democratic president would be less inclined to encourage HSAs than did President Bush. But those individual account devices, along with HRAs, are now embedded in the tax law and have self-generating momentum.

A Democratic administration might reduce the tax advantages associated with some individual accounts. However, any such reduction will, at most, have minimal impact upon the long-term future of the defined contribution paradigm. As noted in earlier, during the Reagan administration, the termination in 1986 of the five year period of near universal IRA deductibility had little impact on the individual account paradigm, given how many people established IRAs during that five year period and the enormous sums contributed to these new IRAs. Similarly, even if a Democratic president and Congress prune the deductions for contributions to individual accounts, enormous sums will have already flowed into individual accounts, further entrenching such accounts in American society and tax policy.

Moreover, the economic and demographic forces depressing the defined benefit system cannot be repealed by Congress. And, as I elaborate in Chapter Six, much of the future debate about the defined contribution paradigm will occur at the

---

[185] *See, e.g.*, Henry J. Aaron, *Social Security: Tune It Up, Don't Trade It In*, in Friedman, *supra* chap. two note 5 at 89–95. *See also* Diamond and Orszag, *supra* chap. two note 29.

state and local levels as state and local policymakers seek to shift funding, investment and longevity risks from public treasuries to public employees, just as private sector decisionmakers have shifted such risks to their employees. Thus, much of the impetus for future expansion of the defined contribution paradigm will not come from Washington.

On balance, then, the defined contribution paradigm as it exists today will frame tax and social policy choice for the foreseeable future.

L. Conclusion: The Significance of Enron

Hence the significance of Enron for tax policy and the individual account paradigm. The Enron scandal provoked Congress to pass securities law and accounting reforms quickly.[186]

If any event were going to stimulate a serious effort to revive the defined benefit paradigm, it would have been L'affaire Enron as thousands of Enron employees, their 401(k) accounts stuffed with Enron stock, saw their retirement savings evaporate.[187] Here, in a very visible nutshell, were the dangers of the defined contribution paradigm, a paradigm under which employees have no guaranteed benefits prefunded in accordance with actuarial standards and are subject to the vagaries of investment, funding and longevity risks.

The plight of Enron's employees was a subject of intense national attention.[188] However, that attention resulted in no action to reverse the rise of defined contribution system. Instead, after Enron, the movement toward the individual account

---

[186] The Sarbanes-Oxley Act of 2002 has, not surprisingly, started to generate a significant legal literature. *See, e.g.*, Larry E. Ribstein, *Market vs. Regulatory Responses to Corporate Fraud: A Critique of the Sarbanes-Oxley Act of 2002*, 28 J. OF CORPORATION LAW 1 (2002); Cunningham, *supra* note 67.

[187] Stabile, *supra* chap. three note 56 at 824 ("As a result, many [Enron] participants lost between seventy and ninety percent of their retirement funds.") Millon, *supra* intro. note 2 at 853 ("Enron graphically illustrates the risks workers face when they over-invest their pension savings in their company's stock.") Reece, *supra* note 56 at 82 ("Most of the sensation concerning the unfortunate employees at Enron revolves around the losses they have experienced in their 401(k) plans.")

[188] *See, e.g.*, Jonathan Skinner, *Professor's Remarks at Hearing on Retirement Security and Defined Benefit Pension Plans*, 2002 TNT 121–70 (June 24, 2002) ("The Enron debacle has focused attention on what is perhaps the most serious charge against 401(k) plans – that they are just too risky for use in retirement planning.")

society continues. It was after Enron that President Bush advanced his proposals for reemployment accounts and for the consolidation and expansion of existing defined contribution devices.

Some members of Congress do pursue legislation to help resuscitate the defined benefit paradigm but their efforts, even if enacted into law, seem likely to have minor effects, at best. The typical post-Enron reform proposal has been to tweak the 401(k) framework, not to resurrect defined benefit plans.[189]

In short, while Enron elicited an immediate congressional response in some areas, it has not resulted in any serious reconsideration of the now-sustained trend toward the defined contribution paradigm. Enron was a watershed event for that paradigm, confirming the permanence and preeminence of the defined contribution format. Since no serious effort to resuscitate defined benefit plans and to deemphasize individual account arrangements was forthcoming after Enron, none is likely to be forthcoming.

---

[189] *See, e.g.*, Regina T. Jefferson, *Post-Enron Pension Reform: Where Do We Go From Here?* in Alvin D. Lurie (ed.), NEW YORK UNIVERSITY REVIEW OF EMPLOYEE BENEFITS AND EXECUTIVE COMPENSATION (2003) at Section 10.05; Reece, *supra* note 56.

CHAPTER FOUR

Why Did It Happen?
And Why Social Security
Accounts Didn't

In this chapter, I explore the causes underlying the defined contribution para-digm as well as the reasons that President Bush, despite the growth of individual accounts for retirement, health and medical savings, has (so far, at least) failed in his effort to introduce individual accounts to the federal Social Security system.

The causes of the defined contribution paradigm are varied: demographic, statu-tory, political, economic, cultural. Exploring those causes suggests that the defined contribution paradigm, though not originally inevitable, is now deeply-rooted. Consequently, the limits and the opportunities of the individual account paradigm will frame tax and social policy choices for years to come.

The first steps on the road to the defined contribution culture were the enactment of ERISA and Code Section 401(k). As we saw in Chapter Three, prior to the adop-tion of these laws, economic and demographic factors were depressing the tradi-tional defined benefit system. These factors—falling union membership; the stagnation and demise of traditional manufacturing and extractive industries; an aging population; the changing, less physically taxing nature of work; the accept-ance of increased employee mobility; the desire of employers to shift to their employees the risks associated with providing retirement income—weakened the conventional defined benefit pension and thereby set the stage for the defined contribution paradigm. However, these economic and demographic factors, by themselves, were not enough to create the defined contribution paradigm as it exists today. It took Congress's adoption of ERISA and Section 401(k) to inaugurate that paradigm.

Congress's initial legislative steps were aggressively exploited and reinforced by the promotional activities of the financial services industry. The birth of the defined contribution paradigm is a story of unintended consequences and path dependency. The first legislative moves toward the individual account framework had a pronounced impact, creating constituencies and interests which reinforced and extended the defined contribution framework—though no one planned it that way.

The origins of the defined contribution paradigm is also a tale of cultural receptivity. Both the congressional creation of individual accounts and the promotional efforts of the financial services industry fell on particularly fertile soil since individual accounts comport well with American cultural norms about private ownership and control. In recent years, those norms have been reinforced by conservative think tanks and interest groups which have promoted defined contribution devices to empower individual account holders, to impose fiscal discipline on elected officials, to convert public employees into investors, and to sensitize the consumers of medical care to the costs of that care. Individual accounts have also proved well-adapted to a world of diverse lifestyles and family arrangements. Moreover, such accounts have worked well for many middle-class and upper-middle class families, giving them a politically potent stake in the defined contribution paradigm.

Even a dominant paradigm has its limits. The defined benefit model still retains resilience with respect to publicly-sponsored retirement programs. Despite the significant inroads of individual accounts into the governmental workplace, public employment remains the last bastion of the traditional, employment-based defined benefit plan. President Bush's efforts to introduce individual accounts to the federal Social Security system have proved unsuccessful to date, leaving that federally-sponsored system in its traditional defined benefit form.

The defined contribution paradigm, initiated in a bi-partisan, almost casual fashion, will prove more politically contentious in the years ahead as focus increases upon public defined benefit arrangements. In contrast, in the private sector, the defined contribution model for retirement, health care and educational savings is entrenched and will continue to expand with little resistance.

A. The Adoption of ERISA and Section 401(k): Unintended Consequences and Path Dependency

The decline of the traditional benefit plan set the stage for the rise of the defined contribution paradigm. However, the decline of the traditional defined benefit pension did not make that rise inevitable. It took affirmative congressional decisions to inaugurate the defined contribution paradigm as we know it today. The first of these were Congress's enactment of ERISA and Section 401(k).

To see the pronounced, if unintended, influence of these early legislative enactments, consider a thought game: Assume, for a moment, a counterfactual world without ERISA and Section 401(k). In this theoretical world, Congress did not create the IRA, did not burden defined benefit plans with ERISA's minimum funding rules or with PBGC premiums, did not authorize self-directed accounts under ERISA Section 404(c), and did not impose upon defined benefit plans limitations on employer stock holdings. Moreover, in this counterfactual world, the debate about constructive receipt and qualified plans which culminated in the adoption of Section 401(k) was resolved differently, i.e., by forbidding all salary reduction contributions to qualified plans

In this alternative world, the economic and demographic forces depressing the defined benefit system would still have done so. However, this world would not be the defined contribution society as it exists today. Indeed, this hypothetical world would lack basic features of that society, e.g., IRAs, 401(k) plans, self-directed accounts. In this alternative universe, individual accounts would be less widespread and less entrenched, economically and psychologically, than they have in fact become.

The first critical steps toward the defined contribution society were a classic instance of the law of unintended consequences. Those who drafted and supported ERISA and Section 401(k) did not seek the sea change that has been the emergence of the defined contribution paradigm. True, these drafters and supporters expected that some (mostly smaller) defined benefit plans, confronted with the burdens and limitations newly-imposed by ERISA, would terminate.[1] However, those who crafted ERISA and Section 401(k) thought they were addressing discrete

---

[1] In the immediate wake of ERISA's adoption, the number of defined benefit plans actually increased. However, after peaking in 1985, the number of such plans has been in steady decline.

problems of tax and retirement policy (e.g., coverage, participation, insuring defined benefits, constructive receipt). They were not self-consciously inaugurating a revolution in how Americans think and act about tax and retirement issues. Moreover, these early steps were not politically contentious. ERISA was passed in bi-partisan fashion by a Democratic-controlled Congress with significant Republican sponsorship[2] and was then signed by a Republican president.

If ERISA and Section 401(k), by initiating almost casually the movement towards the defined contribution paradigm, epitomized the law of unintended consequences, they also catalyzed the phenomenon today labeled "path dependency". The first steps toward the defined contribution society created constituencies and interests which made it difficult to turn back. Those first legislative steps thus had a pronounced impact upon the ultimate shape of the defined contribution society.

Judge Posner has described a course of events as path dependent if "it was an accident that you started where you did and if you had started somewhere else you would have ended somewhere else."[3] If the legislative choices embodied in ERISA and Section 401(k) were not quite "accidents", they nevertheless were not the only plausible choices available and they have certainly brought us to a different place—the contemporary defined contribution paradigm—than where we would have wound up had Congress made other choices (including the choice of no legislation).

Following the enactment of ERISA and Section 401(k), the financial services industry quickly recognized the opportunities created by that legislation and,

---

[2] The definitive study of ERISA's origins is Wooten, *supra* chap. 2 note 41. Professor Wooten's history describes the critical role in ERISA's passage played by Republican Representative John Erlenborn and Republican Senator Jacob Javits. The final conference report on ERISA passed the House with only two dissenting votes and passed the Senate unanimously. *Id.* at 269. In today's partisan environment, it appears remarkable that such important legislation passed Congress with such bi-partisan support.

[3] Richard A. Posner, LAW, PRAGMATISM, AND DEMOCRACY 368 (2003). Professor Hacker's definition of path dependency is more formal but similar in substance: "Small initial differences in circumstances may have large eventual effects as self-reinforcing processes encourage continued reliance on established institutions of social provision." Jacob S. Hacker, THE DIVIDED WELFARE STATE: THE BATTLE OVER PUBLIC AND PRIVATE SOCIAL BENEFITS IN THE UNITED STATES 9 (2002). Scholars have increasingly found useful the concept of path dependency. *See, e.g.,* Eugene Volokh, *The Mechanisms of the Slippery Slope,* 116 HARV. L. REV. 1026, 1035–36, 1043–1044 (2003); Paul Pierson, POLITICS IN TIME: HISTORY, INSTITUTIONS, AND SOCIAL ANALYSIS (2004) at 64 ("the key mechanism at work in these path-dependent sequences is some form of self-reinforcement or positive feedback loop. Initial steps in a particular direction may encourage further movement along the same path.") For a particularly enjoyable article on the notion of path dependency, *see* Charles M. Yablon, *Judicial Drag: An Essay on Wigs, Robes and Legal Change,* 1995 WISC. L. REV. 1129.

through its promotional activities, encouraged individual accounts. The financial services industry thereby became the sales force for the defined contribution paradigm; account holders became important (often affluent) stakeholders under that paradigm. Together, the financial services industry and the individuals and businesses it serves became a formidable political force, making it difficult for Congress to revisit or alter the trend toward a defined contribution society. Congress's initial, unintended steps toward a defined contribution society thus became self-reinforcing, creating constituencies with vested interests in individual accounts, thereby generating a path dependent outcome.[4]

Moreover, the financial services industry itself accommodated to the defined contribution paradigm, adapting to serve the holders of 401(k) accounts, IRAs and other individual accounts. Defined benefit participants do not need financial planners; there is nothing for them to invest since defined benefit plan assets are collectively managed by the plan's trustee as an employer-financed common pool, not by individual participants in separate accounts. It is consequently hard to envision the network of retail financial planners which has emerged in the last generation except to serve the middle-class and upper-middle-class households which for the first time managed their own retirement resources for themselves through individual accounts. There has consequently been a symbiotic relationship between the defined contribution paradigm and the financial services industry as we know it today: The industry reinforced the paradigm even as the paradigm gave rise to the industry.

B.   Cultural Receptivity

The individual accounts established by Congress and the efforts of the financial services industry to promote those accounts fell on particularly fertile soil. Such accounts resonate with some of the strongest-held values of American culture, namely, personal autonomy, private property and self-support.[5] A proponent of introducing individual accounts into the Social Security system has declared that,

---

4   Professor Hacker similarly views the development of the federal Social Security system and of Medicare in path dependent terms. *See* Hacker, *supra* note 3 at 253.

5   *See, e.g.*, David Rieff, *America the Untethered*, N.Y. TIMES MAGAZINE, July 2, 2006, at 11 (reporting that the Pew Resarch Center's Global Attitudes Project found that "while people in most of the world look to government to solve their problems, Americans do not. They are strongly attached to their belief in individual responsibility and unwilling to hold 'outside factors' responsible for failure in life.")

"Ultimately, this is a values issue of people controlling their own money."[6] While he was referring specifically to proposals for adding individual accounts to the Social Security program, his comment was an equally apt characterization of the appeal of such accounts more generally,[7] an appeal which resonates with important themes of American culture, to wit, individual control, private ownership, personal self-sufficiency.

From an historical perspective, there is continuity between the individual accounts of the defined contribution paradigm and earlier federal efforts to expand private ownership of property. Consider, for example, the Homestead Act of 1862[8] by which Congress, in the midst of the Civil War, encouraged settlement of the West by deeding land to individuals willing to develop and live on such land.[9] In theory, Congress could have provided encouragement to settlers in a different form. Congress could, for example, have granted federal land only to large, collective farms. Communities with common ownership were not unknown in the American West.[10] One can thus imagine an alternative history which replaces the image of the solitary homesteader with pictures of American kibbutzim.

But only imagine. It is difficult to envision in practice the Homestead Act, a testament to (among other things) the norm of private ownership, supplanted by federal

---

6   *See* Warren Rojas, *Cato Analysts to Privatization Foes: Give Us Your Best Case*, Tax Notes, March 3, 2003, at 1327, 1328 (quoting Michael Tanner).

7   Martin Sullivan, who is skeptical of MSAs and other health care accounts, has in similar terms noted the appeal of such accounts which enable individuals to control their own health care outlays. *See* Martin Sullivan, *Economic Analysis: The Side Effects of Health Savings Accounts*, tax notes, July 21, 2003, at 301 ("proponents of MSAs emphasize that the accounts would also empower individuals to take control of their health care. Individuals are probably more primed than ever for this type of change.") *See also Employees Want More Health Care Control and Choice, Survey Finds*, BNA Pensions & Benefits Daily, Feb. 26, 2002 ("Employees want more control and choice in health care . . ."); Gratzer, *infra*, note 37 at 109, 122 (HSAs appeal "to Americans' desire to make their own decisions, especially in a matter so important as health.")

8   One-Hundred-and-Sixty Acre Homestead Act, 37 Cong. Ch. 75, 12 Stat. 392 (1862) While the Homestead Act was a fundamental event in American history, the implementation of the Act was not without its problems. *See* Louis S. Warren, buffalo bill's america: william cody and the wild west show 72 (2005) ("Settlers had their own share of tricks. After 1862, the federal government deeded 285 million acres to homesteaders. Half their claims were fraudulent, backed by false identities, fake improvements, or worse.")

9   "(A)ctual settlement and cultivation," in the words of the statute. One-Hundred-and-Sixty Acre Homestead Act, Sec. 2, 37 Cong. Ch. 75, 12 Stat. 392 (1862).

10   Among the most famous of these communities was the Amana Colony in Iowa. *See* National Park Service, *The Amana Colonies*, *at* http://www.cr.nps.gov/nr/travel/amana/intro.htm (last visited March 23, 2006).

---

legislation encouraging collective farming. Such legislation, even if it had been enacted, would not have fit comfortably onto the individualistic, property-owning ideals of American society. In a similar fashion, future historians may look back on the traditional defined benefit plan as something of an anomaly, a form of pooled ownership that ultimately fit less well with American norms of private property and control than do the individual accounts of the defined contribution paradigm.

Similarly, after World War II, the federal government, chiefly through Federal Housing Administration (FHA) mortgage insurance, helped to underwrite the expansion of suburban home ownership which has physically and socially transformed the American metropolis.[11] Again, one can imagine alternative courses which could have been pursued. For example, the federal government, instead of subsidizing most heavily new construction in expanding suburbs, might instead have aimed FHA support predominantly at the renovation of existing urban areas and older structures. It is, however, hard to imagine the federal government's subvention of middle class housing after World War II challenging deeply-rooted norms of private ownership and self support. Public housing in America has always been for the poor.

Here, again, the analogy to the contemporary defined contribution society is suggestive: For middle class and affluent families, the increasingly common forms of retirement savings are 401(k) accounts and IRAs, privatized, self-directed devices which account holders themselves control and largely fund through their own contributions. The bottom half of retirees are relegated to dependence on Social Security, a public defined benefit program whose economic future depends upon the vagaries of democratic politics.

The analogy between the individual accounts of the defined contribution society, on the one hand, and the Homestead Act and FHA-insured mortgages, on the other, is revealing in another respect. In all three instances, public subvention (of farm ownership, home ownership, and retirement savings) occurred in a way which

---

[11]   It is today widely-recognized that FHA's underwriting policies played a key role in the growth of America's suburbs and the decline of central cities. *See, e.g.*, Michael Lewyn, *Campaign of Sabotage: Big Government's War Against Public Transportation*, 26 Colum. J. Envtl. L. 259, 278 (2001) ("For many years, FHA guaranteed home loans only in 'low-risk' areas. FHA guidelines defined low-risk areas as areas that were thinly populated, dominated by newer homes, and had no African-American or immigrant enclaves nearby—areas that disproportionately tended to be suburban.")

reconciled that subvention with Americans' celebration of individualism and autonomy.[12] No one accused the homesteaders of being on welfare because the public assistance to them was tied to capitalist norms of self-support. The homesteaders received government largesse in the form of free public land, but they received that largesse on terms which transformed them into property-owners by dint of their own individual work efforts. Similarly, FHA mortgage insurance was a form of public assistance which facilitated private ownership and which demanded, as a price of such assistance, compliance with cultural norms of self-support, i.e., earning income and saving it via mortgage payments.

So too with the account holders of the defined contribution society who must earn income and then save it through salary reduction or other kinds of contributions to obtain what is conventionally thought to be public support in the form of tax subsidies for these accounts.[13] The defined contribution paradigm thereby reconciles public subvention and private ownership in a particularly American and historically precedented fashion.

To be sure, as the federal government subvented private ownership through its support of homesteaders and homeowners, the federal government also enacted defined benefit pensions for veterans[14] and commenced the ultimate American experiment in defined benefit arrangements, namely, the federal Social Security system. History rarely offers a one-dimensional narrative.

Nevertheless, the United States always has been an ownership society. The defined contribution paradigm is a new, important but by no means inevitable chapter in the story, expanding the portfolios of middle-class and upper-middle

---

12 Professor Moss similarly concludes that American government often intervenes as a risk manager since such intervention is less visible and thus more acceptable to Americans than more apparent forms of government activity. Moss, *supra* chap. two note 3 at 17 ("Less visible than other forms of government intervention in the economy (such as wealth redistribution or direct government ownership), risk management policy may be particularly well suited to the distinctive political and ideological character of the United States: statism for anti-statists, so to speak.") (parenthetical in the original).

13 I dissent from the application of the tax expenditure label to the current tax treatment of qualified plans. This is, however, a decidedly minority position. *See supra* chap. two note 23.

14 *See* Jennifer L. Gross, *Pensions, Civil War* in 3 ENCYCLOPEDIA OF THE AMERICAN CIVIL WAR (2000) (David S. Heidler and Jeanne T. Heidler, ed.) at 1489. *See also* 18(1) UNITED STATES STATUTES AT LARGE 912, Revised Statutes of the United States, Second Edition, 1878, Title LVII; 26 UNITED STATES STATUTES AT LARGE 182, 1890, Chapter 634; Mary Beth Norton et al, A PEOPLE AND A NATION: A HISTORY OF THE UNITED STATES (5th ed. 1998) at 577 ("By 1900, soldiers' pensions accounted for roughly forty percent of the federal budget.")

class households from their homes to the financial instruments such households own via their 401(k), IRA, 529 and other individual accounts. President Bush's ownership society proposals, rather than representing radical innovation, would, if adopted, constitute incremental expansion of the defined contribution paradigm which itself is the product of cumulative incremental choices.

C. International Comparisons

International comparisons confirm the notion that our individualistic culture, which privileges personal ownership and control, underpins the emergence of the defined contribution paradigm in the United States. While our major trading partners confront the same demographic trends as does the U.S. (aging populations straining retirement systems)[15], none has developed a widespread defined contribution network comparable to that of the U.S. For example, neither France[16] nor Germany[17] has to date evolved anything similar to the elaborate web in the U.S. of 401(k) and individual account arrangements. The defined benefit format remains similarly dominant in Canada.[18]

Many factors likely explain different national approaches to retirement policy. The political processes shaping such policy are likely as path dependent in other countries as they have been in the U.S. Stronger unions abroad can also explain the hardier persistence of traditional defined benefit plans outside the United States as perhaps can smaller national populations, greater cultural homogeneity,

---

[15] *See, e.g.*, Frederick Kempe, *Demographic Time Bomb Ticks On*, WALL ST. J., June 6, 2006 at A9; Gillian Tett, *Pensions crisis could hit national bonds*, FINANCIAL TIMES, June 5, 2006 at 18.

[16] *See* Lucy apRoberts, *Comments in* SECURING EMPLOYER-BASED PENSIONS, AN INTERNATIONAL PERSPECTIVE 109–111 (Bodie et al. eds., 1996) (hereinafter INTERNATIONAL PERSPECTIVE) at 109–111 (discussing French "complementary plans.")

[17] *See* Peter Ahrend, *Pension Financial Security in Germany* in INTERNATIONAL PERSPECTIVE, *supra* note 16 at 75 (In Germany, "(i)n general, individuals cannot establish individual retirement accounts and receive a tax deduction.") and at 87–88 (in Germany, "defined contribution plans . . . are not very widespread.") Like the United States, Germany confronts the problem that aging "baby boomers will stress the retirement income system." Peter A. Diamond, TAXATION, INCOMPLETE MARKETS, AND SOCIAL SECURITY 123 (2003).

[18] CUPE, *Comparing Defined Benefit and Money Purchase Pension Plans* (September 30, 2003) *available at* http://www.cupe.ca/www/Pensions/definedvsmoneypurcha (last visited April 14, 2006) ("Statistics Canada reports that over 88% of pension plan members belong to defined benefit plans, and this figure climbs to 95% when looking at public sector workers. The overwhelming majority of pension plan members participate in defined benefit plans. On the other hand, nearly 90% of money purchase plans had less than 100 members, which reflects the fact that they have been the secondary pension option for small employers that are unwilling or unable to take on a defined benefit plan.")

and differing political systems. Nevertheless, greater cultural emphasis on private ownership and control explains in important measure the receptivity of Americans to individual accounts in contrast to the relative indifference (so far, at least) of German, French, and Canadian society to such defined contribution devices.[19]

In an international comparison, Britain and Japan fall between the United States (with its enthusiastic embrace of the defined contribution paradigm) and France, Canada, and Germany (with their relative indifference to date to the lure of individual accounts). Japan has developed defined contribution devices on a limited scale.[20] Britain comes closest to the U.S. individual account experience.[21] Sweden and Italy have switched their national public pension systems to the pseudo-defined contribution format which Americans call the "cash balance" configuration and Europeans call the "notional defined contribution" (NDC) model.[22] But, so far at least, no major trading partner of the United States has embraced individual accounts with the relish of the United States.

Perhaps, over time, the retirement systems of the modern industrial nations will come to resemble one another.[23] For now, however, there is no evidence of a broad

---

[19] One French commentator agrees that national culture helps to explain the difference between the U.S. and the German and French retirement systems. *See* apRoberts, *supra* note 16 at 108 ("Cultural as well as historical factors may help to account for differences between the German and the U.S. system") and at 111 ("There are probably a number of cultural attitudes that can help to explain the French complementary plan system.")

[20] Noriyasu Watanabe, *Private Pension Plans in Japan* in INTERNATIONAL PERSPECTIVE, *supra* note 16 at 124 ("In Japan private pension plans have traditionally been defined benefit plans"), at 126 (Japanese defined contribution arrangements are "of considerably less importance"), and at 129 ("Compared to defined benefit plans, defined contribution plans have a short history.") Robert L. Clark, *Comments* in INTERNATIONAL PERSPECTIVE, *supra* note 16 at 143 ("Japanese pensions are virtually all defined benefit plans").

[21] Anthony M. Santomero, *Comments* in INTERNATIONAL PERSPECTIVE, *supra* note 16 at 70 ("the United Kingdom pension system is predominantly a defined benefit structure" although there "is significant evidence of a trend in the United Kingdom toward defined contribution plans as well.")

[22] World Bank Pension Reform Primer, *Notional accounts: Notional defined contribution plans as a pension reform strategy*, at 1 available at http://siteresources.worldbank.org/INTPENSIONS/Resources/395443-1121194657824/PRPNoteNationalAccts.pdf (last visited April 11, 2006) ("Recent reforms in Italy, Latvia, Poland and Sweden were based on the notional-accounts model.") Sweden has also created a parallel system of mandatory individual accounts. James C. Capretta, *U.S. Should Study Swedish and German Social Security Reforms*, 113 TAX NOTES 173 (2006); John Turner, *Public Policy For Retirement Security in the 21st Century: Comparative Perspectives: Lessons From Other Countries: Individual Pension Accounts: The Innovative Swedish Reform*, 65 OHIO ST. L.J. 27 (2004).

[23] For an indication of the possibility of such convergence, *see* Benjamin Seeder, *German firms change to DC plans*, PENSIONS & INVESTMENTS, Oct. 27, 2003, at 3 ("Several German companies are restructuring, or are considering restructuring, their pension schemes into defined contribution schemes or cash balance plans . . .".)

convergence of retirement policies across national boundaries despite similar demographic and economic challenges. At least part of the reason there has as yet been no such convergence is that different national cultures place different emphases on the values of individual control and ownership which underlie the defined contribution paradigm.

In short, individual accounts today both shape and reflect the norms of American culture. As more Americans experience retirement savings through individual accounts, their expectations are molded by that experience. Those expectations are further reinforced by the promotional efforts of the financial services industry and by the extension of the individual account format to educational savings and medical care. Individual accounts fit comfortably with American norms of private property and control, norms which further reinforce the defined contribution paradigm.

It would be surprising if something as fundamental as a society's tax and retirement policies did not reflect the society's underlying values. On the other hand, values can manifest themselves in different ways. As I interpret the origins of the defined contribution paradigm, cultural predilections for private ownership and control do not, by themselves, explain Americans' embrace of that paradigm. Absent the decisions embodied in ERISA and Section 401(k), individual account devices would not have emerged as they have. However, ERISA and Section 401(k) had the enormous, unintended impact they did because, *inter alia*, individual accounts resonate with the values of American culture.

The cultural receptivity to and reinforcement of the defined contribution paradigm indicate that many (myself included) have underestimated the magnitude of the task of resuscitating the private defined benefit system. We have taken for granted that others find as compelling as we do the desirability of defined benefit plans which allocate investment, funding and longevity risks to employers. We have also inferred that, since ERISA-imposed regulation was an important cause of the stagnation of defined benefit pensions, reducing the regulatory burdens on defined benefit plans today would resurrect such plans.[24]

---

[24] For some of my earlier observations along these lines, see Edward A. Zelinsky, *Pensions and Property Contributions:* Wood, Keystone, *and the Supreme Court,* TAX NOTES, Aug. 3, 1992, at 657 ("In significant measure, the eclipse of the defined benefit plan is attributable to the burdens imposed by the federal government's heavy regulation of such plans . . . . The decline of the defined benefit plan is particularly troublesome at this time, as the aging baby boom generation enters the years when its unprecedented demand for retirement income could best be anticipated through the defined benefit format.")

This perspective underestimates the popular appeal of individual accounts: Many Americans, largely middle-class and upper-middle-class Americans, have experienced such accounts and like them. While ERISA-imposed burdens on defined benefit plans reinforced the demographic and economic forces causing the stagnation of such plans, the reduction of those regulatory burdens would today not stimulate a revival of defined benefit pensions. The contemporary defined contribution system has become entrenched and self-reinforcing, in important measure because that system comports well with American norms about private ownership and control and because more and more Americans now have a vested interest in individual accounts. As Americans undertake successive job changes and consequent rollovers into their IRAs, their IRAs have become the locus of many Americans' financial wealth.

None of this implies that those who have lost defined benefit coverage over the years were or are happy about it. Even before the proponents of behavioral economics taught us about "status quo bias,"[25] most of us understood that people often find change difficult. There are, moreover, solid economic reasons for employees to prefer defined benefit coverage which imposes funding, longevity and investment risks upon their employers, rather than upon the employees themselves. And for many, particularly older, employees, new defined contribution plans are often less lucrative than the traditional defined arrangements such plans replace.

In short, the shift from defined benefit to defined contribution plans entailed significant dislocations and losses for many persons. That this shift occurred notwithstanding these costs is a testament to, among other factors, the cultural strength among Americans of the values of private ownership, personal control and individual self-sufficiency. The comparative de-emphasis of those values in other countries helps to explain why, so far at least, those countries have not incurred these transitional costs to embrace the defined contribution paradigm as Americans have.

Nor does the American predilection for ownership and control imply that all Americans are great investors, in general or in the particular context of their 401(k)

---

[25] *See, e.g.,* Amitai Aviram and Avishalom Tor, *Overcoming Impediments to Information Sharing*, 55 ALA. L. REV. 231, 257 (2004) ("Loss aversion and the status quo bias are fundamental characteristics of human decisionmaking.")

and other individual accounts. As noted in Chapter Two, there is mounting evidence that many, perhaps most, participants in self-directed defined contribution plans invest their respective accounts poorly. This is a major concern of those (myself included) who believe that the shift from the defined benefit to the defined contribution format will work unsatisfactorily for many.

However, the point remains that the transition to the individual account paradigm has been facilitated by the celebration in American culture of private ownership, personal autonomy and individual self-sufficiency. It is hard to imagine the contemporary defined contribution system absent those values.

D. Individual Accounts and Family Diversity

Another reason for the broad acceptance of the defined contribution format is that that format works well in a society of diverse lifestyles and family arrangements. Again, we see the law of unintended consequences at work: No one set out to promote individual accounts as means of adapting to alternative family structures. Nevertheless, such accounts, by privatizing beneficiary designations, work well in a society with varied domestic arrangements, permitting individuals to delineate their own relationships. In contrast, defined benefit plans financed by common pools invariably require employers and, ultimately, the government to determine who are spouses with legitimate claims against such common pools.

Consider in this context the assertion that same-sex domestic partners should participate in employer-sponsored fringe benefit programs, just like heterosexual spouses.[26] Consider also the claim that unmarried participants in domestic relationships should obtain the same fringe benefit coverage as do married persons.[27]

The annuity payments of the traditional defined benefit pension bring these claims into particular focus, especially when such payments include a "subsidized"

---

[26] See, e.g., Julian B. Ferholt, *Children benefit from same-sex partnerships*, NEW HAVEN REGISTER, March 31, 2003, at A4 (arguing that children will benefit from extending, *inter alia*, pension coverage and health insurance to same-sex relationships).

[27] See Edward A. Zelinsky, *Deregulating Marriage: The Pro-Marriage Case For Abolishing Civil Marriage*, 27 CARDOZO L. REV. 1161, 1170–1173 (2006).

survivor annuity, i.e., an automatic payment to a surviving spouse with no reduc-tion of benefits during the life of the participant to pay for that survivor annuity.[28]

Under current law, one must be a spouse to possess a legal entitlement to a statutorily-mandated death benefit. Consequently, those lacking spousal status (because theirs is a same-sex or a heterosexual, but unmarried, partnership) are incented to demand legal recognition of their relationships to obtain survivor annuities. Conversely, employers sponsoring traditional defined benefit pensions are incented financially[29] to resist those demands, since paying subsidized survi-vors' benefits to more people raises the total costs of those benefits, costs which, at least in the first instance,[30] the employer must finance.[31] Ultimately, this tension requires the government to define who is a spouse or otherwise eligible for survivors' benefits.

This tension may be present even if the survivors' benefit paid by a traditional defined benefit plan is unsubsidized. Consider, for example, an employee in ill-health and near retirement. Suppose that that employee's partner is not civilly married to him because they are members of the same gender or because they anticipate that the ill partner will require Medicaid coverage.[32] To protect his part-ner, this hypothetical employee would like to receive his retirement benefit as an unsubsidized joint-and-survivor annuity. While such an annuity pays the retired employee less during his lifetime than he would otherwise receive, it continues after his death at a reduced rate for his surviving spouse. The employer is finan-cially incented to resist this demand by denying spousal status to the employee's partner since the employer's plan saves money by paying a larger annuity to the

---

[28] Internal Revenue Code Section 417(a)(5); ERISA Section 205(c)(5). An unsubsidized survivor benefit entails a reduction in the payments to the participant while alive to compensate the plan (and thus the employer) for the actuarial cost of the annuity continuing to the participant's spouse after the par-ticipant's death.

[29] Notwithstanding the cost, some employers, as a matter of business practice, provide benefits to non-spousal partners. Nevertheless, the point in the text remains valid: As a financial matter, employers are incented to minimize the cost of the benefits they provide and thus seek, in the defined benefit context, to define narrowly who is considered a spouse.

[30] For the long run, employers undoubtedly shift some of these costs to customers in the form of higher prices and to employees in the form of less employment and lower cash compensation. However, such cost-shifting entails its own downsides for the employer.

[31] Zelinsky, *Deregulating Marriage, supra* note 27 at 1171–1172.

[32] On the marriage penalty often imposed by Medicaid, *see id.* at 1207 ("In effect, the well spouse must impoverish himself or herself to obtain Title XIX for the ill spouse.")

employee during his retirement (anticipated to be relatively short) with no further obligation after his death.

These kinds of disputes disappear with defined contribution arrangements since each participant has his own account and may designate whomever[33] he chooses to receive the account's balance on his death. In the defined contribution context, the employer's only concern when a participant dies is administrative, namely, that the beneficiary be easily determinable and available to receive payment. As to the identity of the death benefit payee, the employer is financially indifferent since it is the deceased participant's individual account being distributed, not part of a common pool which the employer is obligated to replenish. In this setting, the polity need not define who is a spouse since entitlement to a death benefit flows, not from status as such a spouse, but from the participant's designation of his own beneficiary.

A similar story can be told as to health care. An employer sponsoring a traditional health arrangement for its employees (whether fee-for-service indemnity insurance or managed care such as health maintenance or preferred provider coverage) has a financial incentive to minimize the claims advanced against the common pool financing those arrangements since the employer bears responsibility for replenishing the pool.[34] Expanding the universe of claimants to include workers' unmarried partners depletes the resources of that employer-financed pool and concomitantly increases the employer's liability to maintain that pool. This liability incents the employer to resist claims for nonspousal coverage.

In contrast, under an MSA or HSA, the employer is indifferent whether the account holder is married or not since the account is the property of the account holder, not part of a common pool which the employer must replenish if distributed to an employee's mate.[35] Thus, the role of the sponsoring employer and its

---

[33] Two qualifications are in order. First, a prior spouse may have an interest under a qualified domestic relations order in his or her former spouse's individual account. Second, a current spouse may also have an interest in his or her spouse's individual account. *See* Internal Revenue Code Sections 401(a)(11), 414(p) and 417; ERISA Sections 205 and 206(d)(3).

[34] Subject, again, to ultimate cost-shifting by the employer onto customers (in the form of higher prices) and employees (in the form of reduced current wages and less employment).

[35] This is not the case with HRAs since, as to such accounts, any unused amounts ultimately revert back to the employer sponsoring the HRA. Note also that the high deductible insurance to which MSAs and HSAs are coupled are defined benefit plans financed by common pools. Thus, as to this insurance, the employer has an interest in minimizing claimants to minimize costs.

agents is ministerial; substantively, the employer has no interest in minimizing payments from the employee's MSA or HSA since the employer has no obligation toward or interest in the solvency of that account.

A defender of defined benefit arrangements would retort that this accommodation of diverse lifestyles is achieved by atomizing individuals and families, removing them from common pools into privatized, account-based plans for financing retirement and health care. This process diminishes the benefits of risk pooling for those who remain in the (now smaller) population still served by such traditional defined benefit arrangements. Fair enough. But, so far at least, the growth of individual account arrangements suggests that what a critic might view as unattractive atomization with attendant adverse selection problems, some (perhaps much) of the American public views as acceptable, if not desirable, privatization.

In short, since defined benefits are financed by common, employer-supported funds, the claimants against those funds (in particular, spouses) must be specified by the plan and, ultimately, by the polity regulating the plan. This is an inherently contentious activity in a society marked by heterogeneous family arrangements. In contrast, individual accounts permit a diverse society to defuse and diffuse conflict by decentralizing decisions,[36] in this case, letting each participant in a defined contribution arrangement decide for herself the identity of her own beneficiaries.

The defined contribution paradigm thus aggravates the fault line between libertarian conservatives (attracted by the power of the individual account holder to dispose of his own resources and determine his own lifestyle and beneficiaries) and many social conservatives (who will find some of the resulting choices disconcerting).

E. The Recent Politicization of the Defined Contribution Paradigm

As observed earlier, the early steps on the path to the defined contribution paradigm—the adoption of ERISA and Section 401(k) – occurred almost casually

---

36   *See, e.g.*, Schuck, *supra* chap. two note 29 at 328 ("a society that relies on decentralized choice gains an incalculable value – political conflict reduction—that goes well beyond the efficiency and autonomy values enjoyed by those who exercise it.")

and in bi-partisan fashion. No one believed they were inaugurating the revolution they in fact were starting. These initial legislative steps toward the defined contribution society were augmented by the promotional efforts of the financial services industry and by the predilections of a culture valuing private ownership, individual control and personal self-sufficiency.

In recent years, individual accounts have been promoted by conservative think tanks and interest groups which have aggressively encouraged such accounts for state and local retirement systems, for federal Social Security, and for medical care. The growth of defined contribution arrangements for public employees is, in important measure, attributable to lobbying by these ideologically-oriented actors and by the financial services industry. Similarly, Congress's recent expansion of tax-advantaged health care accounts from MSAs to HSAs reflects a market-driven, consumer-controlled conception of medical care, a conception fostered by both ideological and self-interested participants in the legislative process.[37]

The upshot is the relatively recent politicization of the defined contribution paradigm. Such politicization of the individual account model will be increasingly evident in the future.

In this context, consider first governmental defined benefit plans for public employees. Such plans are exempt from ERISA's statutory minimum funding standards.[38] Consequently, in states and municipalities with traditional defined benefit pensions, elected officials may pass the burden of pension funding to their successors by promising future benefits to government employees without financing those benefits now.[39] For the short-run, delaying funding until later

---

[37]   *See, e.g.,* John F. Cogan, R. Glenn Hubbard and Daniel P. Kessler, HEALTHY, WEALTHY & WISE: FIVE STEPS TO A BETTER HEALTH CARE SYSTEM 5, 35 (2005) (HSAs "give individuals more control over and choices for their health care"); Sally C. Pipes, MIRACLE CURE: HOW TO SOLVE AMERICA'S HEALTH CARE CRISIS AND WHY CANADA ISN'T THE ANSWER 95, 102 (2004) at ("HSAs address some of the key problems affecting health care in the United States. They control health care costs by making people price sensitive"); David Gratzer, *What Ails Health Care,* THE PUBLIC INTEREST, Spring, 2005 at 122 ("The HSA approach results in great savings, by giving people incentive to think twice about where and how they spend their health dollars"); Penelope Lemov, *The Job of Patients,* GOVERNING, March, 2006, at 45 (For HSA supporters, "[t]he core selling point in that such accounts can turn patients into better consumers by encouraging them to shop around for the best price and ask whether certain procedures are necessary.")

[38]   Internal Revenue Code Section 412(h)(3). *See also* ERISA Section 4(b)(1) (exempting governmental plans from ERISA).

[39]   Perhaps the best known instance of this sort was the decision by Governor Whitman of New Jersey to reduce current pension funding to finance tax cuts. *See* Roger Lowenstein, *The End of Pensions?,* N.Y. TIMES MAGAZINE, Oct. 30, 2005, at 70.

does not hurt current retirees since there is typically enough cash on hand to pay retirees their retirement benefits as they come due. Similarly, active public employees, promised a defined benefit in the future, usually prefer immediate cash wages to current funding of pension benefits payable down the road. And taxpayers generally prefer to delay taxes if they can.

There are countervailing forces which impel elected officials to fund public defined benefit pensions even in times of fiscal hardship. Most importantly, bond rating agencies may downgrade the debt of states and localities which don't finance their pension obligations adequately.[40] However, the counterpressures to underfund are often greater. It is thus unsurprising that the problem of underfunded public defined benefit pensions is significant in many states and municipalities as benefits are promised for the future but not funded today.[41] It is, moreover, a problem for which responsibility is widespread: Public officials promise future benefits without funding them; taxpayers acquiesce to such underfunding; public employees demand increases in their current wages while leaving pension funding for later; public employee unions proclaim their success at obtaining benefits while winking at the underfunding of those benefits.

By definition, underfunding of future benefits does not occur with a defined contribution plan since the state or municipality, like any other employer sponsoring such an individual account plan, is obligated to make a current defined contribution

---

[40] *See, e.g.,* Deborah Solomon, *Public Pensions Press State Budgets*, WALL ST. J., Feb. 23, 2006, at A2 ("Underfunded public-employee pension plans are straining state budgets just as states face other rising expenses and steep debt levels, according to a Standard & Poor's Corp. analysis to be released today.").

[41] *See, e.g.,* Christopher Cooper, *States' Pension Shortfalls Widen Amid an Increase in Tax Receipts*, WALL ST. J., Feb. 28, 2007 at A2 ("The report says states collectively had about $330 billion in unfunded pension obligations in fiscal 2005, the last period for which complete data are available. That is $46 billion more than in fiscal 2004."); Mary Williams Walsh, *Public Pension Plans Face Billions in Shortages*, N.Y. TIMES, August 8, 2006, at A1; Douglas Fore, *Going Private in the Public Sector; The Transition from Defined Benefit to Defined Contribution Pension Plans*, in PENSIONS IN THE PUBLIC SECTOR 273 (Olivia S. Mitchell & Edwin C. Hustead eds., 2001) ("Where public plans are less than fully funded, the amount is substantial . . . ."); J. Fred Giertz, *The Impact of Pension Funding on State Government Finances*, STATE TAX NOTES, Aug. 18, 2003, at 509 ("With the inexorable growth in liabilities, the shortfall could grow to $300 billion by the end of fiscal 2003 if the market remains at the current low level."); Christopher Swope, *Payout Planning*, GOVERNING, Sept., 2003, at 48 ("Some 27 states face pension shortfalls that run more than half as large as their entire state budgets."); Mary Williams Walsh, *States And Cities Risk Bigger Losses To Fund Pensions*, N.Y. TIMES, Oct. 12, 2003 at 1 ("Many state and local governments, facing ballooning pension promises to police officers, firefighters, teachers and other public employees, are rushing to sell bonds to cover the shortfall."); Alan Greenblatt, *Plight of The Benefits*, GOVERNING, April, 2006 at 36 ("Collectively, states are close to $300 billion short of meeting future pension obligations.").

for each employee, not to finance future benefits payable later.[42] Thus, proponents of public sector individual account arrangements can credibly claim that such arrangements require responsible budgeting by precluding officials from promising a benefit payable at a later time which they do not fund (or do not fund adequately) today. Defining the government's funding obligation in terms of current contributions disciplines elected officials who, in the defined benefit context, can push off to tomorrow the financing of benefits promised for the future but who must, in contrast, allocate a defined contribution today.

On a more ideological level, individual accounts turn public pension participants from claimants against prospective tax receipts into investors, stakeholders in their accounts and in the investments those accounts hold. Here again an analogy suggests itself: Margaret Thatcher's government sold public housing to its residents to convert those residents from the recipients of government largesse into private property owners.[43] At least some of the groups promoting public defined contribution plans envision a similar transformation of the interests and outlooks of public pension participants.

In addition, public employee self-directed defined contribution plans are another market for the financial services industry. Moreover, taxpayers who themselves experience retirement savings through 401(k) accounts and IRAs will believe that public employees should also. Indeed, as I discuss in Chapter Six, there will be tension in the years ahead between taxpayers, themselves covered by 401(k) and other defined contribution arrangements, and public employees insisting that they must retain their traditional defined benefit pensions.

Conservative think tanks played a critical role in designing and advocating proposals to augment the Code's MSA provisions with the new HSA. The themes advanced to support such accounts, not surprisingly, reflect the values underpinning the defined contribution paradigm, namely, the empowerment of individual account holders and the benefits which flow from that empowerment.

---

42 General Accountability Office, SOCIAL SECURITY REFORM: INFORMATION ON USING A VOLUNTARY APPROACH TO INDIVIDUAL ACCOUNTS, GAO-03-309 (March, 2003) at 4 ("Defined contribution pensions and individual retirement savings are fully funded by definition.")

43 *See* Margaret Thatcher, THE DOWNING STREET YEARS 604 (1993) ("The extension of home ownership over the last decade had been one of the Government's greatest successes"); Margaret Thatcher, THE PATH TO POWER 243 (1995) ("I had always believed in a property-owning democracy and wider home ownership") and at 245–246 (discussing Conservative Party proposals permitting residents of public housing to purchase their homes).

As I discuss in Chapter Six and in contrast to the bi-partisan origins of the defined contribution paradigm, debate about that paradigm will be partisan and ideologically contentious in the years ahead.

F. Social Security and the Limits of Dominant Paradigms

In light of the entrenchment of the defined contribution paradigm in tax and retirement policy, what explains President Bush's failure to extend private accounts to the federal Social Security system? *Ex ante*, it was plausible to predict that the American people, now inured to the defined contribution model, would embrace individual accounts for Social Security as a logical extension of their experiences with IRAs, 401(k) plans, 529 programs and other individual accounts. Nevertheless, *ex post*, neither Congress nor the American people as a whole supported the introduction of individual accounts into the federal Social Security system—despite the growth of such accounts for private savings for retirement, education, and health care.

The simple explanation for this failure is that even dominant paradigms have their limits. The more detailed explanation identifies five reasons for the failure (so far, at least) of the Bush proposal for individual Social Security accounts, notwithstanding widespread acceptance of individual accounts in other contexts.

First, as a procedural matter, the enactment of private accounts for the federal Social Security system requires an overt and public break with the status quo, namely, explicit congressional votes to alter a popular entitlement program—not an easy thing to accomplish in a democratic society.

This overt break with the status quo contrasts with the incremental, essentially unintended nature of the process by which the defined contribution paradigm emerged in its present form. Had ERISA been understood as causing a shift from the defined benefit model to a world of individual accounts, that change would likely have generated substantial resistance in 1974. Similarly, had Congress's adoption of Section 401(k) been advertised as heralding a switch from the defined benefit model to the defined contribution format, that legislation too would likely have met significant opposition. In normal times, democracies resist open and abrupt change.

In fact, neither ERISA nor Section 401(k) could have been advertised as catalyzing a shift from the defined benefit format to the defined contribution paradigm since few, if any, foresaw this shift. This inability to foresee the long-term significance of ERISA and Section 401(k) facilitated the move to an individual account society. The introduction of the defined contribution paradigm occurred, if not quite by stealth, in successive steps, each of which, by itself, seemed (and was) incremental, though cumulatively these steps constituted nothing short of an unintended revolution in tax and social policy.

There was, in contrast, no way President Bush could introduce private accounts to Social Security in similarly incremental fashion.

A famous piece of FDR lore has him defending in political terms the regressive nature of the FICA payroll taxes financing the Social Security system. According to this tradition, FDR recognized that a sense of "legal, moral and political"[44] entitlement flows from characterizing workers' FICA payments as earmarked "contributions" paid for their own federal pension benefits. "With those [payroll] taxes in there, no damn politician can ever scrap my social security program."[45]

To enact his proposal for individual accounts, President Bush had to confront openly and surmount this long-fostered sense of Social Security entitlement. In contrast, the defined contribution paradigm was introduced through incremental steps, the long-term implications of which were not fully perceived as each was enacted.

Second, in terms of political constituencies, the segment of the American populace most dependent on Social Security for retirement income is also the portion of the populace lacking experience with individual accounts. The defined contribution paradigm is largely a middle- and upper-middle-class phenomenon. The half of the population without significant participation in 401(k) plans, IRAs and

---

[44] *See* Patricia F. Dilley, *Taking Public Rights Private: The Rhetoric and Reality of Social Security Privatization,* 41 B.c. l. rev. 975, 1033 (2000). *See also* Graetz and Mashaw, *supra* chap. two note 29 at 285–286 ("In his effort to enact Social Security and to secure its future, Franklin Roosevelt insisted that the payroll taxes imposed on virtually all employees and their employers to fund benefits to retirees and survivors be called 'contributions.' Individuals were supposed to view their payroll deductions as contributing to their own retirement, not as transferring money to someone else."); Moss, *supra* chap. two note 3 at 201 (noting that, in the design of the federal Social Security system, "FDR himself eventually demanded an exceedingly tight connection between the contributions and benefits of each participant (as in a private annuity contract)") (parenthetical in the original).

[45] Dilley, *supra* note 44.

other such accounts are lower income and lower-middle-class individuals who typically have neither pension coverage nor discretionary income for significant saving, even when such saving is tax-favored. Not surprisingly, many of these individuals proved risk averse in the context of President Bush's proposal, unwilling to trade the familiar security of traditional Social Security for individual accounts with which they have no significant experience.

Thus, debate about President Bush's proposal for Social Security accounts in part reflected the class-based fault lines of the defined contribution paradigm. Confronted with that proposal, most low-income and working-class Americans could not analogize from their experiences with individual accounts since they had no such experiences from which to analogize.

Third, individuals successfully participating in the defined contribution paradigm for private and employment-based savings can logically favor the traditional defined benefit format for Social Security as a secure offset against the risks they assume with individual accounts. Such individuals can view traditional, annuity-paying Social Security as providing an assured[46] baseline retirement income which enables them to absorb the investment, funding and longevity risks of individual accounts. For these individuals, there is a symbiotic relationship between their coverage by traditional Social Security and their participation in individual accounts; the former makes them more secure about the risks involved in the latter. In terms of an overall portfolio for retirement, Social Security as it exists today diversifies these individuals' entitlements, providing a more conservative, fixed income component to balance the risks they assume and the rewards they pursue through their individual accounts.

These individuals don't need more defined contribution accounts; they typically contribute less than the maximum allowed to the accounts they already have.[47]

---

[46] Yes, yes I know: no one has a legally protected right to Social Security. But, the political reality is that many, perhaps most Americans, have a strong (and not unreasonable) sense of entitlement when it comes to the Social Security system by virtue of their perceptions that they have, while working, contributed to the system. For a judicial statement that Social Security does not constitute a legally protected entitlement, *see Lansden v. Marsh*, 961 F. Supp. 1143, 1146–1147 (M.D. Tenn. 1997) (Social Security recipients "have no property interest in the benefits received.")

[47] Karen E. Smith & Eric J. Toder, *Tax Law Changes Increase Deferred Compensation Limits*, TAX NOTES, Dec. 19, 2005, at 1603 ("Of those participating in plans, less than 4 percent contributed the maximum amount in 1990. The share of maximum contributors rose to more than 7 percent in 2001, but the share dropped back to 6 percent in 2003, as many employees did not take advantage of the catch-up provision.")

Instead, these individuals value the security of traditional Social Security to balance their riskier retirement accounts and thus see no need to alter Social Security from its present defined benefit form.

Fourth, when the public and the Congress focused upon the economics of individual Social Security accounts as President Bush advocated them, it became clear that diverting FICA taxes to such accounts would exacerbate, rather than solve, the shortfall between the revenues generated by such taxes and the traditional annuity-style benefits payable by the Social Security system. Such accounts would consequently entail for some, perhaps many, affected individuals a net reduction in Social Security benefits.

This conclusion reinforced the skepticism of both those lacking experience with individual accounts and those who view traditional Social Security benefits as a fixed-income asset offsetting the risks of their individual accounts. Members of both groups correctly came to see the Bush plan as impairing traditional annuity benefits under the Social Security system. Theoretically, the traditional benefits lost through the establishment of individual accounts were to be offset by the investment performance of such accounts. However, reasonably risk-averse individuals could sensibly be skeptical of the net effect of this trade-off. For these individuals, the Bush proposal in the end looked like (and in many cases would have been) a benefit cut as the anticipated reduction in traditional Social Security benefits seemingly outweighed the (uncertain) gains from the investment performance of individual accounts.

In contrast to the unfavorable cost/benefit trade-off presented by the Bush plan for Social Security accounts, when Congress established the other individual accounts of the defined contribution paradigm, it was simply doling out largesse, i.e., creating tax-advantaged opportunities to save. To be sure, these tax-advantaged accounts involve costs for the federal fisc. However, from the perspective of the individual taxpayer and her members of Congress, establishing these accounts was a matter of financial and political gain at no cost—a classic formula for political success. The political calculation for the Bush Social Security proposal was not so lopsided.

Finally, debate about President Bush's proposal for private Social Security accounts was far more politicized than any prior discussion of individual accounts. The ideologically- and politically-charged nature of this debate was foreshadowed by the initial discussions about MSAs and HSAs. In these contexts, proponents of these health care accounts articulated what are today considered conservative themes—individual responsibility and autonomy, consumer sensitivity to and control of medical costs—while opponents of these individual accounts for medical care responded with their counterthemes—the dangers of adverse selection, the benefits of risk pooling.[48] In retrospect, these earlier debates were dress rehearsals for the subsequent and more intense controversy over Social Security accounts.

The polarized, highly-partisan debate triggered by President Bush's proposal for Social Security accounts contrasts with the comparatively casual, bi-partisan fashion in which Congress embraced 401k, IRA and 529 accounts. As I observe in Chapter Six, future discussion about the defined contribution paradigm will focus heavily on public employees' traditional defined benefit coverage and will resemble the contentious debate about Social Security accounts—even as the private sector continues its unimpeded shift toward the individual account paradigm.

Despite President Bush's failure to introduce private accounts to the federal Social Security system, it is too early to proclaim the demise of legislation along these lines. For the near term, it is unlikely that Congress will embrace such legislation. The long run, however, may well be different. Almost a generation elapsed from President Truman's initial call for Medicare to President Johnson's signing of the Medicare statute at the Truman Library.[49] It is not inevitable that a successor to Mr. Bush will similarly sign at Mr. Bush's library legislation establishing individual accounts in the federal Social Security system. However, this possibility cannot be ruled out for the future.

Note in this context the political paradox presented by Congress's decision in 2006 to make permanent the Section 25B tax credit for low income taxpayers who

---

[48] See, e.g., Jonathan Cohn, *Crash Course, Why Health Savings Accounts Will Drive America's Sick Over the Edge*, THE NEW REPUBLIC, Nov. 7, 2005, at 23 ("by luring healthy people and their premiums away from traditional insurance, HSAs would still drain money from the existing system, leaving the unhealthy to make up the cost"); Arnold S. Relman, *The Health of Nations*, THE NEW REPUBLIC, March 7, 2005, at 27 (With consumer-driven health care devises like HSAs, "one of the most important values of insurance – the sharing of risks over a broad population base – would be lost . . .".); Lemov, *supra* note 37 at 48 (Opponents of HSA-based health plans say that such "plans would leach healthy people from the conventional insurance rolls, thus dismantling the shared-risk concept that lies at the heart of health insurance.")

[49] David McCullough, TRUMAN 984 (1992).

contribute to individual accounts for retirement savings.[50] I suspect that many who favor that credit, particularly Democratic supporters of the credit, also oppose individual Social Security accounts, viewing both the credit and traditional Social Security as good for low income households. However, the Section 25B credit, now made permanent, will, over time, incent more lower income and lower-middle-class Americans to participate in individual accounts. The credit may thereby increase popular support for Social Security accounts by extending the defined contribution paradigm down the income scale.

A Thatcherite desire to transform low-income individuals into property owners in large measure explains Republican support for the Section 25B credit. That support also reflected the political calculation that a package of pension proposals including permanency for the credit could attract some Democratic congressmen who would otherwise oppose such a package. Republican support for the credit further reflected a policy-driven vision of universal participation in the defined contribution paradigm and the recognition that, as an economic matter, lower-income and blue-collar households cannot participate in that paradigm without significant subsidy.

However, the desire to make lower-income individuals stakeholders of the ownership society is likely the key reason why Republican tax writers adopted the Section 25B credit and made it permanent. Such a credit, by stimulating individual accounts for low-income individuals, will bring these individuals within the ambit of the ownership society

---

[50]   Internal Revenue Code Section 25B. *See also* Section 812 of the Pension Protection Act of 2006.

CHAPTER FIVE

What Does It Mean? Consumption Taxation, Tax Expenditures, and the Future of the Internal Revenue Code

In this chapter, I place the defined contribution paradigm in the context of contemporary tax policy debates about consumption taxation and tax expenditures. I conclude that, under the most likely scenarios, the individual accounts of the defined contribution paradigm will persist as central features of federal tax law.

A. Cash Flow Taxation and Individual Accounts

Among tax commentators and policy analysts, no topic is more hotly debated today than the advisability of shifting the federal tax base from income to consumption.[1] Prominent voices argue that converting the Internal Revenue Code to a consumption base would enhance efficiency and equity while simplifying the tax law.[2] Under what is commonly denoted a cash flow consumption tax, there would no longer be separate accounts for savings for particular purposes, e.g., retirement, health, education. Rather, every taxpayer (with earned income

---

[1] The literature on cash flow consumption tax is now voluminous. Among seminal contributions to that literature are William D. Andrews, *A Consumption-Type or Cash Flow Personal Income Tax*, 87 HARVARD L. REV. 1113 (1974); Alvin C. Warren, Jr. *Would a Consumption Tax Be Fairer than an Income Tax?* 89 YALE L. J. 1081 (1980); and Michael J. Graetz, *Implementing a Progressive Consumption Tax*, 92 HARVARD L. REV. 1575 (1979).

[2] *See, e.g.*, Bruce Bartlett, EXPLAINING THE BUSH TAX CUTS, 117(6) COMMENTARY 23, 27 (June, 2004). *See also* Alvin C. Warren, Jr., *Three Versions of Tax Reform*, 39 WM. AND MARY L. REV. 157, 166 (1997).

or not) would undertake all of her savings through either or both of two kinds of accounts, i.e., accounts subject to the conventional tax-deferral regime (deduction on contribution, tax-free accumulation of earnings, taxation upon withdrawal from the account) or the alternative pattern today reflected in the treatment of Roth, Section 529 and educational savings accounts (post-tax contributions, tax-free accumulation of earnings, tax-free withdrawals). Under the cash flow consumption tax, there would no longer be distinctions, in theory or in practice, among savings for particular purposes since all savings would receive either of these tax treatments. Likewise, under a cash flow consumption tax, there would be no limits on the amount which any taxpayer could save through such accounts since tax would be deferred[3] on all saved income until such saved income were consumed.[4]

Equally prominent voices opposing a consumption tax base contend that, as a matter of distributional fairness, the federal fisc should tax all income when earned or received, including income which is saved.[5] Since it is more affluent taxpayers who save, exempting saved income from the tax base potentially skews the effective tax burden away from these more prosperous taxpayers towards lower-income nonsavers. Yet others characterize the existing Code as a hybrid tax, in some respects an income tax which taxes income which is saved, in other respects a consumption tax which defers the taxation of saved income until such saved income is subsequently used for consumption.[6]

My survey of the defined contribution paradigm suggests a fourth perspective: For middle-class and upper-middle-class households, the federal government today *de facto* levies a federal cash flow consumption tax since these households can effectively conduct all their financial savings on a tax-deferred (or equivalent) basis via the individual accounts of the defined contribution paradigm. In terms of financial savings,[7] middle-class families save principally for retirement and to

---

[3] Or given the alternative treatment which is equivalent to deferral, assuming stable tax rates.

[4] *See* Engler and Knoll, *supra* intro. note 5 at 62 (2003) ("The principal change required to the existing tax base is the expansion of the current tax treatment of qualified accounts – such as IRAs, 401(k)s, etc. – to all investments, in effect providing an unlimited deduction for new savings.")

[5] Warren, *supra* note 2 ("Income tax proponents have responded that the consumption tax would be regressive and therefore unfair, because higher income individuals save more.")

[6] Edward J. McCaffery, *Tax Policy Under A Hybrid Income-Consumption Tax*, 70 TEXAS L. REV. 1145 (1992).

[7] Financial saving as opposed to saving in the form of housing appreciation and mortgage amortization.

educate their offspring. This saving today occurs largely through tax-deferred devices such as 401(k) accounts, 403(b) accounts, 529 plans, IRAs and cash balance pensions. Under these devices, the taxpayer's saving receives either the traditional tax-deferred treatment of qualified plans and IRAs (deductible contributions, tax-free earnings, taxation on distribution) or the economically-equivalent alternative (nondeductible contributions, tax-free earnings, tax-free distributions). Either way, these families receive consumption tax treatment for their savings. For these families, nothing would in practice change if the Code were transformed into an explicit consumption tax; they effectively live under a federal consumption tax regime today.

Since the families in the bottom half of the income spectrum generally do not undertake financial savings and since middle-income and upper-middle-income households can do their saving on a consumption tax basis through the tax-deferring accounts of the defined contribution paradigm, only the wealthiest taxpayers, who save in excess of the amounts permitted under these individual account mechanisms, are subject to current income taxation on saved income.[8]

A cash flow consumption tax[9] would represent the ultimate extension, indeed the triumph, of the defined contribution paradigm since all savings would occur through individual accounts. If the public does acquiesce to the formal conversion of the Code to an explicit consumption tax, that acquiescence would flow from the public's experience with the defined contribution paradigm, experience which has acclimated the public to the notion of tax-deferred savings accounts. As we have seen, an important dynamic in the evolution of the paradigm has been the incremental expansion of individual accounts. That expansion has, step-by-step, made feasible policies which would otherwise have seemed to have been sharp breaks from the status quo: The IRA begat the MSA which gave rise to the HSA. The conversion of the Code to a formal consumption tax would be the ultimate step in this incremental process, a step for which the public was prepared for a generation by the public's experience with individual accounts such as IRAs, 401(k) and 403(b) accounts, FSAs, and 529 programs.

---

8   Even this statement must be qualified. Much investment income takes the form of dividends and capital gains, taxed at preferential rates. *See* Code Section 1(h). The effective tax rates on some investment earnings can be lowered by deferring tax by avoiding realizations. Yet other investment income, most prominently municipal bond interest, is excluded from gross income. *See* Code Section 103.

9   As opposed to a value-added-tax (VAT), a retail sales tax, or any similar consumption levy.

Consider in this context President Bush's proposals to consolidate and expand the various individual accounts authorized under federal tax law, proposals which have been characterized as radical innovations.[10] In contrast, my analysis indicates that the Bush proposals are quite incremental in nature. While the Bush proposals would enlarge, simplify and combine the extant forms of individual accounts, the resulting changes would expand existing patterns of tax-deferred savings, not initiate new patterns. The Bush proposals thus institutionalize and reinforce the consumption tax features of the Code, rather than break sharply from current law. In sum, President Bush's vision of an ownership society, rather than being a radical departure from the status quo, is an incremental extension of the individual account status quo which itself is the product of cumulative incremental change.

Despite their gradualist nature, the Bush proposals are noteworthy insofar as they would weaken the link between the individual account devices of the defined contribution paradigm and savings for particular purposes. The Bush proposals would thereby move the Code closer to a pattern of generalized deferral for savings as such.[11] As we have seen, in their current incarnation, each form of individual account implements savings for a specific end, e.g., Section 529 accounts effect savings for the costs of higher education; 401(k) and 403(b) accounts implement savings for retirement; MSAs and HSAs are used to save for health costs. The Bush proposals, on the other hand, would largely decouple savings from particular purposes, permitting tax-deferred savings *per se*.[12] Such decoupling would move the Code closer to consumption tax norms by extending tax-deferral to savings as such, rather than conditioning such tax-deferral on the future purpose for which savings are to be used.

---

[10]   *See, e.g.*, Heather Bennett, *Bush To Renew Call For Savings Accounts But Details Await Budget Release*, 2004 TNT 21–6 (February 2, 2004) (quoting assistant secretary of the Treasury for tax policy Pamela F. Olson on the "radical change" sought by the Bush Administration through its savings account proposals).

[11]   This is not the only significant issue raised by the Bush proposals. For example, by increasing the ability of entrepreneurs to save on a tax-deferred basis on their own, the Bush proposals, if enacted into law, would discourage some business owners from establishing qualified plans at the workplace since these owners will themselves no longer need work-based plans to defer tax on saved income. *See* Martin A. Sullivan, *Economic Analysis: Budget Preview: Are LSAs Coming To Town*, 101 TAX NOTES 1255 (December 15, 2003) ("So because RSAs and LSAs would give small employers significantly greater capacity to save for retirement outside of a pension plan, many pension experts believe the enactment of RSAs and LSAs would reduce pension coverage.")

[12]   *Id.*

But here also the Bush proposals are more incremental in nature than first appears. Congress has already moved towards consumption tax norms by attenuating the links between tax deferral and the particular purposes animating tax-deferred savings, thereby pointing towards generalized tax deferral for savings as such. Congress, for example, has chipped away at the notion that retirement savings are just for retirement. In Code Section 72(t), Congress has exempted from the ten percent (10%) penalty tax on premature distributions those qualified plan and IRA distributions used for tax deductible medical expenses.[13] Congress has also exempted from this penalty tax IRA withdrawals used for certain higher education expenses,[14] for limited down payments for first-time home buyers,[15] and for health insurance premiums for certain unemployed persons.[16] The message which emerges from Section 72(t) is that "retirement" savings are properly used for certain pre-retirement needs.

Less explicit but equally revealing is the extent to which Congress has condoned the use of qualified plan and IRA resources for testamentary transmissions of wealth. Congress has thereby signaled that individual account retirement savings may be used for the nonretirement purpose of intergenerational wealth transfer—just as savings under an explicit consumption tax could be used for such intergenerational transfers.

To a degree, the minimum required distribution (MRD) rules of Code Section 401(a)(9)(A) discourage individuals from hoarding their qualified plan and IRA resources for transfer at death to their children. The MRD rules require that payment of retirement amounts must commence after[17] the participant has attained his "required beginning date," the later of age seventy and one-half or the participant's actual retirement date.[18] Thus, an employee, unless he works until he dies,

---

[13] Code Section 72(t)(2)(B).

[14] Code Section 72(t)(2)(E).

[15] Code Section 72(t)(2)(F).

[16] Code Section 72(t)(2)(D).

[17] Code Section 401(a)(9)(C). The precise statutory requirement is that distributions must commence by the April 1st of the calendar year following the calendar year in which occurs the participant's required beginning date.

[18] Code Section 401(a)(9)(C) (i). If the participant owns five percent or more of the employer sponsoring the qualified plan, his required beginning date is age 70 ½, with no option to extend that date by delaying retirement. See Code Section 401(a)(9)(C)(ii).

cannot simply hold intact his individual account[19] to convey it on death, but must begin withdrawals (and pay income tax on such withdrawals) while alive.

In practice, however, the MRD rules are a minimal impediment to the testamentary transmission of individual account wealth. Most obviously, the MRD mandate that distributions must commence after the account holder's required beginning date does not apply to Roth IRAs.[20] Consequently, an individual who views his Roth account as a device for transmitting wealth to his offspring can hold that account intact (generating income tax-deferred earnings) until his death and then leave that Roth account to his descendants. This possibility has not gone unnoticed.[21]

Moreover, in the early years after the required beginning date, the MRD rules permit a testamentarily-inclined account holder to withdraw quite small amounts based on his life expectancy[22] and thereby preserve the balance of the account for his heirs.[23] Thus, even when the MRD rules apply, the individual account of the

---

[19]   The MRD rules apply to conventional IRAs by virtue of Code Section 408(a)(6). The MRD rules also apply to 403(b) annuities and 457 plans. *See* Code Section 403(b)(10) and Section 457(d)(2).

[20]   Code Section 408A(c)(5). Since Code Section 402A contains no exemption from the minimum distribution rules, amounts contributed under the new elective Roth rules for 401(k) and 403(b) plans are subject to the minimum distribution rules. However, in practice, some, perhaps most, of these new Roth 40i(k) and 403(b) contributions can ultimately be rolled over to Roth IRAs where they will not be subject to those rules.

[21]   *See, e.g.*, Barbara Whitaker, *Managing Retirement, After You Really Retire*, N.Y. TIMES, Section 3, Column 1 (October 16, 2005) at 7 ("Many planners recommend putting as much as possible into Roth IRAs, because, among other reasons, they have no minimum mandatory withdrawals at 70 ½ . . . [A]dvisers of often use the term 'stretch IRAs' to describe those intended to last for generations.")

[22]   Code Section 401(a)(9)(B). This portion of the Code is implemented by Treas. Reg. Section 1. 401(a)(9)–5.

[23]   Consider, for example, a widow who has an IRA balance of $100,000 at age seventy-one. The MRD rules require this widow in the current year to withdraw from the IRA and pay federal income tax on $3,774. That is, $100,000/26.5 = $3,774. Thus, if the account earns a return in that year of four percent, the account balance actually increases since the mandated distribution is less than the year's earnings. True, the account will not grow as much as it would have absent the required distribution. On the other hand, the required distribution will not impair the amount available for testamentary transmission.
Moreover, after this widow's death, the IRA balance transferred to her child can, under the MRD regime, be distributed and taxed to that child on a favorable basis. If, for example, the widowed IRA holder dies survived by a forty-year-old child, that child may spread withdrawals from the inherited IRA (and thus defer income taxes) over a period of 43.6 years, reflecting the child's life expectancy. In this fashion, the child may continue favorable tax treatment of the inherited IRA for the remainder of child's lifetime. If the inherited IRA balance is still $100,000 when received by the child, the child, given her life expectancy of over forty years, must, in the first year after her mother's death, withdraw from her inherited IRA only $2,294. That is, $100,000/43.6 = $2,294. If the IRA earns on its investments a minimum rate of two and one-half percent during that year, the IRA balance will actually increase, despite the required withdrawal based on the child's life expectancy.

defined contribution paradigm is a potentially potent device for transmitting wealth at death.

At the most fundamental level, Congress, by condoning lump sum distributions in lieu of annuities,[24] has countenanced the testamentary transmission of individual account wealth. So far, I have emphasized the longevity risk created by lump sums, i.e., the possibility that individuals will outlive their retirement resources. But congressionally-condoned lump sums also create the possibility that retirement resources will outlive the individual. Annuities terminate on the death of the participant (or of the participant's spouse), leaving nothing for the participant's children. In contrast, lump sums create the possibility (in some cases, the likelihood)[25] that, on the demise of the participant (or of the participant's spouse), a lump sum balance will remain for the participant's heirs. Thus, the congressionally-approved movement from annuities to lump sums has increased the utility of individual account devices for testamentary purposes since lump sums carry the possibility of balances transmittable at the participant's death, unlike annuities which terminate upon the participant's demise.[26]

To summarize: Proponents of a federal cash flow consumption tax can plausibly characterize the individual accounts of the defined contribution paradigm as the harbinger of such a tax. For most middle and upper-middle class families, individual accounts already create a *de facto* consumption tax since those families can undertake all of their financial savings on a tax-deferred basis via these accounts.

---

24   Under Code Section 401(a)(11)(B)(iii) and ERISA Section 205(b)(C), a plan exempted from the minimum funding requirements, i.e., a profit sharing plan, can also exempt itself from the requirement that a joint-and-survivor annuity be the presumptive form in which benefits are paid. In practice, this means that lump sums, rather than annuities, can be offered as the presumptive form of benefit payment for participants in 401(k) plans, profit sharing arrangements with salary reduction features. Moreover, defined benefit and money purchase pensions (subject to the minimum funding rules) may permit the waiver of the joint-and-survivor annuity form if the participant's spouse consents. Code Section 417(a) and ERISA Section 205(c). Typically, such waivers enable the participants to receive lump sum distributions.

25   Consider, for example, a two-earner couple which has amassed substantial resources in their respective 401(k) accounts. Assume that they defer withdrawals until their required beginning dates, and that they withdraw at the minimum rate based on life expectancy. There is a substantial possibility that one or both members of this couple will leave a significant 401(k) balance on his or her death.

26   Munnell and Sunden, *supra* chap. three note 36 at 154 ("Bequests are likely to increase as retirees receive more of their pension benefits as lump sums rather than as annuity payments.")

Congress's decision to condone the use of pension and IRA resources for purposes other than retirement—medical care, education, first-time home buying, testamentary transfers—can plausibly be viewed as steps toward an explicit cash flow consumption tax under which all savings, regardless of purpose, receive tax deferral or equivalent treatment. President Bush's proposals would move the Code further towards consumption tax norms, by increasing quantitative limits on the amounts which can be saved on a tax-deferred basis and by weakening the link between tax deferral and particular purposes for saving. The Bush proposals would thereby nudge the Code closer to the consumption tax norm of generalized tax deferral for all saving as such.

B.   Tax Expenditures and Individual Accounts

The debate about the propriety of consumption taxation has paralleled the simultaneous controversy about tax expenditure analysis.[27] Tax expenditure analysis starts from the premise that the Code should tax income[28] and further contends that deductions, exemptions and exclusions constitute "tax expenditures" when these provisions are used, not to measure the taxpayer's income, but to pursue policies extraneous to such income measurement. Proponents of this perspective typically cite the Code provisions concerning qualified plans as a quintessential tax expenditure, a subsidy for retirement savings rather than an appropriate part of a normative income tax.

There are those who dispute in general the utility of the tax expenditure label[29] and those who question in particular the application of that label to the

---

[27]   For a small sample of the now voluminous literature on tax expenditure analysis, see Stanley S. Surrey and Paul R. McDaniel, TAX EXPENDITURES (1985); Boris I. Bittker, *Accounting for Federal "Tax Subsidies" in the National Budget*, 22 NATIONAL TAX J. 244 (1969); David A. Weisbach and Jacob Nussim, *The Integration of Tax and Spending Programs*, 113 YALE L. J. 955 (2004); Edward A. Zelinsky, *Do Tax Expenditures Create Framing Effects? Volunteer Firefighters, Property Tax Exemptions, and The Paradox of Tax Expenditure Analysis*, 24 VIRGINIA TAX REV. 797 (2005) (hereafter, *Framing Effects*); Edward A. Zelinsky, *Are Tax "Benefits" Constitutionally Equivalent To Direct Expenditures?* 112 HARVARD L. REV. 379 (1998); Edward A. Zelinsky, *James Madison and Public Choice at Gucci Gulch: A Procedural Defense of Tax Expenditures and Tax Institutions*, 102 YALE LAW J. 1165 (1993).

[28]   The key premise of tax expenditure analysis—the division of tax provisions into the normative and the subsidizing—can be applied to any tax. In practice, Professor Surrey and his followers have devoted the bulk of their attention to income taxation.

[29]   The most prominent of these opponents is Professor Bittker. *See, e.g.*, Bittker, *supra* note 27.

Code provisions governing qualified plans.[30] What cannot be gainsaid is that tax expenditure analysis is now deeply embedded in the federal[31] and state[32] budgetary processes and in the academic understanding of the tax law[33] and that tax expenditure budgets classify the qualified plan provisions of current law as among the largest subsidies administered through the federal tax law.[34]

From this perspective, the defined contribution paradigm is an elaborate subsidy mechanism, delivering tax expenditures through the income tax to those who contribute to and retain assets in tax-favored individual accounts. The costs and benefits of such tax-based subsidies have been much debated. For purposes of the present discussion, the most salient fact is the distributional implication of those subsidies. Professor Surrey, the founder of tax expenditure analysis, in a powerful sound bite denoted the distributional consequences of tax expenditures as "upside-down,"[35] i.e., tax deductions, exclusions and exemptions provide the greatest subsidies to high bracket taxpayers who, absent such deductions, exclusions and exemptions, pay tax at the highest rates. If the defined contribution paradigm represents a tax expenditure, Professor Surrey's distributional concerns carry force since the prime beneficiaries of the paradigm are families and individuals who can afford to save, the same affluent, high bracket beneficiaries of tax preferences like the mortgage interest deduction.[36]

C.   Individual Accounts and the Likely Futures of the Code

From either the cash flow consumption tax or the tax expenditure perspective, the prospects of the defined contribution paradigm are intimately tied to the

---

[30] *See supra* chap. three note 23.

[31] *See, e.g.,* 2 U.S.C. Section 639(c).

[32] One commentator indicates that thirty-three states today have tax expenditure budgets. Herman P. Ayayo, *Tax Expenditures: Useful Economic Concept or Economic Dinosaur?* 93 TAX NOTES 1152 (November 26, 2001).

[33] *See, e.g.,* William D. Andrews, BASIC FEDERAL INCOME TAXATION (5th ed. 1999) at 401–414.

[34] *See, e.g.,* David Wray, *PSCA's Testimony at W&M Oversight Hearing Pensions,* 98 TNT 87–41 (May 5, 1998) (characterizing "the exclusion of employer contributions to a qualified plan and the earnings on plan assets" as "the largest tax expenditure figure in the tables".)

[35] Surrey and McDaniel, *supra* note 27 at 3.

[36] *See* Code Section 163(h)(5).

future of the Code of which the paradigm is now a central feature. The most likely future of the Code is the continuation of the *status quo*, whether that status quo is considered a proto–consumption tax or an imperfect income tax laden with tax preferences. Under either characterization, the defined contribution paradigm is both an important contributor to and product of the *status quo*. It is unlikely that Congress will upset that *status quo* by jettisoning the individual accounts of the defined contribution paradigm as this would defeat the expectations and raise the taxes of Congress's middle-class and upper-middle-class constituents. As mechanisms which (depending on your premise) afford consumption tax treatment to taxpayers' savings or which give taxpayers expenditure-type subsidies for their savings, individual accounts are now deeply embedded in the tax law and American society.

If the most likely possibility for the Code is the continuation of the *status quo*, the next most probable possibility is the formal conversion of the Code to a cash flow consumption tax, providing generalized tax-deferral (or its equivalent) for all savings. The conversion of the Code to a formal consumption tax would constitute the ultimate triumph of the defined contribution paradigm since all savings would be conducted through individual accounts. If the Code were changed to a cash flow consumption tax, employer-sponsored plans would largely become a thing of the past since any taxpayer could, without limit, replicate for herself the tax results of such plans through her own tax deferred (or equivalent) accounts.[37] There would, accordingly, be no tax-based attraction for employer plans.

Here a paradox arises as, under an explicit cash flow consumption tax, the employer-sponsored plan with the greatest utility, and thus the highest chance of survival, would be the traditional defined benefit pension which, by shifting investment, funding and longevity risk to the employer, performs a unique economic function, desired by some (particularly older) employees. This niche function, attractive to employers seeking older workers, might keep some traditional defined benefit plans alive under a cash flow consumption tax.

---

[37] Professor Forman agrees that a cash flow consumption tax would likely lead to the demise of most employer-sponsored pension plans. *See* Jonathan Barry Forman, *The Impact of Shifting to a Personal Consumption Tax on Pension Plans and Their Beneficiaries*, in Dallas L. Salisbury (ed.), Tax Reform, Implications for Economic Security and Employee Benefits (1997) at 51, 52.

D.   Individual Accounts and Fundamental Reform

The final, and I think least plausible, possibility for the federal tax system is what is today widely, but unhelpfully, denoted as "fundamental tax reform." Indeed, "fundamental tax reform" has become a hollow label since neither the advocates of such "reform" nor the political actors who must enact it agree on what constitutes such reform.[38] That the Senate, otherwise closely divided over the 2003 tax act, easily voted for a commission to study fundamental tax reform indicates that the call for such reform has become an anodyne, indeed empty, slogan. Even if Congress were to enact any of the various proposals labeled as fundamental reform, the network of individual account devices would likely emerge from the legislative process intact, at least for a prolonged transition period, possibly permanently, though the defined contribution paradigm would be undermined decisively by the adoption of either of two fundamental tax reforms—a stand-alone value-added tax (VAT) to replace *in toto* the federal income tax or an expansive accretionist regime which taxes all unrealized appreciation annually including the appreciation in individual accounts.

To assess the impact of fundamental tax reform upon individual accounts as we know them today, I explore the impact upon such accounts of Professor Mitchell Engler's proposal for a "hybrid" consumption tax, Professor Michael Graetz's plan for a national VAT supplemented by a reduced rate income tax on high income taxpayers, an accretionist income tax which taxes unrealized appreciation, and a stand-alone VAT. Together, these four plans are representative of the universe of fundamental tax reform proposals. Examining the impact of each plan upon the defined contribution paradigm suggests the likelihood that, in the face of fundamental reform, individual accounts are likely to survive, at least transitionally, more likely on a permanent basis.

---

[38]   As part of its deliberations leading to the passage of the Jobs and Growth Tax Act of 2003, the U.S. Senate, by voice vote, approved the formation of a "Blue Ribbon Commission on Comprehensive Tax Reform." Lest anyone miss the point, the amendment establishing this Commission was denoted as the "Fundamental Tax Reform Commission Act of 2003." *See* Section 2(a) of the Fundamental Tax Reform Commission Act of 2003, 2003 TNT 96-9 (May 19, 2003).

i.　The Engler "Hybrid" Consumption Tax

Consider first Professor Engler's proposal for fundamental reform, which he denotes as a "hybrid" consumption tax.[39] Under this proposal, labor-based income would be taxed when earned. To the extent the taxpayer uses those taxed earnings for current consumption, no further tax would be due. In this respect, Professor Engler's proposed levy looks, in the context of labor-based income, exactly like the current federal income tax.

However, under the Engler proposal, to the extent the taxpayer saves his after-tax earned income, the amounts saved would continually be credited with the risk-free rate of return as measured by the rate at which the U.S. Treasury borrows. If the taxpayer withdraws funds for consumption up to the resulting total, no tax would be due. When the taxpayer's withdrawals for consumption exceed the cumulative sum of his previously taxed, saved income grossed-up by the tax-free rate of return, the taxpayer would be taxed on that excess.

In the context of the extended debate on the merits of consumption taxation, this is an imaginative proposal—with no chance of public acceptance or political enactment.[40] However, for purposes of the current discussion, let us assume that a president endorsed and a Congress seriously considered the Engler proposal for fundamental tax reform. How would that proposal emerge from the legislative process? My prediction is: with the network of existing defined contribution devices essentially unimpaired.

Consider in particular the problem of transition.[41] How would a Congress debating the Engler proposal treat existing individual accounts? One possibility would be constructive realization, i.e., to tax immediately amounts in existing accounts and, going forward, to apply to these taxed amounts the Engler formula of tax-free withdrawals equal to the sum of such previously taxed amounts plus the

---

[39] Mitchell L. Engler, *A Progressive Consumption Tax For Individuals: An Alternative Hybrid Approach*, 54 ALA. L. REV. 1205 (2003); Engler and Knoll, *supra* intro. note 5.

[40] Professor Bankman agrees. *See* Joseph Bankman, *The Engler-Knoll Consumption Tax Proposal: What Transition Rule Does Fairness (or Politics) Require?* 56 SMU L. REV. 83 (2003) ("It is also not a solution that I think is likely to fly politically, . .") and at 85 ("will seem unfathomable to taxpayers.")

[41] There is, of course, irony here: Professor Engler advances his proposal as a way to transition to a consumption levy, but, in terms of existing individual account devices, the Engler proposal raises its own transition issues.

risk-free rate of return imputed to such amounts. A political nonstarter: Few, if any, legislators will vote to impose immediate taxation upon their constituents' IRAs, 401(k) accounts and other individual accounts.

Another possibility is to modify the Engler proposal to accommodate individual accounts. In theory, for example, the gross-up for the risk-free rate of return could be applied to balances in Roth IRAs, 529 plans and educational IRAs as of a specified transition date. Under this possibility, in lieu of the tax treatment of current law (all withdrawals from these accounts are tax-free), the holders of these accounts would instead withdraw amounts tax-free up to the sum of these balances plus the cumulative credits based on the risk-free rate of return. Withdrawals above that sum would be taxable.

Again, a political nonstarter: Perhaps there would be some brave (or politically secure) members of Congress who would tell their constituents and the financial services industry that the tax rules should be changed for these accounts. I suspect, however, that reliance considerations—holders of these accounts were promised totally tax-free withdrawals—plus the sheer number of affected account holders would preclude legislation imposing tax on withdrawals above the imputed risk-free rate of return.

Consider also the Engler formula in the context of distributions from conventional IRAs and qualified plan accounts. Presumably the amounts in these accounts, having never been taxed, would be taxed *in toto* upon withdrawal. This would require for an extended period the segregation of these accounts (fully taxed on withdrawal) from the new accounts implementing the Engler plan (only taxed to the extent withdrawn earnings exceed the risk-free rate of return). Again, we would find existing individual accounts persisting for a potentially long period.

Consider finally the matter of personal deductions. My guess is that Congress would append to the Engler plan for fundamental reform some personal deductions, for mortgage interest payments, for charitable donations—and for contributions to qualified plans and other individual account devices.[42] If so, even if the Engler proposal (or something like it) developed political momentum, the

---

[42] Professor Engler apparently agrees that, under his proposal, current rules for retirement savings are likely to persist. *See* Engler, *supra* note 39 at 1225 [suggesting that, under his hybrid consumption tax, "like current law, a limited amount of wages saved for retirement could receive cash flow treatment (i.e., taxed only when withdrawn for consumption in retirement,)"] (parenthetical in original).

network of defined contribution devices would likely emerge from the legislative process wholly or largely intact.

ii.   The Graetz Proposal: A High Income Tax Coupled with a Value Added Tax (VAT)

Similar observations are to be made about Professor Graetz's proposal for fundamental tax reform.[43] Professor Graetz proposes a national value added tax (VAT) coupled with an income tax restored "to its pre-World War II status—a low-rate tax on a relatively thin slice of higher-income Americans." Professor Graetz calculates that the federal government could be financed by a VAT levied at between 10% and 15% augmented by "a vastly simpler income tax at a 25% rate to be applied to incomes over $100,000."

In the context of calls for fundamental tax reform, the Engler and Graetz proposals are essentially opposites: The Engler plan entails modification of the existing Code to implement consumption tax norms while the Graetz proposal entails termination of the income tax for most taxpayers. Professor Engler calls for a modified cash flow levy on consumption while Professor Graetz proposes a national VAT, augmented by a low rate income tax on high income taxpayers. Despite these marked differences, these two proposals for fundamental reform share one important characteristic: Both are likely to emerge from the legislative process with existing individual accounts intact, perhaps indefinitely, certainly for an extended transition period.

Consider initially the taxpayer earning over $100,000, subject to Professor Graetz's simplified income tax supplementing a national VAT. Suppose further that that taxpayer has both a Roth IRA and a 401(k) account. Congress is unlikely, under the simplified income tax, to tax distributions from the Roth IRA, given that the taxpayer has already paid tax on his contributions to that IRA and was promised tax-free withdrawals from it. It is also unlikely that Congress will excuse 401(k) distributions to this affluent taxpayer from future income taxes. Thus, for at least an (extended) transition period, Congress will need to maintain

---

[43]   Michael J. Graetz, *100 Million Unnecessary Returns: A Fresh Start for the U.S. Tax System*, 112 YALE L. J. 261 (2002).

the existing network of individual accounts to distinguish between those accounts generating tax-free distributions and those yielding taxable payments.

Less certain (but, I think, probable) would be Congress's decision to permit additional contributions to these accounts. With a flat 25% income tax rate, there will be less political and popular pressure for deductions and exclusions than with the higher tax rates of existing law. But pressure there still will be, particularly when taxpayers and tax writers ponder the possibility that the 25% rate might creep up in the future and the $100,000 threshold might move down.

All things considered, the best prediction for the simplified tax under the Graetz proposal is Congress's continuation of the existing network of defined contribution accounts for high income taxpayers.

What about everyone else? When a taxpayer below the $100,000 threshold receives a qualified plan or IRA distribution, will he be required to pay income tax on that distribution? Congress might say "no" and thereby walk away from the revenue built into current law, forgiving tax on all such distributions to persons earning less than $100,000. Given Congress's willingness to pass the large tax cuts of 2001, 2003, and 2006, that possibility cannot be ignored.

But that decision would be complicated to implement. Consider, for example, the taxpayer who falls below the $100,000 figure in the years his 401(k) amounts accrue but whose income exceeds the $100,000 threshold when those amounts are paid to him. Indeed, it might be the payment of his 401(k) balance as a lump sum which sends the taxpayer over the $100,000 threshold for income tax liability under the Graetz proposal.

The simplest way to address these situations is to continue the existing defined contribution framework and the accounts established under it. On distribution, if a taxpayer triggers the $100,000 level for income tax liability (because of the distribution itself or otherwise), income tax would be assessed. Consequently, we would, at a minimum, live with these accounts for an extended transition period until existing account balances are fully paid out.

Consider as well the possibility that Congress, to favor savings for particular purposes, might vote direct subsidies to retirement, educational and health accounts once the income tax no longer covers the bulk of families and individuals. Such subsidies would resemble the credit under Code Section 25B; an individual entitled to such a subsidy (by virtue of his modest income level or otherwise) would demonstrate that he had made the required contribution to his account and, in return, the Treasury would send a check to him or, perhaps, directly to his account.

I do not know whether such a scenario would come to pass under Professor Graetz's proposal. If it did, the defined contribution society under the Graetz-simplified income tax would bear a striking resemblance to that society as it exists today. But, even if Congress did not vote direct subsidies for individual accounts, those accounts would likely persist, at least for a (probably prolonged) transition period.

iii.   Accretionist Taxation

A third variation of fundamental tax reform is an accretionist income tax which would tax unrealized appreciation annually.[44] Unlike the current federal income tax, which generally requires a sale, exchange, or other realization event to recognize gain or loss, an accretionist tax would tax each taxpayer yearly on the increased value of his assets, whether or not the taxpayer sells, exchanges, or otherwise realizes that increased value. Accretionism, also known as "mark-to-market" taxation, is popular among tax policy mavens. However, it today finds little favor with the public or its representatives.

The impact of an accretionist tax on the defined contribution paradigm would depend critically upon the scope of the accretionist regime, namely, whether that regime would apply to qualified plans and individual account devices or whether unrealized gains would be taxed only outside such plans and accounts. In the latter case, qualified plans and other individual accounts would stand out as tax-favored vehicles, refuges from the rigors of the accretionist taxation of annual appreciation. This would reinforce the defined contribution framework. In contrast, an accretionist regime could subject qualified plans and individual accounts to immediate taxation on their (realized and unrealized) earnings and might also tax participants on their accrued but as yet unpaid benefits. If so, we could expect that, unless directly subsidized, qualified plans and individual

---

44   *See* Edward A. Zelinsky, *For Realization: Income Taxation, Sectoral Accretionism and the Virtue of Attainable Virtues*, 19 CARDOZO L. REV. 861 (1997).

accounts would (except for some niche-defined benefit plans designed to attract older workers) atrophy and die when stripped of tax advantage by an accretionist regime.

iv. A National Value Added Tax (VAT)

A stand-alone federal VAT is a reform scenario which poses a similarly dire threat to the defined contribution paradigm. I agree with Professors Julie Roin and Jonathan Barry Forman that, upon the adoption of a free standing national VAT,[45] most employer plans will disappear as the abolition of the income tax would strip such plans of any tax advantage.[46] Again, the ironic exception would be a relatively small number of traditional defined benefit plans likely to persist under a VAT as niche devices for attracting older workers particularly attuned to the advantages of such plans.

As to other kinds of individual accounts, unless Congress elected to provide direct subsidies to such accounts, these would likely disappear under a VAT, though the insurance industry might still find it desirable to market IIRAs. Thus, among the possibilities for the future tax reform, the stand alone VAT regime is a great, albeit a remote, threat to the defined contribution paradigm in its current form.

E. Conclusion: Individual Accounts and Tax Complexity

The defined contribution system is an important cause of complexity in the current tax law. There is, however, little chance for simplifying this area. Under the likely possibilities for the federal tax law (e.g., continuation of the status quo, movement toward an explicit cash flow consumption tax), the network of individual accounts will, in one form or another, continue indefinitely. Under the less likely possibility of fundamental tax reform, there is a substantial likelihood that, as such reform will actually pass Congress, individual accounts will persist,

---

45   That is, a VAT not supplemented by an income tax along the lines suggested by Professor Graetz.

46   *See* Roin, *supra* chap. three note 97 at 328 ("Given that employer pension plans are expensive to administer, employers and employees may both decide they are better off letting workers save for their own retirement independent of the workplace.") Forman, *supra* note 37.

possibly as permanent features of a reformed federal tax law, almost certainly for an extended transition period.

There are good reasons to be skeptical of the feasibility or desirability of tax simplification.[47] The existence and popularity of the defined contribution paradigm is one reason for such skepticism.

---

[47] It is a commonplace in discussion of tax simplification that there is no constituency for simplification since most everyone has higher priorities, priorities which often make for greater complexity.

CHAPTER SIX

What Is the Future of the Defined Contribution Paradigm?

In this chapter, I explore the future of the defined contribution paradigm, assuming, as I think likely, that the Internal Revenue Code will for the foreseeable future look like it does today, i.e., heavily laden with tax expenditures including what are widely considered to be tax subsidies for retirement savings and for other socially favored objectives. As I observed earlier, the defined contribution society is both a product of and a contributor to this status quo.

In the private sector, the expansion of the individual account paradigm will continue in the years ahead without significant controversy or impediment. In contrast, there will be increasing contention about public employees' defined benefit coverage as governmental decision makers emulate their private sector counterparts by embracing individual account plans to shift investment, funding and longevity risks to public employees. Equally disputatious will be the debate about efforts to expands the use of HSAs, a debate which addresses the fundamental implications of the defined contribution paradigm: the merits of individual ownership and control, the benefits of risk-pooling, the costs of adverse selection, the distributional consequences of individual accounts.

A. The Defined Contribution Paradigm and the Private Sector

The future of the defined contribution model in the private sector is straightforward: In the private sector, the predominance of individual account plans will continue to expand without significant controversy. There is nothing on the horizon to hinder the ongoing shift to individual accounts for private sector retirement, medical and education savings.

The prevalence of 401(k) plans over traditional defined benefit pensions will continue to grow. For many companies, the cash balance pension is turning out to be, not a lasting means of continuing defined benefit coverage, but a temporary way station on the path to 401(k).[1] In terms of health care, the expansion of FSAs, HRAs and HSAs[2] will similarly persist in the private sector. Likewise, the Section 529 account will continue to grow as the predominant device by which Americans save for their children's college educations.[3]

In sum, the individual account paradigm will continue to work well for many Americans, mostly middle-class and upper-middle class Americans. While I (along with others) am concerned that the decline of the traditional defined benefit system will prove problematic for those individuals poorly equipped to assume for themselves investment, funding and longevity risks, it cannot be gainsaid that the defined contribution model will enable some persons to accumulate significant sums on a tax-advantaged basis in their respective accounts for retirement, health care and educational savings. These winners of the defined contribution society will be important (typically affluent, often articulate) stakeholders of that society.

---

[1] Some knowledgeable observers argue that cash balance plans will stabilize, and perhaps revive, as the legal issues surrounding such plans are resolved favorably. Foremost among these issues is whether cash balance pensions pass muster under the pension age discrimination statutes. For "periods beginning on or after June 29, 2005," the Pension Protection Act of 2006 (PPA) decreed that cash balance pensions do not discriminate on the basis of age. Section 701 of the PPA. I believe the erosion of cash balance pensions will continue even if all legal issues concerning such pensions are resolved favorably. For the commentary and case law addressing the status of cash balance plans under pre-PPA law, see *supra* chap. three notes 133 and 134.

[2] The GAO reports that, during 2005, "the number of enrollees and dependents covered by . . . an HRA-based plan or an HSA-eligible plan – increased from about 3 million to between about 5 and 6 million." Other published reports indicate that "(a)t least three million people" may currently have the kind of high-deductible health insurance which permits HSA participation and that some observers expect there to be as many as fifteen million Americans covered by HSAs in 2010. *See* Government Accountability Office, *Consumer-Directed Health Plans* (GAO-06–514) (April 28, 2006), 2006 TNT 104–37; Sarah Lueck, *Tax Breaks to Boost Cost of Bush's Health Budget*, WALL ST. J., Feb. 6, 2006, at A1. *See also* Eric Dash, *Wall Street Senses Opportunities In Health Care Savings Accounts*, N.Y. TIMES, Jan. 27, 2006, at A1.

[3] A potential obstacle to the continued growth of Section 529 accounts was eliminated in 2006 when Congress made permanent the income-tax-free status of cash payments and in-kind benefits received under Section 529 plans. Section 1304(a) of the Pension Protection Act of 2006.

B. The Defined Contribution Paradigm and the Public Sector

As the defined contribution paradigm continues to expand with ease in the private sector, there will be increasing controversy about public employees' defined benefit coverage. A harbinger of this contentious future was the strike in 2005 by the subway and bus employees of the New York Metropolitan Transportation Authority (MTA) and the ensuing controversy about the traditional pensions covering them and other New York City government personnel.[4] MTA employees are today covered by a typical, underfunded public defined benefit plan with a relatively young (age 55) normal retirement age. When MTA employees struck to protect this quintessential defined benefit pension, many taxpaying subway riders found themselves contrasting that traditional pension with their own 401(k) coverage.

The financial risks of defined benefit plans have been an important cause of private employers' shift to 401(k) and other defined contribution retirement plans. It is only natural for state and local governments, confronting the liabilities associated with their traditional defined benefit plans for public employees, to similarly eye individual account arrangements to shift funding, investment and longevity risks to their employees.[5] This tendency will be reinforced by taxpayers' awareness that they have 401(k) coverage at work. The MTA strike and its protracted aftermath suggest how at least some (perhaps many) public employees and their unions will react to proposals to alter their existing pension arrangements.[6]

---

[4] The protracted dispute between the MTA and its employees was ultimately resolved in binding arbitration. *See* Jeremy Olshan, *1-Yr. Train All For Nothing; Arbitrator Hands Transit Union Same Contract It Got After Strike*, N.Y. POST, Dec. 16, 2006, at 5. For earlier coverage, *see* Pete Donohue, *Transit Talk Panel Taps Big-Time Ref*, N.Y. DAILY NEWS, May 24, 2006 at 14. *See also* Steven Greenhouse, *City's Pension Cut Proposal May Set Negotiating Pattern*, N.Y. TIMES, June 6, 2006 at B3; Thomas J. Lueck & Steven Greenhouse, *Transit Union Approves Contract It Rejected Before*, N.Y. TIMES, April 19, 2006, at B3; Thomas J. Lueck & Steven Greenhouse, *A New Transit Strike Is Unlikely. But How About a Deal?*, N.Y. TIMES, March 21, 2006, at B1; Sewell Chan & Steven Greenhouse, *M.T.A. Returns To Harder Line in Labor Talks*, N.Y. TIMES, Jan. 26, 2006, at A1.

[5] *See* Phyllis Feinberg, *Eight states considering shifting to DC plans*, PENSIONS & INVESTMENTS, Feb. 7, 2005 at 3. *See also* Greenblatt, *supra* chap. four note 41 at 37 ("Many state and local leaders are looking to defined contribution and other approaches for answers.")

[6] Professor Secunda has correctly observed that pensions are not a proper subject of collective bargaining under New York's Taylor Law. *See* http://lawprofessors.typepad.com/laborprof_blog/2005/12/did_the_twu_win.html. *See also* NY CLS CIV. S. SECTION 201.4 ("'terms and conditions of employment' . . . shall not include any benefits provided by or to be provided by a public retirement system, or payments to a fund or insurer to provide an income for retirees, or payment to retirees or their beneficiaries. No such retirement benefits shall be negotiated pursuant to this article, and any benefits so negotiated shall be void.")

It is no surprise that public employment is the last bastion of traditional defined benefit pensions since public employment is also the last bastion of unionism. As noted in Chapter Three, for a variety of reasons, unions prefer defined benefit plans to defined contribution arrangements: A defined benefit plan reinforces the collective solidarity of the union by subjecting all participants into a single formula to receive uniform benefits. Such a plan also emphasizes the importance of the collective bargaining services the union supplies to its members since any increase of a participant's retirement income must be achieved through such bargaining, rather than through the participant's superior investment performance with his own individual account. In the case of those public unions which can lobby but not bargain about pensions, defined benefit plans similarly increase the value of such lobbying activities as the means by which union members improve their pensions. When traditional defined benefit plans are jointly governed by both management and union trustees, the union has more economic power than when individual participants make their own decentralized investment decisions 401(k)-style. Since public employee unions are still robust, they are better positioned to resist the conversion to individual account plans than are their private sector counterparts.

Moreover, unionized public employees themselves often have strong reasons to resist the conversion to defined contribution pensions. In many cases, the public defined benefit plans in place are more lucrative than the individual account arrangements which will supplant them. This is invariably true for older, long-term public employees on the verge of earning the lucrative backloaded benefits of a traditional defined benefit pension. These backloaded benefits, the reward for a long career with a single employer, are snatched from older employees by the conversion to individual account plans. Such older, long-term employees are typically active in union governance and therefore well-placed to defend their pension-based interests. Add in status quo bias and the result is a potentially explosive mix for the future as government policymakers look to defined contribution arrangements to minimize taxes and pension outlays and as unions and their public employee members resist.

C.   The Partisan Divide: Promoting HSAs

While President Bush's bid to introduce individual accounts to the federal Social Security system seems moribund, debate about his continuing efforts to promote

HSAs will reprise the themes prominent in both the original debates about MSAs and HSAs as well as the more recent Social Security controversy, i.e., the merits of individual ownership and control, the costs of adverse selection, the benefits of risk-pooling, the distributional implications of individual accounts.[7] The tenor of this debate will be quite partisan, reflecting the stridency of the contemporary political environment. This contrasts sharply with the bipartisan spirit in which the defined contribution paradigm was (inadvertently) launched over a generation ago with the adoption of ERISA and Section 401(k).

At one level, President Bush's outspoken support for HSAs will focus attention upon the fundamental implications of the defined contribution paradigm. At another level, however, the ongoing debate about HSAs will be less important for the individual account paradigm than some of the rhetoric might suggest. Even without Bush's promotional efforts, HSA coverage will expand in the years ahead as will FSA participation.

Moreover, many insurers and employers which do not switch to HSAs will instead embrace HRAs. In the contemporary defined contribution culture, traditional insurers have strong incentives to encourage such HRAs which the insurers them selves sponsor rather than sit on the sidelines and let HSAs and the high deductible insurers which promote them occupy the field of health-related individual accounts. For traditional insurers, the handwriting is on the proverbial wall: They will either adapt to the defined contribution paradigm or will lose business to competitors who do. The upshot is that insurers will find themselves coupling HRAs to

---

[7] For example, former Treasury Secretary John Snow, touting President Bush's proposals to expand the tax advantages associated with HSAs, declares that such accounts "put patients back in charge of their healthcare purchasing decisions." In contrast, the Center for Budget and Policy Priorities criticizes President Bush's HSA proposals for "fragment[ing] the pooling of risk," depriving "less healthy people" of "an adequate pooling mechanism" for medical insurance, and "provid[ing] large tax breaks for the most affluent people." *See* Emily Dagostino, *GAO Study: Younger, Wealthier Individuals More Likely to Use HSAs*, TAX NOTES TODAY, Feb. 3, 2006, 2006 TNT 23–3; Jason Furman, *Expansion in HSA Tax Breaks is Larger – and More Problematic – Than Previously Understood*, TAX NOTES TODAY, Feb. 7, 2006, Lexis 2006 TNT 25–52. *See also* Joint Economic Committee, Democratic Staff, *Administration's Proposed Tax Deduction For High-Deductible Health Insurance: A Boon to the Healthy and Wealthy But No Help for the Uninsured*, TAX NOTES TODAY, Feb. 1, 2006, 2006 TNT 21–36 (HSAs are "a costly tax subsidy" for "the wealthy and healthy" which cause the "vicious cycle" of adverse selection) *Cf.* Katherine Baicker, *Tax Incentives and Healthcare Spending*, TAX NOTES, June 12, 2006 at 1256 ("HSA-based policies are not attractive to just the healthy.")

their conventional health insurance products to adapt to a marketplace where many of their customers think in terms of individual accounts.[8]

D. The Future (Or Lack Thereof) of Money Purchase Pensions

It is likely that, within the defined contribution universe, 401(k) arrangements—profit sharing plans with salary reduction features—will crowd out private sector money purchase pensions. Employers favor profit sharing plans over pensions because of the greater flexibility of the former. Flexibility has been a major cause of the shift from defined benefit pensions to profit sharing arrangements including 401(k) plans. Within the realm of individual accounts, concern for flexibility also impels employers to shift from money purchase pensions (which entail an annual funding obligation) to profit sharing plans (which do not).

Until the enactment of EGTRRA in 2001, the principal impediment to that shift had been Code Section 404 which permits a maximum employer deduction for contributions to defined contribution plans of twenty-five percent of participant compensation. Before EGTRRA, Section 404 also limited deductible profit sharing contributions to fifteen percent of participant compensation.[9] This statutory scheme compelled employers desiring to make the full contribution of twenty-five percent of participant compensation (usually smaller employers and professional firms) to maintain both a profit sharing plan for a contribution equal to the first fifteen percent of employee compensation and a money purchase pension for the additional ten percent contribution. Indeed, employers seeking to contribute more than fifteen percent of participant contribution typically embraced the two plan configuration since any contribution above the fifteen percent cap for profit sharing contributions had to be made to a money purchase pension.[10]

---

[8] For example, when Connecticut eliminated regulatory barriers to the high deductible coverage necessary for MSAs, Anthem Blue Cross and Blue Shield responded, not by embracing MSAs, but with "Personal Care Accounts." Marcia Simon, *Medical Savings Accounts come to Connecticut*, NEW HAVEN REGISTER, June 29, 2003 at E1, E3.

[9] *See* Code Sections 404 (a) (7) (A) (i) and 404 (a) (3) (A) (i) (I) prior to amendment by EGTRRA, P.L.107–16.

[10] Theoretically, the entire contribution could have been made to a single money purchase pension plan. In practice, however, this rarely occurred since employers preferred the flexibility entailed with profit sharing arrangements.

EGTRRA amended Code Section 404 to allow employers to make the entire permitted deductible contribution—twenty-five percent of participant compensation—to a single profit sharing plan.[11] In 2006, Congress made this change permanent.[12] For most employers, this effectively renders money purchase pensions superfluous since the employer can now achieve the maximum deductible contribution with only a profit sharing plan. An employer seeking a deductible contribution greater than fifteen percent of participant compensation no longer need pay the administrative costs for a money purchase pension nor incur the annual funding obligation which such a pension entails.

We can accordingly expect most private sector money purchase plans to be terminated or merged[13] into profit sharing plans now that the full deductible contribution to individual account arrangements can be made to a profit sharing plan alone. While a few employers will find the commitment of a money purchase pension helpful in recruiting and retaining employees, in most situations employers will now view a defined contribution pension as unnecessary, given their ability to make the maximum individual account contribution of twenty-five percent of compensation to stand-alone profit sharing plans. The money purchase pension plan, no longer needed to achieve the maximum contribution permitted under the Code, is thus doomed to extinction.

E. The Paradoxical Future of Pension-Based Redistribution

In 2001, EGTRRA increased the limits on contributions to individual accounts. In 2006, PPA made these increases permanent. The beneficiaries of the now permanent, higher limits on contributions to individual accounts are (and will continue to be) the relatively few affluent employees who bump against these limits because they can afford maximal savings through individual account arrangements. However, the redistributional implications of the defined contribution society are more complex than this observation suggests since redistribution can

---

[11] See Code Section 404(a)(3)(A)(i)(I) after amendment by EGTRRA.

[12] See Section 811 of the Pension Protection Act of 2006.

[13] The IRS contends that, after mergers are affected, the funds previously be held by the money purchase pension plans must remain subject to the distribution rules pertaining to such plans. See Rev. Rul. 94–76, 1994–2 C.B. 46.

be more carefully targeted with individual accounts than with defined benefit arrangements.

Historically, the chief means of channeling pension savings to rank-and-file workers has been the principle of nondiscrimination: To qualify for income tax exemption under Code Section 401, a pension or profit sharing plan cannot discriminate in favor of highly-compensated participants.[14] As it has developed, the principle of nondiscrimination is incoherent in theory and ineffective in practice, usually failing to direct significant pension savings toward rank-and-file participants.[15] Indeed, today even those sympathetic to the underlying purpose of the nondiscrimination principle—channeling tax-based pension assistance to rank-and-file workers—have relatively little good to say about that principle in practice.[16]

In contrast, in a world of individual accounts, assistance can be targeted directly to particular persons and to their respective accounts based upon income levels and other individual characteristics deemed relevant. In this context, consider again Code Section 25B which provides a tax credit to low-income taxpayers to subsidize their contributions to defined contribution plans. This credit is carefully aimed at its intended audience, lower income taxpayers, and can be so aimed because individual accounts permit public largesse to be targeted to particular individuals meeting specified criteria.

On the other hand, a subsidy flowing into a common pool funding a defined benefit plan is subject to the claims of owner-employees, managers and other higher income workers who often drive the design of such plans for their own benefit. This, in a nutshell, is the principal critique of the perceived tax expenditure as a means of ensuring retirement savings for less affluent workers: The subsidy is largely diverted to those who do not need it.

---

[14] Code Section 401(a)(4).

[15] *See supra* note chap. three note 136.

[16] *See, e.g.,* Orszag and Stein, *supra* chap. two note 27 at 632; ("We also find ourselves in agreement with Professor Zelinsky that the current nondiscrimination rules poorly bear the weight of the rules' complexity and the ability of sophisticated pension planners to exploit that complexity to tilt the benefits of plans to the advantage of favored highly paid employees.") *See also* Halperin, *supra* chap. two note 2 at 52–57 ("benefits testing should be allowed only in limited circumstances, rather than as a matter of course.")

Individual accounts, in short, can efficiently facilitate public subsidy of retirement savings, like the Section 25B credit, targeted to the intended beneficiaries and their respective accounts.

But there is the further paradox that assistance (like the Section 25B credit) narrowly tailored to low income individuals, while more efficient in terms of redistribution, may be less viable in terms of political survival. A common defense of Social Security in its current form is that its subsidization of lower-income workers is tied to and is thus protected by a middle-class entitlement.[17] While no one would accuse the current formula for calculating Social Security benefits of elegance,[18] that formula, by linking redistribution favoring less affluent workers to a middle-class entitlement, gives the political protection of the latter to the former.

Hence, the paradox that less efficient redistribution (like a tax subsidy channeled through the nondiscrimination principle to low income defined benefit participants) may, for the long run, be more viable politically than an more efficient subsidy (like the Section 25B credit) which, while more precisely targeted at the poor, lacks ties to a middle class entitlement.

F.   Conclusion: The Permanent Eclipse of the Defined Benefit Pension Plan

A final prediction for the future: There will be no resurrection of traditional defined benefit pension plans. The advocates of such plans will (and should) continue to press for a reduction of the overregulation of such plans. But even if such advocates succeed in pruning the regulatory burdens on traditional pension plans, there will be no wholesale return to the classic defined benefit paradigm. Since that return did not occur in the aftermath of Enron, it will not occur. We are now simply too far down the path to a defined contribution society for there to be a realistic chance of a return to the traditional defined benefit norm.[19]

---

17   See, e.g. Aaron in Friedman, *supra* chap. two note 5 at 84 ("Social Security has linked pensions for everyone to social assistance for low earners.")

18   For a particularly concise description of the current Social Security benefit formula, see John B. Shoven, *Social Security Reform: Two Tiers Are Better Than One*, in Friedman, *supra* chap. two note 5 at 31–33.

19   A potentially interesting development is the defined benefit-style Section 529 program organized by a consortium of private colleges. Since this program has just commenced, it is too early to tell if it will avoid the problems of the comparable, defined benefit state-sponsored prepaid tuition arrangements. *See* Ira Carnahan,

In the name of strengthening the traditional defined benefit system, in 2006 Congress passed and President Bush signed into law yet another set of amendments to the complex minimum funding rules.[20] However, under even the most optimistic scenario, this legislation will not reverse the long-term decline of the traditional defined benefit pension. The fundamental shift to the defined contribution paradigm is now deeply-rooted and self-reinforcing. The resurrection of the classic, annuity-paying defined benefit plan is highly unlikely. Such a resurrection, if it could be achieved, could only be provoked by radical measures, e.g., depriving individual accounts of their tax benefits. There is no possibility that a president would propose or that a Congress would enact such draconian measures with the pain they would entail for literally millions of individual account owners who are today stakeholders in the defined contribution paradigm.

Pay Now, Learn Later, FORBES (August 11, 2003) at 98; Elleen Alt Powell, *Independent colleges launch tuition savings program*, NEW HAVEN REGISTER (September 8, 2003) at A8; J. Christine Harris, *New Section 529 Plan For Private Colleges Faring Well, Says Plan Director*, 2003 TNT 178–12 (September 15, 2003).

[20] *See* PPA Sections 102 and 103 (revising the ERISA version of the minimum funding rules) and PPA Sections 111, 112 and 212 (revising the Code version of the minimum funding rules). These amendments take effect for plan years beginning after December 31, 2007. The new PPA version of the minimum funding standards are to be found in the Internal Revenue Code in Sections 412 and 430 through 432, inclusive, and in ERISA Sections 301 and 302.

CHAPTER SEVEN

What Should We Do?

A. Clarifying Premises

In this last chapter, I explore our choices for molding the defined contribution paradigm as it evolves and identify which of those choices I think are best. Since those choices necessarily rest on premises about the defined contribution paradigm and the persons affected by that paradigm, let me try to make my premises as explicit as I can.

First, I think that heavy-handed paternalism in matters of private retirement savings is unwarranted and generally counterproductive, but that there is room to improve individuals' decisions about retirement savings if that is done in a reasonably careful and subtle way. There is today in the academy no more heated debate than whether man is the rational, competent utility-maximizer of traditional economic theory (capable of pursuing his own interests) or the cognitively-impaired being of behavioral economics (potentially benefitting from a heavy dollop of paternalism). The answer for my analysis is that he is both. Standard economic theory is a powerful predictor of human behavior because, in many settings, people are rational self-maximizers, responding to incentives and disincentives in methodical, consistent and sensible ways. The power of the behavioralist perspective is not that it shows us man can be irrational—we have always known that. Rather, the great contribution of Tversky, Kahnemann, and those who have followed in their footsteps is to demonstrate that irrationality, when it occurs, often occurs in systematic and predictable (if not sensible) ways—although, even when most people are behaving illogically, many are not.[1]

---

[1] For example, even when most people respond differently to logically identical choices because of the manner in which such choices are framed, some people do not succumb to the framing effect but make rationally coherent decisions. In yet other instances, framing effects fail to materialize. *See, e.g.,*

On balance, I conclude that, in the context of the private retirement system, the strongest forms of paternalism are not warranted (many people do behave rationally)[2] nor is heavy-handed paternalism likely to succeed (people can opt out of the system if its restrictions chafe too much). Most obviously, if 401(k) plans are perceived as overly restrictive, employees can decline to participate in them.

On the other hand, there is room for improving the retirement savings choices of many people if the rules are formulated and implemented with reasonable care and subtlety. Retirement is a complex topic; consequently, individuals who can make rational decisions about simpler aspects of their lives are less than optimal decisionmakers in this complicated area. Feedback from retirement savings decisions is long delayed—the value of retirement savings undertaken when an individual is in her thirties will not be manifest for most of the individual's working career. Aging is the ultimate nonrepeat game—the sixty-five-year-old who suddenly realizes that he did not save enough when younger does not get a second chance. Furthermore, as this example suggests, individuals' preferences may be time-inconsistent—current consumption can look more valuable when one is younger than it does with benefit of hindsight.[3]

In short, we must search for essentially noncoercive ways of guiding individuals' retirement savings decisions, nudging them over any cognitive hurdles without succumbing to the temptation of overbearing paternalism.[4]

Second, in this area, there is a need for greater sensitivity to the costs of regulation than has occurred in the past. The dilemma retirement policymakers face (reflective of a broader problem of regulation generally) is that each particular act of regulation can be justified as responding to a compelling concern. Cumulatively, however, the aggregation of regulations (each plausible on its own) makes for a legal framework of daunting complexity which deters the creation and maintenance of the plans being regulated. To paraphrase a Vietnam-era axiom, overregulation winds up killing retirement plans in order to save them.

David Fetherstonhaugh and Lee Ross, *Framing Effects and Income Flow Preferences in Decisions about Social Security*, in Aaron, *supra* chap. two note 11; Zelinsky, *Framing Effects*, *supra* chap. two note 11.

[2]   *See, e.g.*, William G. Gale, *Comment*, in Aaron, *supra* chap. two note 11 at 120 ("the so-called `evidence' against the life-cycle model presented in the review of the literature in the paper is unpersuasive").

[3]   On procrastination and time-inconsistent preferences for retirement savings, see Ted O'Donoghue and Matthew Rabin, *Procrastination in Preparing for Retirement*, in Aaron, *supra* chap. two note 11.

[4]   Professors Sunstein and Thaler come to similar conclusions. *See* Sunstein and Thaler, *supra* chap. two note 8.

The interaction of the defined benefit minimum funding rules and the PBGC illustrates this dynamic. There are plausible arguments both for legislating funding standards for defined benefit plans and for insuring basic benefits. But there are substantial costs to such regulation as well, i.e., inflexibility, impenetrability, administrative and professional fees, insurance premiums. Because the PBGC, as the ultimate guarantor of basic pension benefits, is at risk when plans are underfunded, the PBGC has a compelling interest in ever more stringent versions of the minimum funding rules to minimize the PBGC's own exposure. The upshot is that the funding problems of defined benefit plans have not been eliminated. Rather, those problems have been shifted in large part to the PBGC. And Congress, confronted with the possible need to bail out a bankrupt PBGC, has responded to entreaties to reduce the PBGC's exposure by repeatedly tweaking the minimum funding rules further,[5] most recently in 2006.[6] This, in turn, continues the cycle of regulation with its costs and the resulting discouragement of the formation and continuation of defined benefit pensions.

After all is said and done, are we better off with the enormously-complex minimum funding standards and the PBGC? At best, the answer is unclear. In retrospect, other, less intrusive responses to the problem of defined benefit underfunding (e.g., better disclosure)[7] look like potentially productive paths not taken.

There is a cautionary tale here about embarking on a comparable course regulating individual account plans: Well-meaning mandates, each arguably justifiable individually, cumulatively can overburden the plans those mandates are designed to improve. In the final analysis, employers' decisions to maintain and establish defined contribution plans are voluntary; if the costs of such plans outweigh the perceived benefits, employers will abandon such plans or will not establish them in the first place. The same is true of accounts maintained by individuals. If the rules are too onerous, some (perhaps many) will eschew them.

Third, the defined contribution paradigm has its advantages, not least that it exists, that it corresponds to Americans' cultural norms about individual ownership and

---

5   See also GAO, *Single Employer, supra* chap. two note 48 ("Concerns about PBGC finances also resulted in efforts to strengthen the minimum funding rules incorporated by ERISA in the Internal Revenue Code.")

6   See supra chap. six note 20.

7   An approach belatedly embraced in the Pension Protection Act of 2006. *See* PPA Section 501, adding to ERISA new Section 101(f).

control, and that it works well for many Americans, particularly middle-class and upper-middle-class Americans. I have emphasized my concern (shared with many others) that the individual account paradigm shifts risks—investment, funding and longevity—to many employees poorly suited to handle those risks, employees who would have been better served by traditional defined benefit pensions.

But there is no chance—today, for the foreseeable future, probably indefinitely—of revitalizing such traditional pensions. Indeed, in the post-Enron era, the absence of any serious effort to revive traditional defined benefit plans is the Holmesian[8] dog that did not bark. Any program for the future must start with the acknowledgment that the private retirement system going forward will predominantly reflect the defined contribution paradigm.

Finally, I start with the premise that it confuses, rather than helps, to label current law *vis-a-vis* qualified plans as a tax expenditure. Mine, of course, is a decidedly minority position within the pension community.[9] It is, however, a position which, with the passage of time, looks better and better.

Under the provisions of current law, tax-deferred saving within qualified plans is typically more attractive than is taxable saving outside such plans. This advantage to accumulating within qualified plans underpins the conventional characterization of the Code as creating a qualified plan tax expenditure.

However, the provisions of current law can be understood, not as an effort to subsidize pension and profit sharing arrangements, but as a plausible (perhaps the best) selection from among the range of practical alternatives for taxing such arrangements. Considering such criteria as administrability and taxpayer liquidity, a Congress seeking not to underwrite qualified plans but to tax them correctly, could plausibly decide upon the features of current law as the best of the feasible possibilities.[10] Indeed, Professor Wooten has demonstrated that, as a

---

8   Sherlock, not Oliver Wendell. *See* Arthur Conan Doyle, *Silver Blaze* in THE ADVENTURES AND THE MEMOIRS OF SHERLOCK HOLMES 277, 296 (Penguin Books 2001) (1894) ("That was the curious incident . . .". (internal quotation marks omitted)).

9   Orszag and Stein, *supra* chap. two note 27 at 670. ("We are among those people who subscribe to the opposite view, which Professor Zelinsky in an understatement labels conventional wisdom: that the tax regime for qualified plans varies from the normative features of an income tax and thus can be justified only as a tax expenditure.")

10   *See supra* chap. three note 23.

matter of history, this is what occurred.[11] Those who crafted the existing income tax treatment of qualified plans did not seek to subsidize such plans, but, rather, sought to tax such plans and their participants correctly.

Moreover, in the years since Professor Surrey first propounded the "tax expenditure" label, there has been a noted shift in political and academic opinion towards the ideal of consumption (rather than income) taxation.[12] In a world characterized by a strong consensus that income is the desired tax base, those labeling current law as a tax expenditure for qualified plans plausibly invoked an idealized version of that base. Under that idealized income tax base, all savings would be taxed currently as they accrue—a theoretical treatment far from the reality of current law under which the taxation of qualified plan savings is delayed (often for a long time) until the participant actually receives his plan distribution.

However, starting from the premise that consumption (not income) should be taxed, the Code's treatment of qualified plans no longer looks like a subsidizing departure from the theoretical income tax norm that all savings should be taxed immediately. Rather, from the premise of consumption taxation, the Code's treatment of qualified plans looks more like the harbinger of a consumption tax under which all saving would be treated as are qualified plans today, i.e., tax-deferred until withdrawn for consumption.

In short, placing the label "tax expenditure" on the present tax treatment of qualified plans is conclusory and problematic. Perhaps most seriously, that label obscures the nature of the decisions which are embedded in current law and which we confront for the future. The "tax expenditure" label allows paternalistic pension regulation to be defended without confronting its paternalistic nature. Rather, subsidy rhetoric allows such regulation to be characterized merely as the government guaranteeing that it receives something for its tax-based assistance.[13]

In contrast, I think that, if we choose to be paternalistic, we should be open and explicit about that choice, not obscuring such paternalism by subsidy rhetoric.

---

11 Wooten, *supra* chap. three note 23.
12 *See supra* chap. five notes 1 through 6, inclusive, and accompanying text.
13 Orszag and Stein, *supra* chap. two note 27 at 650. ("[M]ost analysts and policy-makers agree that qualified pension plans generate tax expenditures. As such, non-discrimination rules and other forms of regulation are warranted.")

B.   The Program

From these premises, I propose the following program:

i.   Do No Harm

The most important imperative for the future is to do no harm. That leads me to skepticism about numerous suggestions which are plausible (indeed, anodyne) at first blush but which, upon further reflection, appear problematic. Consider, for example, the now widespread consensus that, in a world of individual accounts, 401(k) and IRA holders need investment education.[14] From this consensus, it is a short step to mandating that employers provide such education.

But not so fast. Education is not costless. Someone must pay for it. Either employers will absorb the costs of investor education for their employees or those costs will be passed onto employees via lower wages and/or lower employer contributions. However, there is, as yet, no hard evidence that mass investment education of 401(k) participants would in practice accomplish enough to justify its not inconsiderable costs. Important voices are skeptical that such education would be efficacious.[15]

Consider again in this context the research about framing effects.[16] Perhaps the most interesting finding of the Tversky-Kahnemann school is that, when confronted with their substantively inconsistent decisions, many (often well-educated) persons persist in viewing their choices as correct even though they conflict with each other. At a minimum, this suggests that good investment education is not always easy and certainly not costless.

Before mandating such education, we need rigorous proof that the results are likely to justify the expense. Without such data, a mandate for employer-provided investor education looks suspiciously like a windfall for the providers of that mandated education.

---

14   *See* Zanglein, *supra* chap. two note 4; Lawrence, *supra* chap. two note 4.

15   *See, e.g.*, Swensen, *supra* chap. two note 18 at 4. ("Even with a massive educational effort, the likelihood of producing a nation of effective investors seems small.")

16   *See supra* note 1 and chap. two note 11.

Similar observations are to be made about proposals for mandatory annuitization, i.e., for requiring that, in lieu of lump sum distributions, participants must purchase annuity contracts with their qualified plan or IRA balances. Again, at first blush, such proposals are a plausible response to the problems of longevity risk and adverse selection. If everyone is required to purchase an annuity with their respective individual account balances, the adverse selection problem disappears since everyone (whether likely to be long-lived or not) must buy an annuity. Moreover, since everyone must buy an annuity, it is probable that, in at least some contexts (e.g., large 401(k) plans), plans will negotiate for annuity contracts on a centralized basis, thereby minimizing administrative costs and sales fees. As the market for annuities expands, competitive pressures will force the insurance industry to pass onto purchasers the resulting economies of scale.

But there is a potential flaw in this happy scenario, and it is a big one: Mandatory annuitization may deter some, perhaps many, employees from participating in defined contribution plans or individual retirement accounts by imposing a restriction such employees consider onerous. By way of example, let us assume that a thirty year old employee, with no history of saving in a qualified plan or otherwise, is deciding whether to participate in her employer's 401(k) plan. Retirement for this young employee seems far away. Saving for retirement ties up her resources for a seemingly distant eventuality.[17] However, under current law, there are important safety valves which reassure the thirty-year-old that funds put into a 401(k) plan are not falling into a black hole. The plan may permit preretirement distributions on account of hardship.[18] The 401(k) arrangement may also authorize loans to participants.[19] Perhaps most importantly, the employee knows that she will receive a lump sum distribution from the plan when she changes jobs.

In its simplest and strongest incarnation, mandatory annuitization would eliminate these possibilities for accessing retirement resources early by permitting withdrawals only on retirement and only in annuity form. For our hypothetical thirty-year-old, this would restore the black hole quality to her employer's plan and may thereby deter her from participating.

---

17   Congressional Budget Office, *Utilization, supra* chap. one note 10 at 2. ("Young workers tend both to be single and to have low income; with retirement far in the future, they may be less concerned about saving for that distant day.")

18   *See* Code Section 401(k)(2)(B)(i)(IV) (authorizing distributions from 401(k) plans "upon hardship of the employee" from cash-or-deferred amounts contributed by the employee).

19   *See* Code Section 72(p)(2) (authorizing participant loans within certain limits).

In response to these concerns, one can envision less stringent proposals for mandatory annuitization, e.g., requiring such annuitization only after age fifty. But, under that regime, many participants may take distributions in their late forties to avoid forced annuitization—even though they would have left their retirement savings untouched in the absence of the annuitization requirement. Under this scenario, mandatory annuitization might actually cause greater preretirement consumption of plan distributions than would otherwise be the case. This, of course, would not be the first instance of qualified plan regulation generating unintended consequences.

Likewise, proposals for PBGC-type insurance for defined contribution plans are attractive when considered in isolation and without weighing their possible secondary effects.[20] But someone will be required to pay for this insurance. If we charge employers or their 401(k) plans for those costs, as well as the expenses of investment education and the burden of mandatory annuitization rules, we change the cost/benefit calculation of such plans for employers and participants, perhaps to the detriment of maintaining such plans or participating in them.

If, on the other hand, government-sponsored insurance for defined contribution plans is a voluntary program, we must confront the failure of the private sector to provide such insurance. That the commercial insurance market has not generated such coverage suggests that publicly-provided defined contribution insurance is likely to flunk the test of the market also and will eventually require subsidization either from the public treasury or from the universe of defined contribution plans. Neither alternative seems attractive.

In short, "do no harm" is not a bromide but, rather, is a caution to avoid the repetition of the overregulation of the defined benefit format. In constructing the elaborate rules in which defined benefit pensions are now enmeshed, each step along the way was, in isolation and ignoring its ripple effects, plausible and well-intended. However, the cumulative network of regulation deters the creation and maintenance of such defined benefit plans. We should be reluctant to replicate this experience with defined contribution arrangements.

The adage to do no harm leads me to skepticism about several, obviously well-intended requirements imposed by the PPA on those 401(k) plans which permit

---

20   *See, e.g.*, Regina T. Jefferson, *Rethinking the Risk of Defined Contribution Plans*, 4 FLA. TAX. REV. 607 (2000) (proposing voluntary insurance coverage for defined contribution plans).

participants to self-direct the investment of their respective accounts. Such plans must now furnish participants with statements quarterly about their accounts.[21] In addition, PPA requires the Secretary of Labor to promulgate standards for the default investments to which participants' assets will be devoted in the absence of affirmative investment instructions from such participants.[22]

Everything else being equal, it is hard to object to regulation which provides more information and protection to participants. The problem is that not everything else is equal. No regulation is costless. Employers, particularly smaller employers, are sensitive to the costs of establishing and maintaining qualified plans. As we learned in the case of defined benefit plans, the pathway to overregulation is paved with good intentions.

ii. Amend Section 401(k) to Require Elections Out

While I would eschew many well-meaning, but potentially counterproductive, changes to the rules governing defined contribution plans, I would amend Section 401(k) in one important respect: to require employees to opt out of 401(k) participation. Most 401(k) plans require the employee to elect plan coverage; absent such an election, the default rule for most plans is nonparticipation.

There is now substantial evidence that the opposite approach, making participation the default rule,[23] dramatically increases employees' coverage under 401(k) arrangements.[24] Employees who procrastinate about opting in also procrastinate about electing out. Hence, there is much to be gained by defining a Section 401(k) plan as an arrangement from which the employee must affirmatively withdraw by electing current cash salary rather than an equivalent plan contribution on his behalf.

---

21 *See* PPA Section 508 adding to ERISA new Section 105(a)(1)(A).

22 PPA Section 624 adding to ERISA new Section 404(c)(5).

23 The IRS specifically approved automatic enrollment 401(k) plans under which participation is the default rule if the employee makes no election. *See* Rev. Rul. 2000–8. *See also* Prop. Treas. Reg. Section 1.401(k)-1(a)(3)(ii). And, as is discussed in the text, Congress in 2006 removed some of the perceived impediments to automatic enrollment for 401(k) plans. *See* Patrick Purcell, *Automatic Enrollment in 401(k) Plans*, Congressional Research Service, Order Code RS21954 (Jan. 16, 2007) available at 2007 TNT 34–187.

24 *See supra* chap. two note 8.

In 2006, Congress blessed automatic 401(k) enrollment, by providing an optional statutory framework for employers who desire automatic enrollment for their 401(k) plans.[25] However, it is sensible to go further, by requiring of all 401(k) plans that eligible employees participate in such plans unless they affirmatively elect to receive current cash salary rather than an equivalent contribution to the plan.

Unlike the reforms I reject as potentially imposing significant burdens on employers and participants, defining the Section 401(k) default rule as participation does not constitute overbearing paternalism. Under such a rule, the employee can choose to depart from the plan and thereby take current cash compensation in lieu of a plan contribution on his behalf. Moreover, a 401(k) default rule which puts employees in the plan unless they affirmatively elect out might be as or more easy for employers to administer than the default rule which requires employees to opt into the plan. This suggests that, over time, many, perhaps most, 401(k) sponsors will, on their own, gravitate towards the rule under which plan participation is presumed unless the employee elects out.

On balance, however, I favor legislating such a default rule, thereby accelerating the trend to such a rule. A compelling analogy is presented by the Code's withholding provisions for lump sum qualified plan distributions. Today, federal income taxes are generally withheld from a qualified plan distribution[26] unless the distributee elects a "trustee-to-trustee" rollover, i.e., a direct payment of the distribution to an IRA or another qualified plan.[27] Substantively, this withholding rule does not affect the ultimate tax consequences of the distributee's choices: If the employee undertakes a traditional rollover, tax is withheld from the distribution. If the rollover is properly completed, the previously withheld taxes are subsequently refunded on the employee's federal income tax return for the rollover year. Under the no-withholding rule, the employee making a trustee-to-trustee rollover instead pays no tax on his rolled over lump sum and thus receives no refund. Except for liquidity[28] and time-value-of-money concerns, there is no substantive difference between, on the one hand, paying tax and receiving a refund or, on the other hand, avoiding withholding *ab initio*. Either way, there is ultimately no tax due.

---

[25]   Section 902 of the Pension Protection Act of 2006.

[26]   Code Section 3405(c).

[27]   Code Section 401(a)(31).

[28]   If the employee making a traditional rollover desires to transfer the full amount of his distribution to an IRA or a qualified plan, that employee must transfer from his own or borrowed resources an amount equal to the taxes withheld.

But, as behavioralists tell us, there may be a difference in how these two possibilities are perceived by many individuals. Even one skeptical of the vocabulary of framing effects might agree that the rule which suspends withholding on trustee-to-trustee rollovers highlights the tax benefits of rollovers and therefore inclines more distributees in that direction—as opposed to the delayed reward of a subsequent refund at filing time.

Similarly, there is now enough experience and study to indicate that putting participants into 401(k) plans, unless they affirmatively elect current cash compensation instead, overcomes some of the cognitive barriers (or, more accurately, uses those barriers) to increase employees' participation in such plans.[29]

iii.   Reduce Scheduled Social Security Benefit Levels

Under the defined contribution paradigm as it exists today and for the foreseeable future, there is a *de facto* division of responsibility between private retirement plans and the federal Social Security system. We have assigned to the federal government the task of providing, via Social Security, basic, traditional, annuity-paying defined benefit coverage, particularly to low income individuals. In contrast, the private retirement regime predominantly places risk and reward upon the individual account holder. Proposals to introduce individual accounts to the Social Security system would alter this division of responsibility by installing individual accounts in that system and thereby diluting its defined benefit quality.

I am skeptical of such proposals. In the main, the half of the workforce covered by private retirement plans already has opportunities for employer-sponsored individual accounts. Most of these individuals contribute to their respective accounts less than the permitted maxima. For these individuals, accounts under the Social Security system would be duplicative, if not redundant. Many of these individuals might respond to Social Security accounts by making offsetting reductions in the contributions to their private accounts.

Moreover, I am doubtful about the wisdom of diminishing the defined benefit nature of Social Security for the other half of the population which lacks private

---

29   Professors Sunstein and Thaler come to a similar conclusion. *See* Sunstein and Thaler, *supra* chap. two note 8.

plan coverage. In my judgment, the risks thereby imposed on these individuals outweigh the potential rewards for them.

However, the benefit levels now scheduled to be paid by Social Security are not financially sustainable at prevailing FICA tax rates. Since I see no prospect of increasing those tax rates (and, in any event, am unenthusiastic about increasing those rates given their regressive impact),[30] the only way to restore fiscal balance to the Social Security system is to reduce that system's projected benefit payments. Indeed, it should be (and often is)[31] the advocates of the defined benefit nature of Social Security who, to preserve it, would bring the current Social Security system into actuarial balance by reducing its benefit commitments.

Here, again, the behavioralist perspective has useful lessons: Economically equivalent benefit reductions may be perceived differently when achieved through different formulas. For example, delaying social security benefits (while keeping nominal annual payments the same) is economically equivalent to starting a lower level of benefits earlier. As Professor Diamond observes, "changing the age of full benefits is a benefit cut, plain and simple."[32]

Nevertheless, pushing back the early and normal retirement ages at which individuals may collect social security benefits seems more politically palatable than is an economically equivalent reduction of annual payments commencing earlier.

---

[30] It is true that, considering Social Security benefits and taxes together, the overall package is somewhat progressive in incidence. That, however, does not allay my qualms about increasing FICA taxes, an increase which imposes its heaviest burden on low-income persons and deters their work efforts.

[31] See, e.g., Aaron, *supra* chap. three note 185 at 89–94. Peter A. Diamond and Peter R. Orszag argue that scheduled Social Security benefit increases can be scaled back in a fashion which simultaneously helps to restore the actuarial balance of the Social Security system, maintains current benefits for existing retirees and near retirees, and authorizes benefit increases for future retirees (just not as great as the benefit increases scheduled for them under current law). See Diamond and Orszag, *supra* chap. two note 29 at 28, 83, 87–88, 93, 167–170, and 183. In their particulars, my conclusions are somewhat different than those underpinning the Diamond-Orszag proposal. Specifically (and contrary to that proposal), I believe that at least some near retirees (i.e., those like me in our early and middle fifties) should be forsaking some Social Security benefits we are scheduled to receive and that the politically palatable way to do this is to push back normal retirement age for us while that age is still a decade or more away. However, in its broad outlines, the Diamond-Orszag proposal demonstrates that reducing scheduled Social Security payments is critical to the maintenance and continuation of Social Security as a solvent defined benefit plan.

[32] Diamond, *supra* chap. four note 17 at 127.

After all, who can deny the reality that ages like 62,[33] 65,[34] and 67[35] carry different connotations for the Woodstock generation than they did for our parents?[36]

iv.   Expand the Coverage of the Section 25B Credit and Make the Credit Refundable

The advocates of incorporating individual accounts within Social Security implicitly raise an important issue: the nonparticipation in the defined contribution paradigm by the half of the population (largely lower-income individuals) who lack qualified plan coverage. The federal government's principal device for encouraging low-income individuals' IRA and 401(k) contributions is today the saver's tax credit of Section 25B. In 2006, Congress wisely made the credit a permanent feature of the Code.[37]

However, the 25B credit suffers from two important limitations. First, the credit only applies to retirement contributions. If saving for medical or educational outlays is a higher priority for a particular low-income taxpayer, the Code provides no assistance for those kinds of saving.

Second, the credit is nonrefundable. An individual without federal tax liability receives no assistance from the credit since he has no liability to offset the credit. There is, moreover, no provision for carrying over to future years any unused Section 25B credit. In some cases, it is likely the individual with no federal tax obligation who most needs assistance with his savings.

Accordingly, I recommend that the coverage of the Section 25B credit be expanded to subsidize, not just retirement contributions, but to reward contributions to HSAs, educational savings accounts and Section 529 programs if the taxpayer

---

33   The early retirement age for social security old-age benefits. *See* 42 U.S.C. Section 416(l)(2).

34   The social security normal retirement age for most individuals who were sixty-two years old before January 1, 2000. *See* 42 U.S.C. Section 416(l)(1)(A).

35   The age to which Social Security normal retirement is scheduled to be changed over time. *See* 42 U.S.C. Section 416(l)(1)(E).

36   An article in the magazine published by AARP declares that "Sixty Is the New Thirty." If so, delaying Social Security payments to age seventy (70) seems rather modest. *See* Martha Sherrill, *Sixty is the New Thirty*, 46(6A) AARP, THE MAGAZINE 52 (November/December, 2003).

37   Section 812 of the Pension Protection Act of 2006.

prefers any of these instead.[38] In addition, I recommend that the credit be made refundable.[39] If that option is deemed too costly, I would instead recommend that individuals without federal income tax liability be permitted to carry forward unused Section 25B credits for a reasonable period, say, five years.

v. Apply the Ten Percent Limit on Employer Stock to Defined Contribution Plans

Diversification of retirement savings is good. Of course, sometimes a fortune can be made by pursuing a single investment: Bill Gates and the Walton families have done well with undiversified portfolios. But most of us will not become Microsoft or Wal-Mart billionaires and, for us, diversification is a sensible investment strategy.[40] ERISA reflects the value of diversification both by imposing upon plan fiduciaries a general obligation to diversify the plan assets under their control[41] and by preventing defined benefit pension trusts from investing more than ten percent of their total assets in employer stock.[42]

In terms of diversification, it is particularly troubling for an employer or for the employee herself to invest the bulk of the employee's retirement assets in the employer's stock since the employee's job, and thus her current compensation, is already tied to her employer's economic fate. Concentrating the employee's retirement investments in the employer (whether that concentration is imposed upon the employee or represents the employee's choice) creates an economic form of double jeopardy, further entwining the employee's finances with the employer's future performance.

---

[38] President Bush's budget for 2008 suggests broadening the 25B credit to reward low-income individuals' contributions to Section 529 accounts. Wesley Elmore, *Tax Cut Permanence, Health Insurance Deduction in Budget*, 114 TAX NOTES 599, 600 (2007).

[39] Professor Forman agrees that the Section 25B credit should be made refundable. However, he would expand the credit by raising the statutory income limits and thereby make more taxpayers eligible for the credit. In contrast, my priority would be to expand the range of accounts generating creditable contributions. Forman, *supra* chap. three note 73 at 234.

[40] *See, e.g.,* Swensen, *supra* chap. two note 18 at 16–20. ("The act of diversification provides a free lunch of enhanced returns and reduced risk, increasing the likelihood that an investor will stay the course in difficult market environments.") Lawrence, *supra* chap. two note 4 at 3. ("Diversification is a cornerstone principle of prudent investment practices.")

[41] ERISA Section 404(a)(1)(C).

[42] Code 4975(d)(13) and ERISA Sections 407 and 408(e).

Some employees can win from this kind of undiversified approach—just as some people can win the lottery. But, as a matter of retirement policy, diversification is the more sensible course, as the statute declares.[43]

It is thus today anomalous that the ten percent limit on employer stock does not apply to defined contribution plans. This exemption from the ten percent ceiling can best be understood historically. When ERISA was adopted, defined benefit plans predominated. The typical money purchase pension or profit sharing plan supplemented a defined benefit arrangement. Even if the defined contribution plan was loaded with employer stock, that concentration was expected to be balanced by the diversified assets held in the employer's defined benefit plan. Today, in contrast, with defined contribution plans the main (typically sole) retirement savings vehicles for most employees, there is no longer a diversified pool of defined benefit assets to offset heavy concentrations of employer stock in 401(k) or other individual accounts.

With an appropriate transition period so that plans can sell their excess employer stock holdings in an orderly fashion, the ten percent limit on employer stock should apply to all defined contribution plans.[44] Employers would still be free to grant employees stock as current compensation and to award stock options. However, the undiversified individual account, bloated with employer stock, should, in the post-Enron era, become a thing of the past. Given employers' evident determination, even after Enron, to permit heavy concentrations of employer stock in 401(k) accounts,[45] ERISA's ten percent cap should be extended to defined contribution arrangements also.

C. Conclusion

Pension cognoscenti have frequently remarked on the stagnation of the defined benefit system and the concomitant rise of defined contribution plans. I suggest

---

[43] *See* Gretchen Morgenson, *Lopsided 401(k)'s, All Too Common*, N.Y. TIMES, Section 3 (Money & Business), October 5, 2003 at 1. ("After Enron collapsed, Congress discussed limits on the amount of company stock that can be in a 401(k), but the issue died. Now, almost two years later, investors in many 401(k) plans remain dangerously overexposed to their companies stock.")

[44] This would entail the phase-out of ESOPs.

[45] *See, e.g.*, Fred Williams, "More employers allow unlimited company stock," 31(22) PENSIONS & INVESTMENTS 1 (October 27, 2003) ("87% of plan sponsors allow unlimited allocation of participant assets in company stock, compared to 59% in last year's survey.")

that, over the last generation, something even more fundamental has occurred, something which can justly be called a paradigm shift. Americans today experience and conceive of retirement savings in the form of individual accounts. Such accounts are primary instruments of public policy, not just for retirement savings, but increasingly for health care and education as well. Many of the defined benefit pensions which have and will survive will, through the cash balance format, mimic defined contribution arrangements.

The causes of the defined contribution society are deeply-rooted and now self-reinforcing. This explains why, in the aftermath of Enron and the well-publicized losses of the Enron 401(k) participants, there has been neither a popular or political backlash against the defined contribution paradigm nor a concerted effort to resuscitate defined benefit pensions. Tinkering at the margins will not rejuvenate the now-stagnant defined benefit system, given the magnitude of the forces— economic, demographic, historical, regulatory and cultural—underlying that stagnation and the concomitant emergence of the individual account framework. Among these forces, individual accounts comport well with American norms of private property and control.

Contemporary efforts—in Congress, in the executive branch, among commentators—to revive the defined benefit format are ultimately like my grandmother's[46] chicken soup in times of ill-health: They can't do any harm; they might help a little. It would be sensible to relieve defined benefit plans from the opaque morass of overregulation now enveloping them. But under the best of circumstances, we should not expect the restoration of the *status quo ante* for defined benefit pensions. The now-dominant defined contribution paradigm is today entrenched in American tax and social policy.

In this context, President Bush's ownership society proposals represent incremental extension of the defined contribution paradigm which itself embodies thirty years of cumulative incremental changes.

While the decline of the traditional defined benefit plan and the corresponding emergence of contemporary individual account arrangements have worked well for many, the movement from the defined benefit framework to the defined

---

[46] This refers to my paternal grandmother. The cooking of my maternal grandmother likely did kill.

contribution paradigm will, for the long run, prove problematic for some, perhaps many, employees by shifting from their employers to them the invest-ment, funding and longevity risks associated with retirement savings. However, in a post-Enron world, there is no realistic chance of resuscitating the classic, annuity-paying defined benefit plan; we are simply too far down the defined contribution road. Since L'affaire Enron did not trigger a reassessment of the contemporary defined contribution paradigm, there is no foreseeable possibility that such a reassessment will occur. The best we can do is try to make that para-digm work.

Index